# International Safeguards and Nuclear Industry

# International Safeguards and Nuclear Industry

edited by MASON WILLRICH

Henry D. Smyth

Bernhard G. Bechhoefer

Mason Willrich

Paul C. Szasz

Edwin M. Kinderman

Victor Gilinsky

Theodore B. Taylor

Lawrence Scheinman

Published under the auspices of
THE AMERICAN SOCIETY OF INTERNATIONAL LAW

The Johns Hopkins University Press, Baltimore and London

The Johns Hopkins University Press, Baltimore, Maryland 21218
The Johns Hopkins University Press Ltd., London

Library of Congress Catalog Card Number 72-12360
ISBN 0-8018-1458-8

Library of Congress Cataloging in Publication data
will be found on the last printed page of this book.

Supported primarily by a grant to The American Society of
International Law from the Research Applied to National
Needs Directorate (RANN) of the National Science Foundation.

# Contents

# Foreword

The Treaty on the Non-Proliferation of Nuclear Weapons (NPT), which entered into force on March 5, 1970, is a major attempt to reduce the risk of nuclear war. Under the NPT, each non-nuclear-weapon party agrees not to manufacture nuclear weapons or other nuclear explosive devices. In order to facilitate verification that its Treaty obligations are being fulfilled, each non-nuclear-weapon party is also required to accept the application of safeguards on all peaceful nuclear activities within its territory or control. The safeguards required are those developed in accordance with the International Atomic Energy Agency (IAEA) system.

The IAEA/NPT safeguards system is intended to ensure that nuclear material destined for use in peaceful activities, such as the generation of electric power, is not diverted to use in nuclear weapons or other explosive devices. A few kilograms of special fissionable material successfully diverted from the hundreds of thousands of kilograms that will soon be present in worldwide nuclear industry would be sufficient to create a nuclear explosive powerful enough to destroy a small city. The need for an effective system of international safeguards against diversion of such material from civilian industry is clear and urgent.

This book contains an extensive study of the IAEA/NPT safeguards system and the problems which it must deal with now. The study was conducted with the need for greater public understanding of the issues involved very much in mind. It should be, we think, comprehensible to general readers who have little or no previous technical knowledge of the nuclear field.

First, a foundation for detailed analysis is provided. In Chapter 1 Henry D. Smyth explains why international safeguards are needed and suggests criteria which should be used in the development and evaluation of a safeguards system. In Chapter 2 Bernhard G. Bechhoefer traces the history of the development of international safeguards from the far-reaching Baruch Plan in 1946 to the 1971 revision of IAEA safeguards after conclusion of the NPT. In Chapter 3 Mason Willrich describes nuclear industry in terms of the cycle of operations involved in the use of nuclear fuel to generate electric power, its implications for international and internal security, and the present and projected civilian nuclear capabilities of nations throughout the world. Following this basic introduction, safeguards against nuclear diversion are described and analyzed. In Chapter 4 Paul C. Szasz examines the IAEA/NPT system in detail. In Chapter 5 Edwin M. Kinderman outlines the development of a national system of safeguards in the United States. Various possibilities for nuclear diversion by national governments are discussed by Victor Gilinsky in Chapter 6; possibilities for diversion by non-governmental groups are described by Theodore B. Taylor in Chapter 7. The industrial implications of safeguards are investigated by Dr. Kinderman in Chapter 8, and their overall political implications are considered by Lawrence Scheinman in Chapter 9. In Chapter 10 Mason Willrich sets forth the conclusions of the group as a whole.

This book is the result of a study conducted under the auspices of The American Society of International Law's Panel on Nuclear Energy and World Order, with support from a grant by the National Science Foundation. The members of the panel were drawn from various disciplines—law, the natural sciences, and the social sciences—and from government, private industry, the academic community, and research organizations. Their names are listed in an appendix to this volume. The purposes of the panel are to stimulate and assist original research on important international policy issues and, by a process of informal discussion, to give each member of the panel new insights into his own work in the nuclear field. A list of publications assisted by the panel is set forth in the appendix.

In June 1971 the panel established a working group, under the direction of Mason Willrich, composed of the authors of this volume. The task of this group was to analyze and evaluate the IAEA/NPT system of international safeguards which had just emerged from multilateral negotiations conducted over many months. The group met a number of times, and draft papers were produced. These drafts were reviewed and criticized at a meeting of the full panel in December 1971; the working group then met to refine each author's contribution.

Individual chapters represent a variety of points of view and reflect the diverse experience and knowledge of their respective authors. Nevertheless, each author's work has been thoroughly scrutinized, especially by other members of the working group. We hope that, as a result, the book presents a coherent analysis of a complex and important international problem.

On behalf of the working group and the panel, we wish to express our appreciation to The American Society of International Law and the National Science Foundation for supporting this study. As Project Director and Panel Chairman, respectively, we also wish to express our gratitude to the working group members who gave so much time and creative effort to the study.

Mason Willrich
*Project Director and Editor*

Bennett Boskey
*Chairman*

# Part I
## Introduction

# CHAPTER 1

# The Need for International Safeguards

## HENRY D. SMYTH

### THE TWO FACES OF NUCLEAR ENERGY

The destruction of two cities in Japan, each shattered and burned by a single nuclear bomb, ended World War II in August 1945. This bombing not only ended the war but revealed to the world the presence of a new and dramatically powerful source of energy. The fission of uranium had been announced to the scientific community in 1939, and its possible peaceful and military uses were soon recognized. Five years of secret development had shown how nuclear fission reactions could be made to occur either explosively, as in a bomb, or more slowly, as in a reactor, to produce a continuing source of heat convertible to electric power. Since 1945 there have been many nuclear explosions for weapons testing and some for exploring possible peaceful uses of such explosions themselves. No nuclear bombs have been used in warfare, but large stockpiles of such weapons and of nuclear materials have been built up in the United States and in a few other countries.

In 1945 demands for electric power were already growing rapidly, and resources of fossil fuel were beginning to be recognized as limited. Therefore the advent of a new source of energy, uranium, was welcomed with enthusiasm. Development of nuclear power plants was pushed vigorously in the United States and elsewhere, but only after twenty years or more did uranium fission begin to be of significance in the power picture. Nuclear power plants are now increasing rapidly and require increasing amounts of nuclear material for fuel.

Even before the nuclear bombs were dropped on Japan, many responsible people connected with their development recognized that a new dimension of horror was being added to warfare and privately urged plans for their control. Almost immediately after the war ended the United States took the initiative in proposing international control of nuclear materials and facilities. Such proposals recognized the close relation between the technology of nuclear weapons for war and the technology of nuclear power plants for peace. The dilemma was clearly posed: how can the dangers of nuclear war be reduced while the benefits of the peaceful uses of nuclear energy are exploited? Some progress has been made, but the current rapid increase of nuclear power plants planned or in being makes the need of control more urgent and the achievement of it more difficult than ever before.

### Nuclear Power Plants

Production of the large amounts of electric power required by the modern world is done most efficiently in big central stations. Basically, such stations convert chemical energy or nuclear energy into heat, which is converted into steam, which drives generators which produce electric current. This is a clumsy, indirect process, wasting some 60 to 70 percent of the energy inherent in the original fuel, whether it be coal, gas, oil, or uranium—but it is the best we can do at present.

The waste heat produced by all steam-electric power plants must be dissipated, and this creates the problem of so-called thermal pollution. This type of pollution has become important more because of the enormous capacity of modern power plants than because some of them are nuclear, though a nuclear plant does produce more waste heat than a fossil fuel plant of the same size. In contrast, toxic pollution of the atmosphere from plants burning coal is much more serious than from nuclear plants. The routine discharge of small amounts of radioactive substances from nuclear plants can be and is controlled by proper design and operation. Exactly what limits are acceptable remain controversial. The nuclear plant must also be protected from accidents which might release a large amount of radioactivity from the core of the reactor.

Although very much concerned about these dangers, the general public remains remarkably relaxed about the product of nuclear power plants that concerns us in this book. Every nuclear power plant of the type now being built produces plutonium. Plutonium is a nuclear explosive. Even a small amount of plutonium in the hands of a terrorist group would be dangerous, and a supply of it is a major step toward a stockpile of nuclear bombs which a nation might use to wage nuclear war.

## Nuclear War

The effects of nuclear war would be the direct destruction of whole cities or complexes of cities and the widespread fallout of radioactive debris. Fallout will not recognize national boundaries. Distance may attenuate its intensity, but neither rivers nor mountain ranges nor oceans will prevent its dissemination through the earth's atmosphere. A minor nuclear war where only a few weapons are dropped may seriously endanger only the combatant nations and their close neighbors. A major nuclear war will endanger the whole world.

These are the dangers that have confronted us ever since Hiroshima and Nagasaki. So far they have been avoided: nuclear bombs have not been used in war since 1945. While we must hope and pray that no more will ever be used, this can be assured only by eliminating war or by eliminating nuclear weapons. Regrettably, the attainment of either of these objectives appears unlikely in the near future.

Some argue that the danger of nuclear war is less now than it was ten or fifteen years ago because of the apparent lessening of international tensions and the growing realization that nuclear war is not likely to be profitable to either side. Others argue that nuclear war is becoming more probable because of increasing stockpiles of nuclear weapons, the increase from one to five in the number of countries having nuclear weapons (the United States, the Soviet Union, the United Kingdom, France, and China), and the spread of nuclear power plants with their inevitable production of plutonium. Debate between these two schools of thought seems somewhat academic. As long as the probability of nuclear war is finite, we should try to reduce it.

## THE PRESENT STATUS OF NUCLEAR POWER

It is now of only historical interest to question whether the potential peaceful benefits of nuclear fission are sufficient to justify the dangers inherent in the spread of nuclear technology. Once the feasibility of nuclear bombs had been demonstrated, it would presumably have been impossible to prevent the eventual spread of nuclear technology to many countries. Acceptance of this view was implied in President Eisenhower's Atoms for Peace speech in 1953 and in subsequent U.S. policy. In effect, U.S. policy since 1953 has been to promote the technology of peaceful uses of nuclear energy, but at the same time to establish controls to prevent diversion of that technology to military use.

Numerous nuclear power plants have recently begun to operate or are under construction, located both in countries that have nuclear weapons and in those that do not. All these power plants produce plutonium. The Treaty on the Non-Proliferation of Nuclear Weapons (NPT) emerged from years of negotiation in the summer of 1968. By March of 1970 enough countries had become parties to the treaty to bring it into effect. Under the NPT, the parties to the treaty without nuclear weapons pledge not to develop or obtain them from other countries. Furthermore, these parties undertake to allow inspection of their peaceful nuclear activities to ensure that materials are not diverted from these activities to the manufacture of nuclear explosives. Such inspection is to be undertaken by the International Atomic Energy Agency (IAEA), an international organization established in 1956, with headquarters in Vienna, Austria, and a membership of more than one hundred countries.

By the spring of 1971, the IAEA had completed a revision of its "safeguards system" and had prepared a document to be used as a basis for the necessary safeguards agreements between the NPT parties and the IAEA. As of this writing, a number of such agreements have been negotiated. However, several important nations are delaying their adherence to the NPT, awaiting the outcome of other negotiations now in progress, principally those involving the members of the European Atomic Energy Community (Euratom).

In summary, the current question is what will be done through the NPT or otherwise to inhibit the diversion of nuclear material from peaceful purposes to the production of nuclear weapons.

## WHAT ARE SAFEGUARDS?

If I were a student of the English language I would be tempted to write a scholarly essay on the increasing use of the word "safeguard." We hear it in TV commercials advertising a deodorant, in testimony before Congress by Department of Defense officials supporting ABM systems, and in many other contexts. Even in talk about nuclear energy, the word is used in several different senses. The U.S. Atomic Energy Commission insists that nuclear power plants must set up safeguards against pollution, worries about safeguards for the health of workers in plants handling radioactive materials, and may even declare how it is safeguarding the peace of the world by making more nuclear weapons. Though such multiple use of the word is confusing, I find a certain logic running through the various meanings. Let me provide a general definition before explaining the kind of safeguards that are the subject of this book.

The purpose of any safeguard or system of safeguards is to prevent some unwanted event or at least to reduce the likelihood of its occurrence—an umbrella is a safeguard against getting wet. The manufacture and use of automobiles are surrounded by an elaborate system of safeguards, including many types of inspection—but people are still killed by automobiles. Not only do automobiles endanger individual drivers, passengers, and pedestrians, but their large numbers in our cities produce smog which is both unpleasant and unhealthy.

The public has become increasingly concerned by the unwanted effects of automobiles and many other technologies of modern society. Belatedly, we are recognizing that our environment must be safeguarded against both immediate danger and ultimate destruction. Perhaps this concern has been stimulated by astronauts' photographs showing the limited size of the Earth, on which we all must live. Whatever the cause, general public concern needs to be translated into action, into establishing safeguards against the consequences of many technologies of modern life, old ones long neglected and new ones more readily dramatized. In particular, we need safeguards against the consequences of the discovery of nuclear energy and its uses in war and peace, a discovery often called the greatest technological breakthrough of modern time. To put this problem in perspective, I compare it with a much earlier discovery of even greater importance, about which we know almost nothing.

Surely the greatest technological breakthrough of all time occurred when prehistoric man learned how to use fire for his own purposes. Fire can be both beneficial and destructive. In using it, man had to learn how to control it, to prevent its spread. He did not always succeed, and he still fails to do so occasionally. The great Chicago fire of 1871 is supposed to have been started by Mrs. O'Leary's cow. In modern parlance, we can say that Mrs. O'Leary's system of domestic safeguards was inadequate or, what is more probable, was carelessly implemented. In Chicago even in 1871 there was a municipal safeguards system to prevent fires from spreading, the fire department. It, too, proved inadequate to meet the unusual conditions of long-continued heat and drought, wooden buildings, and a hot wind from the west. It is not clear whether the technology of fire fighting was insufficiently advanced to meet these conditions, or whether the planners of the fire department failed to anticipate the conditions that occurred, or whether the fire department was starved for men and equipment by the city fathers in the interest of economy. In other words, we do not know whether the safeguards system was inadequately designed or enfeebled for lack of financial support.

I have called the Chicago Fire Department a "municipal safeguards system," but of course fire departments are only one part of the system of safeguards against destruction by fire which men have developed over the centuries. There are building codes, restrictions on domestic heaters, ordinances controlling burning of brush or rubbish, inspection of public places like theaters, alarm systems, fire extinguishers, sprinkler systems—a whole system of regulations, instrumentation, and equipment aimed at preventing fire or limiting its spread. If we examine the components of this system of safeguards against destructive fire, we recognize that they serve three purposes: prevention, detection, or limitation.

The safeguards or systems of safeguards described in this book are concerned with preventing, detecting, or limiting the diversion of nuclear material from legitimate peaceful uses to illicit production of nuclear explosives. More specifically, in Chapters 5 and 7, where the prevention of theft of nuclear material by dissident groups or criminal organizations is discussed, it is clear that the safeguards system should involve physical protection such as vaults, locks, and guards as an important component. The safeguards systems described elsewhere in this book are primarily systems for keeping track of nuclear material. Accounting methods supplemented by sampling, analysis, and inspection are used to detect diversion of nuclear material from authorized use. Though not aimed directly at preventing diversion, such a positive system for detecting violations of the provisions of the Non-Proliferation Treaty can be expected to inhibit such violations and limit their extent.

## THE IAEA AND SAFEGUARDS

The dangers inherent in the use of nuclear energy for peaceful purposes were clearly foreseen in 1956 by the drafters of the statute of the IAEA. Article II of the statute states: "The Agency shall seek to accelerate and enlarge the contribution of atomic energy to peace, health and prosperity throughout the world. It shall ensure, so far as it is able, that assistance provided by it or at its request or under its supervision or control is not used in such a way as to further any military purpose."

The statute provides the legal basis for the establishment of a safeguards system, but the measures necessary to meet its objective took a long time to develop. There were many technical and political difficulties to be surmounted. Fortunately, the spread of nuclear power plants has also been slow, so that the need for international safeguards has become urgent only recently. Also, the Non-Proliferation Treaty, depending as it does on the IAEA safeguards system, has come along at about the right time. The revision and codification of the IAEA system required by the NPT has been done in the light of ten years' experience with safeguards on a gradually increasing scale.

One characteristic of the IAEA safeguards system under the NPT is the emphasis it places on the use of national safeguards systems. If a national government failed to keep a close record of the nuclear material within its borders, the IAEA would have to set up elaborate accounting and inventory procedures which would be both expensive and intrusive. Consequently, it is in the interest of any country adhering to the NPT to have a strong national system of material control. Such a system not only provides safeguards in the IAEA sense but serves other purposes of prudent management as well.

The criteria for a national safeguards system and an international system are similar, but the emphasis differs. Before discussing such criteria, it is well to review the technological sequence that must be present in a fully developed nuclear industry (this subject is fully discussed in Chapter 3, and is merely outlined here).

## THE NUCLEAR FUEL CYCLE

1. The uranium ore is mined.

2. The uranium contained in the ore is concentrated and purified.

3. The proportion of the uranium-235 isotope is increased in an isotope enrichment plant. This step can be bypassed, but nuclear fuel containing slightly enriched uranium is now considered economically desirable in most circumstances.

4. The purified, enriched uranium is put into whatever form is desired as fuel for a nuclear power reactor.

5. The fuel is loaded into a reactor. After a period of operation often lasting as much as a year, the irradiated fuel is removed. By that time the fissionable uranium is partly used up, and other nuclei, including plutonium, have been produced, making fresh fuel desirable.

6. The spent fuel from the reactor, containing plutonium and other highly radioactive elements, is chemically reprocessed to separate the various elements.

7. The separated elements are stored, the residual uranium and plutonium for possible recycling and the other radioactive elements for possible special uses or merely to prevent random dissemination.

In actual practice, some of these seven steps may be combined in one plant or, on the other hand, broken up into substages.

As nuclear material moves through the fuel cycle, it varies in physical form (gaseous, liquid, or solid), in chemical composition, in isotopic ratio, and in degree of radioactivity. The general trend is toward increasing money value (e.g., enriched uranium is worth more than natural uranium) and increasing radioactivity (e.g., the spent fuel coming out of a nuclear power plant is far more radioactive than the fuel initially loaded).

The difficulty of determining amounts of material flowing past various points in the cycle varies greatly. For example, fuel assemblies being loaded into a reactor can be counted. They can be counted again when they are taken out—it's easy, just like putting thousand-dollar bonds in a safe deposit box and taking them out again. But something happens in the reactor; some uranium is converted into plutonium and into other elements. No change may be apparent in the outer protective sheathing in which the nuclear material is sealed, but the composition of the material is changed. The reactor operator would like to know the new composition, as would the manager of the chemical reprocessing plant that will handle the spent fuel, as would the nuclear material control officer. Satisfactory methods for getting this information are gradually being worked out, but it is a difficult technical problem. Similar difficulties arise in other steps of the fuel cycle.

The incentives to overcome such difficulties are different for the different groups of people that are involved. The plant management wants to avoid health hazards or loss of valuable material; the national government's supervisory agency wants to protect the environment and the health of the workers and to prevent illicit diversion of material to a black market. The international community shares the concern of the national government, but it also wants to be sure that the government itself is not engaged in diverting material to a nuclear weapon program.

Management can design the layout of its plants and the procedures of its operations to minimize loss of material and optimize conditions for inventory; it can insure physical protection of material by locks, vaults, guards, and instrumentation; it can make precise measurements of amounts of material at various points in the process; it can punish sloppy operation.

A national supervisory agency can check on the measures taken by the management, make independent analyses of effluents from the plant and of materials flowing past certain points. Above all, national authorities have police power, either through licensing or contracting processes or by direct regulatory laws. Consequently, if there are discrepancies between reports from plant management and direct inspections by a national authority, action can be taken.

An international agency has only such power as may be conferred upon it by international agreements. The Non-Proliferation Treaty gives the IAEA the right and the obligation to detect diversion of material to illicit use for the manufacture of nuclear explosives and to announce the evidence of such a diversion. The agency has no police power, but the NPT does give it authority to verify by independent inspection the reports it receives of the amounts and location of nuclear material in a country that is a party to the treaty.

In the preceding paragraphs, I have outlined some of the technical problems involved in detecting the diversion of nuclear material from legitimate channels to illicit uses and have mentioned in general terms the organizations involved. The application of these general ideas in actual practice requires many compromises, as experience in the United States has shown.

## EXPERIENCE OF THE U.S. ATOMIC ENERGY COMMISSION

One might suppose that prudent management would want to minimize the amount of material that goes up the stack, down the drain, or into the scrap pile in any of the seven stages of the nuclear fuel cycle, particularly in the later stages. After all, 1 kilogram of plutonium is worth more than $9,000. Not only is money being wasted but hazards may be created. A good manager wants to know where every gram of material that comes into the plant finally ends up. This is not so easy, and is certainly much harder than for banks to check dollars in against dollars out. Furthermore, accounting for every gram of material can be very expensive, both as a result of high direct costs and because of interference with the smooth operation of the plant. From the point of view of management, a compromise must be made. Such a compromise may not always be satisfactory from the point of view of the national government.

There have been a few bad experiences with management in the United States. Although there has been no evidence of diversion, there have been a few cases where amounts of material have disappeared that were far above the reasonable errors that could result from technical difficulties of operation or analysis or accounting. If this merely meant loss of profits to the company involved, it would be a matter of private concern, but the implications of such a loss are much wider and involve the national government.

As we have pointed out, the national government has responsibilities for health, for conservation of scarce materials, and for prevention of possible diversion of material to illicit uses, as well as some concern for the economical operation of the plant. In the United States, the Atomic Energy Commission (AEC) is the organization primarily charged with these responsibilities.

## IDEAL AND ACTUAL SAFEGUARDS

Ideally, the AEC would like to know where every gram of fissionable or radioactive material in the country is at any moment of time, extending the ideal for the manager of a single plant to the country as a whole. It is manifestly impractical to attain this goal: a perfect material control system is technically impossible to develop (even banks make mistakes), and its interference with operations and its high cost would make it unacceptable to industry. If the AEC tried to enforce such a system, there would be no nuclear energy industry.

Yet there must be a national safeguards system stringent enough to be effective in reducing almost to zero the probability of loss or diversion of significant amounts of material. Its regulations should insist on physical protection of the nuclear material at all stages and require inventories of material at appropriate stages. There must also be provisions for review of these inventories and for inspections to assure that the regulations are being carried out. Such reviews and inspections must be carried out by government employees of unassailable integrity. In short, the system must satisfy two criteria: technical effectiveness and credibility.

Two other criteria that must be considered are cost and acceptability. They are to a degree antithetical to the first two, as has been implied, but actually in the United States the necessity for good management in terms of the value of the material and of

necessary health and safety measures is well recognized and generally accepted. Additional measures to safeguard against diversion
as well are not usually troublesome in most parts of the fuel cycle,
nor are the additional costs very great. In the past one has heard
little complaint against such provisions per se.

Obviously the AEC must make a compromise between maximum technical effectiveness and credibility, on the one hand, and
the limitations imposed by cost and acceptability of control measures, on the other. This is hard enough in a national system but
much more difficult in an international safeguards system, as we
shall see.

## INTERNATIONAL SAFEGUARDS SYSTEMS

The basic objective of a national safeguards system is to prevent
robbery or embezzlement. The additional objective assumed by an
international safeguards system is to inhibit or detect nuclear
diversion that might be authorized by a national government or by
a dissident group in such a government. An international organization charged with administering a safeguards system in a number
of countries will need the same kind of data required by a national
authority administering a materials accounting system. Similarly,
it must verify the accuracy of those data. In establishing an
international system of safeguards, the same criteria must be borne
in mind as have been mentioned for a national system, but so
many new factors enter into the weighing of the criteria that the
picture is substantially different. To prepare for detailed discussion in later chapters, some major problems are discussed below.
For simplicity they are reviewed in terms of the IAEA.

### Technical Effectiveness

The IAEA does not own any nuclear facilities, nor does it engage
in or control the operation of any of the steps in the fuel cycle
from mine to storage of residual material. It does not own any
substantial amount of nuclear material. Its rights to administer
safeguards arise from bilateral agreements between it and countries
which are parties to the NPT or from pre-existing arrangements,
usually involving a country that has imported nuclear materials
and equipment and the country that has supplied them.

How, then, can the IAEA get the data it needs? The obvious way is to get them from the country involved. If that country does not have an adequate materials accounting system, the agency must insist that such a system be set up. If such an attempt is not successful or only partially successful, the technical effectiveness of the IAEA system will be impaired. Increasing the intensity of inspection would help, but the credibility of the international system might still be weakened.

## Credibility

There are also credibility problems separate from those of technical effectiveness. Credibility is enhanced if there is some degree of adversary relationship between the IAEA inspectorate and the national staff. It would normally not be desirable to send a man to inspect country X who was a national of that country. By the same token, it would be unwise to send an inspector who would automatically be considered hostile by reason of his nationality.

The credibility of a regional safeguards system, such as that of Euratom, has been doubted on the ground that the members of Euratom are close allies and that there is consequently no adversary relationship. Others claim that the Euratom system is equivalent to a national system and is therefore of limited credibility. Supporters of the system argue that clearly most Euratom member countries want other members without nuclear weapons thoroughly safeguarded. The NPT gives the IAEA clear authority and responsibility to verify the effectiveness of national or regional systems by review of reports and by such actual inspections as may be appropriate. The question of whether a regional system is to be regarded as equivalent to a national system or to an international system is a difficult one which must be resolved by negotiation.

To summarize, assuming technical competence at all levels, credibility still depends on the nature of the organizations involved; for example, on whether they are industrial corporations, national governments, groups of allied governments, or international organizations of wide membership. In its fifteen years of existence, the IAEA, with a membership including almost every important nation, has built up a good reputation by its activities in many fields, including its voluntary safeguards system. Reasonable cooperation among its members should give the new system developed for NPT a high degree of technical and political credibility.

## Financial Costs

In a national system of material control, some governmental authority usually has the responsibility for determining how elaborate the system can be without incurring unreasonable costs. Actually, the costs are quite low in relation to the value of the electric power produced in a nuclear power plant. In an international organization like the IAEA the situation is more complex. There are really three questions: the total cost of IAEA safeguards, the distribution of that cost among the members of the agency, and the division of costs between the agency and a particular country for safeguards under NPT in that country.

The Board of Governors of the IAEA has debated these questions at great length over the last several years. The general concern has been that the total cost should not be so great as to be out of proportion to the budget items for other activities of the agency, nor should it make the total agency budget an unreasonable burden on the member states, which pay for it by assessment. Present estimates of the probable costs of the safeguards system under the NPT are much lower than earlier guesses and are apparently acceptable. The reduction is partly the result of the emphasis on the use of national systems in the revised IAEA procedures.

The second problem was how to lessen the financial burden for small states unlikely to develop nuclear programs requiring safeguards. A formula has been worked out which recognizes the principle that non-proliferation is of importance to all members of the agency and yet sets a ceiling on the amounts to be paid by the smaller states. The total amounts of money involved are small. As to the division of costs between the agency and the state under safeguards, what might be called national accountability costs will be paid by the state concerned and verification costs by the agency. These cost arrangements are discussed further in Chapter 4.

## Acceptability

The power of national governments to control activities within their borders varies enormously from country to country. Even totalitarian governments have to pay some attention to public opinion, or at least to the opinion of certain segments of the public. In the United States the AEC has the legal authority to require an adequate system of safeguarding nuclear material, but, as I have suggested, the exercise of such authority may be self-defeating if the proposed system is unreasonably complex and expensive. An international body like the IAEA has limited legal power. Although the non-nuclear-weapon states, parties to the NPT, are required by that Treaty to accept IAEA safeguards, no details of the system of safeguards are specified. The problem of acceptability for an international safeguards system is clearly more difficult than for a national system.

We sometimes think of international controls as impossible to achieve. Of course this is not so. We are not yet able to prevent the outbreak of war, but there is a long history of international agreements controlling activities in many fields. Examples range from the agreement to protect the sea otter (signed by the United States, the Soviet Union, the United Kingdom, and Japan in 1911) to the nuclear test ban treaty of 1963. As the interdependence of the nations of the world not only increases but becomes more obvious, more and more international agreements will be made, and the need of some means of enforcement will become clear. The notion of absolute sovereignty and independence will become obsolete.

Nevertheless, the idea that an international organization has the right to inspect perfectly legitimate industrial activities within the borders of a country is a radical one. It is designed to ameliorate a new and terrible danger—nuclear war. It is a tribute to the wisdom of the statesmen of the world that so many of them have recognized the danger and have accepted unusual measures to lessen it. Unfortunately, such wisdom is not universal. Acceptance of the NPT and of the IAEA safeguards system that it incorporates is not yet sufficiently complete to ensure the effectiveness of the Treaty, though a good start has been made.

The drafters of the Treaty and the IAEA group working on the safeguards system have been well aware of such objections to acceptance as danger of compromising industrial secrets, possible interference with plant operation, excessive cost, and infringement of sovereignty. The system chosen must provide affirmative answers to two questions:

1. Is the safeguards system mild enough to be acceptable to

the individual countries which already are, or are considering becoming, parties to the NPT?

(2.) Is the safeguards system strong enough to be acceptable to the community of nations as likely to deter the spread of nuclear weapons, as intended by the NPT?

## Can the Criteria Be Met?

An international safeguards system must meet the four criteria that have been discussed: technical effectiveness, credibility, reasonable cost, and acceptability. To clarify the problem, consider two extreme cases. The IAEA could insist on keeping its own records of the flow of nuclear material through the fuel cycle and on making its own inventories of stockpiled material in each country. It could have resident inspectors at every one of the seven steps in the fuel cycle from ore to storage of residual material. Such a system would be technically effective and highly credible if the Agency itself maintained a good reputation, but it would be so expensive that the member nations of the IAEA would refuse to pay for it and so intrusive that countries with substantial nuclear installations would be unwilling to accept it. At the other extreme, the staff of the Agency inspectorate could sit in Vienna reading reports from national authorities without ever verifying their accuracy. Such an arrangement might appear technically effective on paper, but its credibility would be very low indeed. Of course the cost would be low and the system would be happily accepted by individual countries, but the community of nations could hardly be expected to view it as a significant deterrent to the spread of nuclear weapons.

The task of the IAEA in preparing for its role under the NPT has been to strike a balance between these two extremes. In approaching this task the Agency has had the benefit of ten years of experience with a more limited safeguards system. Such a system was first established in 1960 and has been extended and revised several times since. At present the Agency is administering safeguards in some thirty countries. Most of the installations involved are small, but certain large power reactors in Japan, India, the United Kingdom and the United States are included.

The IAEA is generally recognized as one of the most effective international organizations. Two factors, often cited as contributing to its success, are its limited objectives and the composition and broad authority of its Board of Governors. In April 1970, a few weeks after the NPT formally came into effect, the Board of Governors established a committee to review the IAEA safeguards system in the light of the Treaty. This committee was open-ended, that is, representatives of any of the 102 member states could participate in its deliberations. The Safeguards Committee met first in June 1970 and continued to meet in a series of sessions, each usually lasting two or three weeks, until March 1971. There were eighty-two sessions and, of course, innumerable bilateral or group discussions outside the meeting room, including at least one on Sunday at the swimming pool in the Prater. In an average session almost fifty countries would be represented, with a hard core of perhaps thirty-five to forty important countries always there.

The spirit and atmosphere of these meetings were remarkable. The problems before the group were recognized as difficult and important and were debated thoroughly and vigorously, with a minimum of irrelevant rhetoric. The Agency staff provided drafts of the necessary documents, defended them clearly and reasonably, and accepted innumerable amendments, which, in their turn, were fully debated.

Article III of the NPT provides that each non-nuclear-weapon state adhering to that Treaty shall negotiate an agreement with the IAEA for the administration of safeguards with regard to peaceful nuclear activities in its territory or under its control. The specific objective of the Safeguards Committee was to draw up a document which would guide the Agency in negotiating such agreements. The document, approved by the Board of Governors, was published by the Agency in May 1971 and is called the Negotiating Instructions.

The details of this document are discussed in later chapters of this book, and only some general comments will be made here. No one suggests that this is perfect or that the IAEA/NPT safeguards system it proposes will be 100 percent effective technically. The proposed international safeguards system depends heavily on the adequacy of national systems, and the provisions for reports and inspections are considered by many experts to be close to the minimum necessary for a viable system. If the parties to the NPT negotiate the necessary agreements with the IAEA in the same spirit shown by their delegates to the ad hoc Safeguards Committee, all will be well, but if they refuse to set up an adequate national system or balk at the suggested programs of inspection, negotiations may fail.

## CONCLUSION

If the negotiations avoid the two dangers mentioned in the preceding paragraph, we will have a system of safeguards under the NPT that is a good compromise between effectiveness and credibility on the one hand and cost and acceptability on the other. Such a system will offer any country little excuse for staying out of the NPT on the ground that the safeguards system is either offensive to its national sensibilities or useless.

The negotiators of the NPT and the staff and membership of the IAEA have made a substantial step forward in the realm of international cooperation. Whatever the ultimate outcome, their example will remain important. If the governments of the world will recognize the desirability of limiting the spread of nuclear weapons and of verifying that limitation by a reasonable system of safeguards, they will adhere to the NPT and thus take a significant step away from nuclear war.

# CHAPTER 2

# Historical Evolution of International Safeguards

## BERNHARD G. BECHHOEFER

### INTRODUCTION

After the use of nuclear weapons against Japan in 1945 at the end of World War II, the United States might have pursued a policy aimed at stopping all further development of peaceful uses of nuclear energy because of the inherent dangers of a holocaust. On the other hand, following the advice of some scientists and politicians, it might have immediately disclosed to the world its nuclear secrets, despite the dangers. However, the United States embarked on an intermediate course—continuing nuclear research with the ultimate, though not immediate, objective of using nuclear energy solely for peaceful purposes. Therefore, a system of safeguards to prevent or at least to detect the diversion of nuclear material from peaceful to weapons uses became a fundamental ingredient of the U.S. nuclear program.[1] This chapter outlines the main steps in the evolution of a broad theoretical objective into a limited but nonetheless important operational reality.

Critics will point out that agreement on an international safe-

---

[1] Richard G. Hewlett and Oscar E. Anderson, Jr., *The New World* (University Park: Pennsylvania State University Press, 1962), pp. 373, 407, and chap. 12.

guards system has been developed only by continuously narrowing the areas and scope of control. Supporters will emphasize that the system, as presently envisioned in the International Atomic Energy Agency and the Non-Proliferation Treaty, is far more desirable than no system at all.

The IAEA/NPT safeguards system is one important result of a vast and mainly constructive effort to reduce the danger of nuclear war, reflecting changes in the world political atmosphere. It is significant not only in its present accomplishment, but also in its promise for the future.

## THE BARUCH PLAN AND THE SOVIET RESPONSE

The first resolution on atomic energy adopted by the United Nations General Assembly in January 1946 established the United Nations Atomic Energy Commission, which "shall make specific proposals: . . . for control of atomic energy to the extent necessary to ensure its use only for peaceful purposes; . . . for effective safeguards by way of inspection and other means to protect complying States against the hazards of violations and evasions."[2] This resolution was jointly sponsored by the United States, the Soviet Union, the United Kingdom, France and Canada and was adopted unanimously.

Thereafter, on June 14, 1946, Bernard Baruch, the U.S. delegate to the Commission, submitted a plan which provided for complete international control of the exploitation of atomic energy and complete accountability for nuclear material.[3] This involved international ownership of all major nuclear installations. Under the original proposals, it is clear that the objective of the accountability system was not limited to timely detection of the diversion of nuclear material for military uses but extended to the prevention of such diversion.[4]

The Soviet representatives, as anticipated, objected to the vast international machinery required to carry out such a concept:

[2] *International Control of Atomic Energy, Growth of a Policy,* Department of State Publication 2702 (Washington, D.C.: State Department, 1946), p. 127.

[3] *Ibid.,* p. 49.

[4] The First Report of the UNAEC refers to the necessity of "safeguards necessary to *Detect and Prevent* diversions from declared Activities" (italics supplied) (*First Report of the United Nations Atomic Energy Commission to the Security Council,* Department of State Publication 2737 [Washington, D.C.: State Department, 1946], p. 14).

"The Soviet Union does not intend to make the fate of its national economy dependent on U.S. financiers, industrialists, and their underlings who seek to bind other countries and in particular the Soviet Union hand and foot."[5] Even Mr. Baruch conceded in his later years that acceptance of the U.S. plan implied a limited world government. Despite its traditional objections to any curbs on national sovereignty, however, the first Soviet proposals to deal with safeguards, presented on June 11, 1947, went much farther toward an international control system than any subsequent Soviet proposals until 1957.[6] Though far less comprehensive than the Baruch Plan, the Soviet proposals prohibited all military nuclear activities and, as for civilian industry, called for (1) inspection and investigation on an international basis; (2) accounting; (3) rules for technological control of plants; (4) information relating to the activity of atomic energy plants; and (5) submission of recommendations both to governments and to the United Nations Security Council. These safeguards would cover all significant nuclear installations in all states. Certainly, such a system went far beyond that presently contemplated under the IAEA/NPT framework, yet in 1946, all the members of the UNAEC except the Soviet Union agreed that such a system was not an adequate basis for effective international control of the development and exploitation of nuclear energy.

After the Soviet Union conducted its first nuclear test explosions in 1949, its enthusiasm for controlling nuclear weapons diminished, and its statements each year drew closer to the propaganda slogan of "ban the bomb." Moreover, it gradually moved away from its 1947 proposals so that there was no fixed target which modifications in U.S. positions could approach.

In public, the United States was itself slow to recede from the Baruch Plan. In 1952 a U.S. working paper on verification hinted at some flexibility in the requirements of a nuclear safeguards system. Somewhat later Benjamin V. Cohen, the U.S. disarmament representative, restated the Baruch Plan, substituting a concept of

[5] *Third Report of the United Nations Atomic Energy Commission to the Security Council,* Department of State Publication 3179 (Washington, D.C.: State Department, 1948), p. 51.

[6] This proposal was a part of the relaxation of Soviet policy which made possible the negotiation at about this time of peace treaties with Hungary, Finland, and other states (William Reitzel, Morton A. Kaplan, and Constance G. Coblentz, *U.S. Foreign Policy, 1945-1955* [Washington, D.C.: Brookings Institution, 1956], p. 239).

international operational control for the requirement of international "ownership" of significant nuclear facilities.[7] In private, however, the U.S. government position was changing rapidly with the anticipated perfection of thermonuclear weapons.

## ATOMS FOR PEACE

On December 8, 1953, four months after the Soviet Union had exploded its first thermonuclear device, President Eisenhower delivered to the UN General Assembly an address comparable in dramatic impact to Mr. Baruch's original call to "make a choice between the quick and the dead."[8] Eisenhower acknowledged the impact of the emerging thermonuclear impasse. He then went on to propose an international program to develop the peaceful uses of the atom which would help the world "shake off the inertia imposed by fear and . . . make positive progress towards peace." The progress visualized was a start towards diminishing "the potential destructive power of the world's atomic stockpiles." This would be accomplished if "the governments principally involved begin now and continue to make joint contributions from their stockpiles of normal uranium and fissionable materials to an International Atomic Energy Agency. . . . The proposal has the great virtue that it can be undertaken without the irritations and mutual suspicions incident to any attempt to set up a completely acceptable system of world-wide inspection and control."[9] The Atoms for Peace proposal thus envisioned a far less stringent safeguards system than that being advocated by the United States in the disarmament negotiations.

Although the Statute of the IAEA, with its safeguards provisions, became the subject of negotiations separate from the Disarmament Commission negotiations,[10] the relationship of any IAEA safeguards system to arms control and disarmament cannot be ignored. Eisenhower had committed the United States to per-

[7] Bernhard G. Bechhoefer, *Postwar Negotiations for Arms Control* (Washington, D.C.: Brookings Institution, 1962), pp. 193-94.

[8] *Atomic Power for Peace,* Department of State Publication 5314 (Washington, D.C.: State Department, 1953), pp. 1-4.

[9] *Ibid.,* pp. 10-12.

[10] It is more than a coincidence that the disarmament representative in 1954, the Honorable Morehead Patterson, and his deputy, the author of this paper, in 1955 became, respectively, representative and deputy in the first IAEA negotiations.

mitting international distribution of fissionable material before the system visualized for arms control was perfected. However, the drafting of the IAEA Statute preceded the public declarations by the United States and the Soviet Union of their views on the relationship of IAEA safeguards to disarmament.

Carrying forward a new policy to develop the peaceful uses of nuclear energy required basic changes in U.S. law. The Atomic Energy Act of 1954 authorized an immediate broader program "to encourage widespread participation in the development and utilization of atomic energy for peaceful purposes to the maximum extent consistent with the common defense and security and with the health and safety of the public."[11] The government was authorized to enter into an "international atomic pool" with a group of nations, and thus the way was paved for the United States to become a member of a future IAEA. The Act also authorized the United States to enter into "agreements for cooperation" with other nations regarding peaceful uses of nuclear energy. Every such bilateral agreement was required to contain, among other provisions, a guarantee by the cooperating nation that no equipment or material transferred under the agreement would be used for nuclear weapons or any other military purpose. Moreover, the Act effected basic changes in the relationship between government and private industry within the United States. It authorized for the first time the private ownership of major nuclear facilities and the possession under license of special fissionable material (plutonium, uranium enriched in the isotope 235, or uranium-233). (Legislation authorizing private ownership of special fissionable material was enacted in 1964.) The international nuclear activities of private enterprise were sanctioned, but only if they were carried on under the umbrella of a government-to-government agreement that included the recipient government's peaceful uses guarantee.

## DEMISE OF THE BARUCH PLAN

Within the U.S. government it had long been recognized that, at some time, the amount of special fissionable material produced and accumulated for nuclear weapons would be so great that no

[11] Joint Committee on Atomic Energy, *Atomic Energy Legislation through 91st Cong., 2d Sess.* (Washington, D.C.: JCAE, 1972), pp. 252, 255.

system of inspection could assure a satisfactory degree of accountability for past production. When that time arrived, the goal of
eliminating nuclear weapons from national arsenals with reasonable assurance of compliance by all powers possessing such weapons would become merely an expression of hope, rather than a
realistic arms control measure. Thereafter, the nuclear-weapon
powers would have to retain some nuclear weapons as part of their
arsenals, even under a large-scale nuclear disarmament scheme.

President Eisenhower's Atoms for Peace speech to the United
Nations did not specifically state that the day had arrived when
total accountability for the production of special fissionable material was unrealistic, but it unmistakably implied such a development. Soviet statements over the next few months contained the
same implications. However, both governments hesitated to state
directly that elimination of nuclear weapons was no longer a
realistic possibility in view of the propaganda impact of "ban the
bomb."

Nevertheless, in private meetings of the Subcommittee of Five
of the UN Disarmament Commission from May 13 to June 22,
1954, the United States moved away from the Baruch proposals.
This step was first embodied in a paper outlining an international
control organization for both conventional and nuclear disarmament with far less authority than the control organ proposed in
the Baruch Plan. The U.S. representative stated that the control
organ and safeguards system envisaged in the paper "would be as
applicable to a program based upon the Soviet Union concepts as
sketched over the past seven years, as it is to the U.S. program."[12]

Over a year later, on May 10, 1955, the Soviet representative
stated: "[T]here are possibilities beyond the reach of international control for evading this control and for organising the clandestine manufacture of atomic and hydrogen weapons, even if there is
a formal agreement on international control. In such a situation,
the security of the States signatories to the international convention cannot be guaranteed, since the possibility would be open to
a potential aggressor to accumulate stocks of atomic and hydrogen
weapons for a surprise atomic attack on peace-loving States."[13]

[12] UN Document DC/SC.1/PV 9, May 25, 1954, in United Nations Disarmament
Commission, *Official Records: Supplement for April, May and June 1954*, pp. 5, 6.

[13] Philip Noel-Baker, *The Arms Race* (London: Stevens, 1958), p. 225.

This Soviet change of policy was a belated response to the earlier statements of the U.S. and U.K. representatives virtually abandoning the Baruch Plan.[14]

## DRAFTING THE SAFEGUARDS PROVISIONS OF THE IAEA STATUTE

### First Stage: Without the Soviet Union

In early 1954, following the Atoms for Peace proposal, there was a series of secret communications between the U.S. and Soviet governments, but no progress was made toward forming the IAEA.[15] Thereafter, the United States decided that negotiations among the states principally involved in nuclear energy should commence without the participation of the Soviet Union. The states principally involved were the United States, the United Kingdom, Canada, France, Belgium, South Africa, Australia, and Portugal. This group included all non-Communist states which were then producing uranium.

In March 1955 Morehead Patterson, the U.S. representative, submitted to the negotiating group a draft of a proposed IAEA Statute using some of the nomenclature of an earlier British draft but differing widely in substance from anything suggested in earlier international discussions. The U.S. proposal, with relatively few changes, developed into a draft which was submitted to the Soviet Union on July 29, 1955, and, with minor changes, was made available for comment to the eighty-four members of the UN or its specialized agencies on August 22, 1955, the last day of the first Atoms for Peace Conference in Geneva.[16]

In preparing its draft, the United States deliberately set about to allay Soviet fears and to lay the groundwork for the Soviet Union's participation in the negotiations. The two areas most likely to give rise to controversy were the establishment of the machinery to control the organization, including the voting formu-

---

[14] Sir Philip Noel-Baker told the author that his conclusion had been confirmed by discussions with the highest officials in the Kremlin.

[15] The communications were by mutual agreement made public on October 6, 1956 (State Department Press Release 527).

[16] Paul C. Szasz, *The Law and Practices of the International Atomic Energy Agency*, IAEA Legal Series 7 (Vienna: IAEA, 1970), pp. 28, 29.

la, and the safeguards provisions. The machinery which the United States proposed in effect assured control of the organization by the states "most advanced" in nuclear energy.

The United States developed the concept of IAEA "projects." States wishing to obtain assistance from the Agency in developing the peaceful uses of nuclear energy would apply for a project. After approval of a project, the applicant state would submit to the safeguards necessary to assure that the nuclear material involved would be used only for peaceful purposes. This meant that the obligations of a state to submit to safeguards would not arise from membership in the Agency, but would take effect only if it applied for and received Agency assistance. States with large nuclear resources presumably would not request Agency assistance and, therefore, would not be subject to the Agency safeguards system. This concept of Agency projects was essential to the establishment of an IAEA because the states with nuclear weapon programs would never have joined if participation had subjected their programs to Agency scrutiny. Despite this limitation, the Agency would be in a position to develop safeguards machinery which might be expanded if a disarmament agreement were reached in the future.[17]   Later drafts of the IAEA Statute permitted application of Agency safeguards "at the request of the parties, to operations under any bilateral or multilateral arrangement, or at the request of a state, to any of that state's activities in the field of atomic energy." The most important safeguards activities of the IAEA have stemmed from such voluntary requests, rather than from Agency projects. However, this added potential did not change the fundamental principle that Agency safeguards would be applied only if a state consented, either by requesting Agency assistance or by specifically requesting the application of safeguards. The proposed scope of IAEA safeguards shows that the United States was no longer insisting on a universal system of control over nuclear material but would find useful a safeguards system applicable to only a small fraction of the total of such material. "This limited concept of controls, of course, constituted an abandonment of the bold Baruch Plan."[18]

A corollary of equal importance related to the extent to which

17 *Ibid.,* p. 539. For a fuller account see Bernhard G. Bechhoefer, "Negotiating the Statute of the IAEA," *International Organization* 13 (1959):50-51.

18 Szasz, *Law and Practices,* p. 585.

a system of safeguards was to be elaborated in the IAEA Statute. Several of the negotiating groups took the position that the Statute should merely set forth (as in Article II) the objective of safeguards: namely, to ensure that nuclear material provided by the Agency or under its control would not be used in such a way as to further any military purpose. This necessarily implied the application of a safeguards system as part of any contract for an Agency project. On the other hand, if the Statute avoided any elaboration of the safeguards system until contracts were drafted covering individual projects, states unfamiliar with atomic energy matters could complain that they were induced to enter the Agency under false pretenses. They would have no warning that, in order to secure Agency assistance, they must submit to extensive Agency inspection.

At this stage of the negotiations, a compromise was reached between the two viewpoints. The elaboration in the Statute of specific safeguards was sufficient notice that states obtaining project assistance would have to submit to them. However, the Statute's safeguards provisions would have to be further developed in order to provide an adequate system. Any attempt to specify the safeguards in greater detail at this stage was deferred, for two reasons: first, time was short and the negotiating team's manpower resources were strained; second, it was feared that, by attacking the safeguards system, the Soviet Union would reap propaganda benefits among states such as India, where the entire safeguards concept was unpopular.[19]

A further U.S. move towards the Soviet position was to make the safeguards provisions in substance, and even in some of the wording, extremely close to the Soviet proposals of June 11, 1947. The Western nations could not have suggested these safeguards provisions without abandoning their main objection to the 1947 Soviet proposals, which was that they failed to provide for an international control organization which would be able "not only to detect violations, but also to prevent and correct them."[20] Thus, the IAEA Statute left the question of forcible sanctions primarily to the United Nations or to a state or group of states. The bridge-building efforts were successful. On October 1, 1955,

[19] Bernhard G. Bechhoefer and Eric Stein, "Atoms for Peace," *Michigan Law Review* 55 (1957):766.

[20] See n. 4 above.

the Soviet government declared that "the draft statute with certain amendments could be used as a basis for drawing up the IAEA
Charter."

### Second Stage: With the Soviet Union

*Working Level Meeting.*  The next stage of the negotiation of the
Agency Statute was the so-called Working Level Meeting of Twelve
States. The eight Western-oriented states participating in the first
stage were joined by the Soviet Union, Czechoslovakia, India, and
Brazil. Despite the formal suggestion by the Soviet Union that
control be accomplished "with due observation of sovereign
rights," this phase of the negotiations produced an elaboration and
strengthening of the safeguards provisions, making possible later
growth of the system. The IAEA's rights were spelled out in
connection with chemical reprocessing of irradiated material and
disposition of special fissionable material recovered during chemical reprocessing. A provision, without precedent in previous international agreements, permitted IAEA inspectors to "have access at
all times to all places, persons and data necessary to account for
special fissionable materials and fissionable products." However, as
a concession to states objecting to the stringency of the safeguards
system, the full range of control measures foreseen in the Statute
would not automatically be applied to Agency projects and other
safeguarded arrangements; only such measures as were relevant
and included in an agreement with the Agency were to be used. [21]
Thus the presence of the Soviet Union in the negotiations did not
result in a weakening of the safeguards provisions.

*Conference of Eighty-One States.*  An international conference of
eighty-one states and observers from seven UN specialized agencies
met at UN headquarters in New York from September 20 to
October 26, 1956, and unanimously adopted as the IAEA Statute
the draft approved at the Working Level Meeting, with relatively
minor changes. The safeguards provision proved to be the most
controversial feature of the Statute.

Two joint amendments were submitted by Ceylon, Egypt,
India, and Indonesia. [22]  One would have removed source material

---

[21] Szasz, *Law and Practices,* p. 33.

[22] Ambassador J. Wadsworth, "Report on the Conference of the Statute of the
IAEA" (unpublished manuscript, 1956), pp. 4, 5.

(natural uranium and thorium) from Agency accountability; the other would have crippled the Agency's ability to prevent the accumulation of national stockpiles of weapons-grade fissionable materials produced as byproducts in Agency-assisted projects. The sponsors of the amendment claimed that this curtailment of Agency authority was necessary to prevent burdensome, unnecessary, and possibly dangerous interference by the Agency in the economic growth of member states, especially the poor and undeveloped members most in need of Agency assistance. The Soviet Union supported these amendments.

Following an extensive debate, Canada, the United Kingdom, and the United States introduced two clarifying and qualifying amendments. One clearly limited accountability for source materials to those used or produced in Agency projects. The other made it explicit that in deciding upon retention by member states of byproduct fissionable material or its deposit with the Agency, the Agency should be guided by only two criteria—whether the material was to be used for peaceful purposes and whether it was to be used in such a way as not to endanger health and safety. As the result of willingness on both sides to negotiate differences, agreement was achieved on unimpaired and textually improved safeguards provisions, which were unanimously approved by the conference.

*Report of the Preparatory Commission.* The foundation for a safeguards program was laid in the Report of the Preparatory Commission submitted to the First IAEA General Conference in September 1957. The Report set forth the following principles of implementation:

(a) The safeguard procedures should keep pace with the development of the Agency's activities, starting with problems related to the transport and storage of source and special fissionable materials and extending to the use of these materials in Agency-sponsored projects and to their subsequent treatment;

(b) The safeguard procedures should be adapted to the specific character of each individual project and the degree of potential risk of material diversion. The safeguards should ensure adequate accountability in accordance with the statutory provisions, including both physical security and material accountability measures to the extent required.[23]

[23] *Report of the Preparatory Commission of the IAEA* (New York: IAEA, 1957), pp. 21, 22.

This Report marked the last step toward an effective IAEA safeguards system that was to be taken for a number of years.

## PAUSE

After adoption of the Preparatory Commission Report by the First IAEA General Conference, the Soviet Union took the position that all further development of the safeguards system should take place in the agreements for its implementation. In other words, the Agency was not to carry on further safeguards planning until there was some indication that it would in fact have safeguards duties.[24]

By the time the IAEA was established in October 1957, it was clear that, in its early years, the Agency would have no substantial safeguards functions. The United States had already entered into a large number of Agreements for Cooperation with individual states and groups of states to furnish limited amounts of nuclear material for peaceful uses by such states. Transfers of material under these agreements would be directly from the United States to the cooperating state. All the agreements provided for substantially the same safeguards as those envisaged in the IAEA Statute, but they were to be administered by the U.S. Atomic Energy Commission.

Development and use of this U.S.-administered safeguards machinery diminished the likelihood of the IAEA's obtaining custody of special fissionable material or becoming a major supplier of nuclear assistance. That possibility was virtually eliminated by legislation governing participation in the IAEA which assured that the price of nuclear material to cooperating nations would be less if they dealt directly with the United States than if they obtained U.S. material through the IAEA.[25] The United Kingdom and the Soviet Union also entered into limited bilateral agreements with a few states to furnish nuclear material directly to them. One of the main functions of Agency safeguards—safeguarding material in its own custody or supplied by it to Agency projects—was thus severely truncated, although the United States had indicated its intention to substitute gradually the IAEA for the United States as the authority to administer safeguards.

[24] State Department Press Release 527, October 6, 1956, pp. 28-30.
[25] IAEA Participation Act, P.L. 85-177 (71 Stat. at Large 458).

At the same time, the other major IAEA safeguards function—accounting for nuclear material in projects where one or more states had requested the Agency to assume responsibility for safeguards—was slow to develop. There were two main reasons for this, both apparent at the end of 1957. First, it would be a number of years before nuclear power could compete economically with power generated from conventional fuel sources. Moreover, the breakthrough to economic nuclear power would come with large generating plants located in industrial areas. The most important of these areas would probably be the United States, the United Kingdom, and the Soviet Union, where the IAEA would have no safeguards functions unless they were requested by the respective countries. The other important area would be Western Europe, where the industrialized states had already established their own organization, the European Atomic Energy Community (Euratom), to facilitate nuclear cooperation on a regional basis. Euratom was given responsibility to administer analogous safeguards under the Agreements for Cooperation between it and the United States. Thus the only nuclear operations in the smaller states for a number of years would be research reactors. Because of the small quantities of special fissionable material involved in most of these reactors, safeguards functions would be minimal.

The second reason why an extensive IAEA safeguards program lost momentum arose out of the disarmament negotiations. In the discussions of the Subcommittee of the Disarmament Commission in 1957, agreement seemed possible between the Soviet Union and the Western powers on a package of proposals, including a prohibition of further nuclear explosions, a limited reduction of conventional armaments, and progress toward a halt in further production of special fissionable material for use in nuclear weapons (described as the "cutoff"). The last agreement would have required extensive safeguards machinery in states with nuclear weapons along the lines provided in the IAEA Statute, and it would have been logical for the Agency to perform such functions. In early 1957 it seemed possible that the United States and the Soviet Union would agree on the immediate prohibition of tests of nuclear weapons, conditional only on progress towards a cutoff of production of nuclear material. On August 29, 1957, however, the Western powers submitted a much broader package of measures which were described as "inseparable," a package which the Soviet

Union rejected emphatically. Thus the one arms control measure which would have required rapid development of extensive safeguards machinery for accounting for nuclear material disappeared from the disarmament negotiations.[26]

The emphasis on safeguards by the United States was never welcomed by the more powerful non-nuclear-weapon states, particularly India. Obvious propaganda benefits accrued to the Soviet Union in opposing further development of an IAEA safeguards system in the years immediately after establishment of the Agency. Moreover, Soviet opposition was completely consistent with the position taken in the Report of the Preparatory Commission that "the safeguards procedures should keep pace with the development of the Agency activities."[27] Therefore it was no surprise when, in 1958, the Soviet Union and Indian delegates to the IAEA attempted to exclude from the IAEA budget any provision for staffing the safeguards function. While the United States mustered sufficient votes to defeat this effort, progress toward IAEA safeguards was minimal for several years.[28]

However, in 1958 Japan applied for Agency assistance in obtaining nuclear fuel for a research reactor, thereby agreeing in principle to submit to IAEA safeguards.[29] Despite the nominal extent of the safeguards required, the Japanese request undercut the claims that the IAEA would have no safeguards duties at all to perform for many years.

In 1962, the United States adopted the policy of transferring from its own Atomic Energy Commission to the IAEA the responsibility for administration of safeguards with respect to its bilateral agreements for cooperation in the peaceful uses of atomic energy. The United Kingdom and Canada adopted similar policies. However, U.S. agreements for cooperation with the six members of Euratom—Belgium, France, the Federal Republic of Germany, Italy, Luxembourg, and the Netherlands—were not included within the transfer policy. Instead, in an effort to strengthen Euratom,

26 United Nations, General Assembly, *Official Records,* 12th Sess., Annex Agenda Item 24 (September 23, 1957), p. 10. See also President's Special Committee on Disarmament Problems, "USSR Note to Japanese Government," December 5, 1957.

27 *Report of the Preparatory Commission of the IAEA,* par. 84, p. 22.

28 Allan D. McKnight, *Atomic Safeguards: A Study in International Verification,* UNITAR Series 5 (New York: United Nations, 1971), p. 45; George W. Keaton and George Swartzenberg, *The Year Book of World Affairs* (London: Stevens, 1965), p. 65.

29 Szasz, *Law and Practices,* p. 420; McKnight, *Atomic Safeguards,* p. 46.

the United States adopted a "fold-in" policy whereby bilateral agreements with Euratom member states were not renewed and nuclear cooperation with these states was continued through the Euratom supply channel. Since over 70 percent of the total amount of nuclear material supplied to foreign countries went to the Euratom members, the result of the fold-in policy was to expand the coverage of the Euratom safeguards system even more than the IAEA system, at a time when Euratom's own members were less than enthusiastic about further development of that institution.[30]

Progress towards a significant IAEA safeguards system during the next decade can be measured in two ways: by the continuous development and refinement of the documents setting forth safeguards procedures and by the assignment to the IAEA of increasingly complex safeguards functions, primarily as a result of a U.S. initiative. This progress was greatly facilitated by a shift in the attitude of the Soviet Union from opposition to cooperation.

## DEVELOPMENT OF IAEA SAFEGUARDS PROCEDURES

The IAEA safeguards system was not established until March 30, 1961, when the Board of Governors approved an instrument which became known as the First Safeguards Document.[31] The complex negotiations leading to this document commenced when a Secretariat draft was submitted almost two years earlier.[32] The First Safeguards Document was followed by the so-called Inspectors Document, which prescribed procedures for the selection of Agency inspectors and for the conduct of inspections.

In May 1962 the IAEA Director General brought to the attention of the Board of Governors the inadequacies of the First Safeguards Document, and in particular the fact that it was not applicable to large reactors with capacity over 100 megawatts (thermal), thus excluding power reactors. After extremely complex negotiations, on February 26, 1964, the Board gave its final approval to an extension to reactors above 100 megawatts of the system contained in the First Safeguards Document. The system as

[30] Mason Willrich, *Non-Proliferation Treaty: Framework for Nuclear Arms Control* (Charlottesville, Va: Michie, 1969), pp. 63, 64.

[31] IAEA, INFCIRC/26, March 30, 1961.

[32] Szasz, *Law and Practices*, p. 551.

extended was substantially unchanged except for a provision for continuous inspection of the large reactors.[33]

Until the extension of the Agency's safeguards system to large reactors, the Soviet Union had voted consistently against any step to develop a safeguards system. The first signal of a change occurred in June 1963, when it abstained from the Board action which provisionally approved the extension of the First Safeguards Document.[34] Commencing with this change in position, the Soviet representative to the IAEA, Dr. Vasily Emelyanov, and the U.S. representative, Dr. Henry D. Smyth, generally agreed that negotiations be kept on a sound technical and business-like basis.

When the extension was approved, the Board realized that further revision was required, and it established a Working Group under the chairmanship of Dr. Gunnar Randers of Norway to review the safeguards applicable to large power reactors. By the time that the work of this group was completed, the atmosphere of the negotiations had markedly improved, and the Soviet Union was strongly supporting improvement of the system. The IAEA General Conference and the Board of Governors adopted the Working Group recommendations almost unanimously. In April 1965 the revised and greatly improved document known as The Agency's Safeguards System (1965) came into effect.

In June 1966 the Board of Governors adopted provisions for extending safeguards to chemical reprocessing plants;[35] in June 1968 it adopted provisions for safeguarding nuclear material in conversion and fuel fabrication plants.[36] Thus far, the development of IAEA safeguards had been confined mainly to expanding the initial system to cover more of the principal facilities throughout the nuclear fuel cycle. At this writing specific procedures are lacking only for enrichment plants, but proposals are pending to extend the system to them as well.

The next step was the revision of the entire system to meet the requirements of the Non-Proliferation and Tlatelolco treaties. In April 1970 the IAEA Board of Governors established the Safeguards Committee to advise it on the content of the safeguards agreements under the Non-Proliferation Treaty. Primarily through

[33] IAEA, INFCIRC/26/Add. 1, February 26, 1961.

[34] McKnight, *Atomic Safeguards,* p. 62.

[35] IAEA, INFCIRC/66/Rev. 1.

[36] IAEA, Annex II to INFCIRC/66/Rev. 2.

hard work and a desire to reach an agreement, by March 10, 1971, the Committee had successfully resolved the many controversial problems which faced it. As a result, the Board of Governors approved the Committee's work, in the form of a set of provisions, "The Structure and Content of Agreements Between the Agency and States Required in Connection with the Treaty on the Non-Proliferation of Nuclear Weapons."[37] The Board has instructed the Director General to use these provisions as a basis for negotiating safeguards agreements between the IAEA and non-nuclear-weapon parties to the NPT. A detailed analysis of the Negotiating Instructions is contained in Chapter 4 of this volume.

## EXPANSION OF IAEA SAFEGUARDS FUNCTIONS

The development of improved safeguards procedures and techniques was paralleled by an increase in the Agency's safeguards tasks. As previously noted, in 1962 the United States adopted a policy of transferring to the IAEA the responsibility for administering safeguards with respect to its bilateral agreements for nuclear cooperation with countries outside Euratom, as these agreements were renewed. The safeguards budget increased from less than $20,000 in 1959 to $358,860 in 1965. By 1965 forty-six reactors in twenty-one states were under IAEA safeguards. However, all of these were research reactors using and producing only small amounts of special fissionable material. Therefore, the safeguards techniques were relatively simple.[38]

A major step occurred in 1964, when the United States agreed to place under Agency safeguards the Yankee Power Reactor, a 175-megawatt, light-water, enriched uranium reactor located in Massachusetts. The United Kingdom shortly thereafter invited Agency inspection of two identical gas-cooled, natural uranium reactors. A much more difficult safeguards task devolved upon the IAEA when the United States agreed in 1966 that spent fuel from the Yankee reactor would be subject to Agency safeguards during its chemical reprocessing at the plant of Nuclear Fuel Services in New York.

When the IAEA first undertook to inspect power reactors in

---

[37] IAEA, INFCIRC/153, May 1971.
[38] International Atomic Energy Document GC(9)/299, June 1965, p. 43.

1965, it had in its employ only eight inspectors. While inspecting a power reactor does not require a large number of personnel, the inspection of a chemical reprocessing plant is quite another matter. The second inspection of the Nuclear Fuel Services facility in 1969, which was partly a training exercise, took sixteen full-time inspectors six weeks.[39] In 1971, the IAEA had some twenty-five full-time inspectors, with other skilled personnel available for individual assignments, and the budgeted cost of safeguards had increased to $1,762,000.[40] As of June 30, 1971, the IAEA was applying safeguards to nine power reactors, sixty-six other reactors, ten conversion plants, fuel fabrication plants, and chemical reprocessing plants, and eighty-five other separate accountability areas.[41]

## ADVENT OF ECONOMIC NUCLEAR POWER

Until the early 1960s it appeared that future production of special fissionable material in civilian nuclear programs would remain quite small in relation to the amount contained in existing weapons stockpiles. Then in December 1963 the Jersey Central Power and Light Company, an investor-owned utility, announced its intention to build a 560-megawatt power reactor at Oyster Creek. Jersey Central contracted to purchase this reactor from the manufacturer without any financial assistance from the U.S. government solely because, on the basis of the bid price, it promised to produce cheaper electricity than a power plant of similar size using fossil fuel. This dramatic event triggered a vast increase in nuclear power plant orders on a worldwide basis. The deadline for establishment of a functioning worldwide system of accountability for nuclear material has thus moved up and is now estimated as somewhere between 1980 and 1985.[42] Unless a comprehensive

---

[39] The first inspection, which was more of a training course than an inspection, utilized more observers than the total plant personnel (T. C. Runion and J. R. Clark, "The First International Inspection of a Chemical Processing Plant," unpublished talk to the Atomic Industrial Forum, March 1968).

[40] McKnight, *Atomic Safeguards,* pp. 56, 57; IAEA, *Annual Report, 1 July 1970-30 June 1971,* GC(XV)/455 (Vienna: 1971), p. 58.

[41] IAEA, *Annual Report, 1 July 1970-30 June 1971,* p. 47.

[42] David Wainhouse et al., *Arms Control Agreements* (Baltimore: Johns Hopkins Press, 1968), p. 14; McKnight, *Atomic Safeguards,* xiii, xiv; Leonard Beaton and John Maddox, *The Spread of Nuclear Weapons* (London: Chatto and Windus, 1962), p. x.

safeguards system is fully operational by that time, there seems to be no feasible way to work out an international control system to provide adequate assurance that a number of states are not developing nuclear weapons. In other words, we would have not only the possibility but the probability of "proliferation unlimited."

## THE MLF AS AN OBSTACLE TO THE NPT

In August 1963 the United States, the Soviet Union, and the United Kingdom at long last reached agreement on a Treaty Banning Nuclear Weapons Tests in the Atmosphere, in Outer Space, and Under Water. By that time it had become apparent that limiting test explosions would not be sufficient to prevent proliferation of nuclear weapons. Therefore, the more important effort in preventing such proliferation would be the direct approach taken in the Non-Proliferation Treaty.[43] The positive momentum imparted to the arms control negotiations by the test ban treaty and by the statements of both the United States and the Soviet Union that the test ban was a first step toward meeting the problem of nuclear proliferation appeared to indicate early agreement on the next step—the Non-Proliferation Treaty. Moreover, the rapid increase in civilian nuclear power clearly established the need for the United States and Soviet Union to accelerate the pace of negotiations toward such a treaty.

Throughout much of the 1960s, however, the United States was engaged in promoting among its allies in Western Europe the so-called Multilateral Nuclear Force (MLF). The MLF proposal involved a nuclear-armed fleet of surface ships, control being shared among the participating NATO countries, with the United States retaining a veto over any decision to launch nuclear weapons. To the Soviet Union, the MLF appeared to grant the Federal Republic of Germany access to nuclear weapons and thereby to create a major security threat.[44] To be sure, the United States went to great lengths to explain the technical arrangements which would prevent Germany from having its finger on the nuclear trigger. However, these technical explanations and the entire concept of the MLF was too complex to be convincing to world

[43] For discussion of the problem see Chalmers Roberts, *The Nuclear Years* (New York: Praeger, 1970), pp. 62-74.

[44] See *ibid.*, pp. 71, 72.

public opinion. Indeed, the MLF appeared to be pure gimmickry to many U.S. allies in the West and even to a large segment of the American public. Unquestionably, the considerable force of the MLF proposals stalled the negotiations on the NPT for several years. Despite a number of promising proposals showing a narrowing of differences, East-West arms control negotiations did not advance toward an NPT until the end of 1966, when the United States finally abandoned its plans for an MLF within the North Atlantic Alliance.

## THE ATTITUDES OF NON-NUCLEAR-WEAPON STATES

On August 24, 1967, the United States and Soviet Union reached agreement on the substance of a draft NPT, except for Article III dealing with safeguards. On January 18, 1968, the United States and the Soviet Union presented identical drafts, including Article III, to the Eighteen Nation Committee on Disarmament. These drafts were discussed in the United Nations, and the United States and the Soviet Union agreed to incorporate into the final texts some of the most important changes requested by the non-nuclear-weapon states.[45] These changes did not, however, touch the safeguards article.

Regarding safeguards, the strongest objection of the non-nuclear-weapon states was that the NPT would create an unequal and discriminatory system under which only states without nuclear weapons would be required to submit all their peaceful nuclear facilities to IAEA inspection, while the nuclear facilities of states with nuclear weapons remained free of international safeguards. To meet this objection, the United States declared its intention, when safeguards were applied under the Treaty in non-nuclear-weapon states, to "permit the International Atomic Energy Agency to apply its safeguards to all nuclear activities in the United States—excluding only those with direct national security significance."[46] The United Kingdom made a parallel policy declaration.

[45] Willrich, *Non-Proliferation Treaty*, pp. 63, 64.

[46] Address by President Johnson, December 2, 1967, *Department of State Bulletin* 57 (1967): 862, 863; *Documents on Disarmament, 1967*, U.S. Arms Control and Disarmament Agency pub. 46 (Washington, D.C.: U.S. Arms Control and Disarmament Agency, 1968), pp. 613, 615.

Another objection of the non-nuclear-weapon states was based on fears that commercial secrets and other proprietary information concerning civilian nuclear processes and facilities would be compromised by international inspections. This objection was met through statements of intention to implement the IAEA safeguards system in a manner that would minimize the dangers of disclosures of proprietary information.

Probably the most important concession made to the non-nuclear-weapon states took the form of strengthened statements in the Preamble of the NPT and in Article VI regarding negotiations on measures to achieve "at the earliest possible date the cessation of the nuclear arms race" and "effective measures in the direction of nuclear disarmament." Other substantial concessions to them were contained in Article IV, which accords all parties "the inalienable right" to develop nuclear energy for peaceful purposes and, to that end, the right to participate in "the fullest possible exchange" of materials, equipment and information; in another concession Article V requires the nuclear-weapon parties to make available, under certain international procedures, the "potential benefits of any peaceful applications of nuclear explosions."

Throughout the discussions in the United Nations the Soviet Union maintained simply that it would not accept any international inspection of its peaceful nuclear activities, despite the U.S. and U.K. offers. Therefore, the choice was between a treaty which applied safeguards on peaceful nuclear activities in a discriminatory way (in addition to being inequitable with regard to the obligation not to acquire nuclear weapons) or no treaty at all. The non-nuclear-weapon states accepted, many grudgingly, the former alternative, and on June 12, 1968, the UN General Assembly adopted a resolution commending the Treaty by a vote of 95 in favor, 4 opposed, and 21 abstentions.[47]

The restraint which marked the UN deliberations on the NPT was absent in the so-called Conference of Non-Nuclear-Weapon States, which took place in Geneva from August 29 to September 28, 1968. It resulted from a resolution passed by the UN General Assembly in November 1966 expressing impatience with the slow progress in the negotiations of the Eighteen Nation Committee on Disarmament. Allan McKnight, the first Inspector General of the

[47] Willrich, *Non-Proliferation Treaty*, pp. 64, 102.

IAEA, characterized this Conference as "a forum for the non-nuclear-weapon States to express their resentment, first, at the Mosaic manner in which the two superpowers had produced the Non-Proliferation Treaty, and second, at the absence in the treaty or outside it of any real 'balance of obligations' to be assumed by the nuclear-weapon States and particularly by the United States and the USSR."[48]

During the Conference of the Non-Nuclear-Weapon States a number of proposals were advanced which could have destroyed the basic accords which made possible the Non-Proliferation Treaty. Some states insisted that safeguards be imposed on the nuclear-weapon states, as well as on the non-weapon states. Some wished iron-clad security assurances from the nuclear-weapon powers far beyond those already provided. Others demanded an immediate international program of peaceful nuclear explosions, presumably financed by the nuclear-weapon states, for the benefit of the non-weapon states. Still others complained of the composition of the Board of Governors of the IAEA and actually succeeded in obtaining the eventual modification of the IAEA Statute to gain greater representation on the Board for developing countries. Fortunately, the Conference's bark was greater than its bite. The actual resolutions did not substantively impair the progress achieved in the NPT and the IAEA toward a safeguards system. Nevertheless, it became clear that unless the Non-Proliferation Treaty were followed by progress toward limitation of existing nuclear weapon systems, thus reducing the menace of nuclear war, the life span of the NPT was likely to be relatively short.


## CONCLUSION

Our historical narrative shows the correctness of the view that, in an area of negotiation involving technical issues, progress comes first through political accords and then through their implementation by increasingly complex technical agreements. It would follow that further progress toward an international system of safeguards, which has the essential characteristics of credibility

---

[48] McKnight, *Atomic Safeguards,* p. 86.

and acceptability suggested by Dr. Smyth in Chapter 1, must take place through building on the areas of agreement already attained.

A pessimistic, but oversimplified, evaluation of the results of twenty-five years of international negotiations on nuclear safeguards would be that agreement on a system was obtained only by drastic, though gradual, reduction in its scope—that safeguards will apply to only a small fraction of the special fissionable material potentially useful for weapons purposes, and that, even in this limited area, international controls will not prevent diversions of nuclear material but will merely create a capability for detecting such diversions.

Such an evaluation overlooks the changing factual circumstances which underlay the negotiations. For a number of reasons, the initial safeguards system proposed by the United States and to a lesser degree that proposed by the Soviet Union were unnecessarily broad. Uranium and thorium are not rare resources, as was supposed in 1946, and therefore these source materials could not readily be subjected to the strict accountability contemplated in the Baruch Plan. Technological developments have permitted somewhat less intrusive safeguards techniques more satisfactory not only to the Communist states but to many other countries. Thus the reduction in scope of international safeguards arose from a reappraisal of the requirements for an effective system, coupled with a recognition of the urgency of adopting an acceptable system prior to the vast expansion of nuclear power programs, with the resultant production of rapidly increasing quantities of plutonium in widely scattered regions. In short, the reduction in scope of the safeguards system represented not a capitulation, but a realistic reappraisal.

An optimistic evaluation of the twenty-five years of negotiation, on the other hand, would begin with the fact that the United States and the Soviet Union have reached agreement on the objective of lessening the danger of nuclear war. This underlying accord has been slowly but steadily translated into concrete actions calculated to attain a shared objective. Further, the nuclear-weapon states have been able to convince most of the non-nuclear-weapon states that specific steps toward nuclear arms control can lead to a safer world for all.

Any such euphoric description of the negotiations must be

qualified by the fact that the agreement of the non-nuclear-weapon states to the Non-Proliferation Treaty (as previously to the Limited Nuclear Test Ban Treaty) expressly depends on further steps by the nuclear-weapon powers to limit their own nuclear capabilities. Therefore, both the NPT and the safeguards system which the IAEA is developing are steps toward a much broader future goal. It is hoped that increasing comprehension and acceptance of such broad goals within the world community may permit progress toward an international safeguards system which is sufficiently rapid to keep pace with the inevitable worldwide dispersion of enormous amounts of material with nuclear explosive potential.

# CHAPTER 3

# Worldwide Nuclear Industry

## MASON WILLRICH

### INTRODUCTION

We are now in the early years of a major technological innovation in the production of electric power. As a result of large research and development efforts sustained in several nations for the past two decades, a variety of nuclear power reactors are available commercially for the generation of electricity. The world's operational nuclear power capacity was only 16,000 megawatts in 1970. It is forecast at about 300,000 megawatts by 1980, which is roughly equivalent to the entire electric generating capacity of the United States in 1970. Though concentrated in industrially advanced areas, this use of nuclear energy will not be confined to any geographic region, level of economic development, or political ideology.

In generating electricity with nuclear energy, heat derived from fission in nuclear fuel is generally used to convert water into steam.[1] The steam is then used to drive large turbine-generators.[2]

---

[1] Gas turbines are incorporated into some nuclear power plant designs, but they have not been widely adopted thus far.

[2] Direct conversion of the energy released in the fission process into electricity does not appear practical as a method of producing large amounts of electric power for

A nuclear power plant is in many respects comparable to a conventional plant which obtains steam by burning one of the fossil fuels—coal, oil, or natural gas. Regardless of the fuel used as the primary energy source, the electricity produced in both nuclear and conventional generating plants is fed into the same transmission and distribution systems.

The quantitative difference in energy content between nuclear and fossil fuel is enormous. Fission of one gram of uranium or plutonium produces the same amount of heat as combustion of more than 3 tons of coal or nearly 700 gallons of fuel oil. A handful of uranium pellets used as fuel in a nuclear reactor produces the same amount of electric power as 85 tons of coal, 15,000 gallons of fuel oil, or nearly two million cubic feet of natural gas. Because of the compactness of nuclear fuel, its transportation costs—often a decisive factor in the choice among competing fossil fuels—are small. The cost of nuclear fuel can thus be relatively uniform throughout the world, whereas costs of the fossil fuels will vary widely. However, unlike the fossil fuels, nuclear fuel requires intensive processing through a complex sequence of interrelated steps, both preceding and following energy production in a reactor. These steps comprise what is called the nuclear fuel cycle.

The purpose of this chapter is to provide the basic information necessary for an understanding of the security problems—both international and internal or domestic—arising out of the development of civilian nuclear industry. The technological and economic characteristics of the nuclear fuel cycle are outlined, the security implications are set forth, and finally, the present and projected worldwide distribution of nuclear resources and industrial capabilities is described.[3]

---

commercial use, nor does direct conversion of energy derived from other sources. Fusion perhaps holds the greatest promise in this regard. However, the scientific feasibility of controlled fusion has not yet been demonstrated, although progress has been made toward that goal recently.

[3] The data used in this chapter are drawn mainly from my book, *Global Politics of Nuclear Energy* (New York: Praeger, 1971), pp. 11-37, 67-73, and extensive source notes. These data have been updated by reference to *The Nuclear Industry—1971*, WASH 1174-71 (Washington, D.C.: AEC, 1971); and *Hearings on AEC Authorizing Legislation for Fiscal Year 1973 before the Joint Committee on Atomic Energy*, 92d Cong., 2d sess. (1972).

## TECHNOLOGICAL AND ECONOMIC CHARACTERISTICS

### Fissionable Material

The essential ingredient of any nuclear capability, whether for civilian or military purposes, is fissionable material. When the nucleus of a fissionable atom absorbs a neutron, it has a high probability of splitting, or fissioning, into two smaller nuclei, with the consequent release of a significant amount of energy and the emission of two or three neutrons. The emitted neutrons may be absorbed by other fissionable nuclei, the result being a sustained nuclear chain reaction.

Throughout this book the term "special fissionable material" means uranium enriched in the isotope 235, uranium enriched in the isotope 233, and plutonium of any isotopic composition. Thus, we have adopted the definitions contained in Article XX of the Statute of the IAEA. Special fissionable material, as we use the term, has basically the same meaning as "special nuclear material" in the U.S. Atomic Energy Act. The two special fissionable materials of primary interest are uranium-235 and plutonium-239. These are the fissionable isotopes of uranium and plutonium that are most desirable and commonly used both in the fuels for nuclear power reactors and in the explosive materials for nuclear weapons.

The element uranium, as it occurs in nature, is composed primarily of the isotopes uranium-235 and uranium-238, signifying that the nucleus of the latter contains three more neutrons and hence has a slightly larger atomic mass than the former. The natural element contains 99.3 percent uranium-238 and 9.7 percent uranium-235. Thus uranium-235 is an extremely small fraction of natural uranium. The nucleus of an uranium-238 atom has a high probability of absorbing a neutron without subsequent fission. Neutron absorption causes a series of nuclear transmutations in uranium-238. The end result is an atom of plutonium-239, a synthetic element that is fissionable. Other isotopes, plutonium-240, 241, and 242, are produced in varying quantities by similar nuclear processes. Thus, when uranium is used as nuclear fuel to generate electric power, plutonium is an important byproduct. The problem of plutonium-240, which fissions spontaneously, is discussed below. Thorium is the only other important source of fissionable material that occurs in nature. Thorium-232 will convert upon neutron capture into uranium-233, a special fissionable material. Either uranium-235 or plutonium might be used to start the conversion of thorium into special fissionable material, but uranium-235 is preferred. Thus, a thorium-232-uranium-233 fuel cycle parallels the uranium-238-plutonium fuel cycle.

## The Nuclear Fuel Cycle

As previously noted, electricity is the end product of the fission process which occurs in nuclear fuel in a power reactor. Depending on the type of reactor fuel used, the cycle of operations involved in nuclear generation of electric power includes five or seven major steps. In the case of natural uranium, these steps include mining and milling of uranium ore, fuel element fabrication, fuel irradiation in a reactor, spent fuel reprocessing to separate residual uranium and produced plutonium from radioactive waste products, and recycling or storage of recovered material and storage of radioactive wastes. Enriched fuel requires two additional steps: conversion of uranium into gaseous form and increasing the concentration of uranium-235 atoms above that contained in natural uranium, a process called "enrichment." Each step in the nuclear fuel cycle entails distinctive physical or chemical processes. The required materials and facilities vary in availability and technological complexity.

*Power Reactors.* A number of different components perform basic functions in a nuclear power reactor. A source of neutrons initiates the fission process in nuclear fuel elements. A moderator slows the neutrons released in fission so that they are more likely to cause further fission. A coolant prevents the fuel elements and other reactor components from melting and also removes the heat for use in power generation. Control rods or other control devices made of material that readily absorbs neutrons are used to start, stop, and control the rate of fission during reactor operation.

One major type of power reactor uses as fuel slightly "enriched" uranium, in which the uranium-235 content has been increased to 2 to 5 percent. Another type uses natural uranium containing only 0.7 percent uranium-235. Slightly enriched uranium fuel permits more fissions in a given volume of material than natural uranium. The capital cost of an enriched uranium reactor is less than a natural uranium reactor with a comparable power-generating capacity. However, as described below, enriched uranium fuel is much more difficult and expensive to produce than natural uranium fuel. Reactors which use slightly enriched uranium fuel are now recognized to have an economic advantage over reactors designed to use natural uranium fuel, in most circumstances.

The high-temperature, gas-cooled reactor (HTGR) is another type that has recently become available for commercial use in the generation of electric power. This reactor uses as fuel highly enriched uranium, in which the content of uranium-235 has been increased to over 90 percent. This material is interspersed with thorium, and the valuable byproduct is uranium-233 rather than plutonium.

The fast "breeder" reactor, which is capable of producing more special fissionable material than it consumes, is under intensive development in a number of industrially advanced countries and may become available for commercial use in the 1980s. This type of reactor uses either highly enriched uranium or plutonium as the fuel core. The core is surrounded by a blanket of uranium-238 that is converted in the course of reactor operation into plutonium. The objective is to develop a reactor that can generate electric power economically and at the same time produce a net gain of special fissionable material. Although present reactors using natural or slightly enriched uranium fuel extract only 1 to 2 percent of the energy potentially available in uranium, fast breeder reactors should make it possible to obtain 60 to 90 percent.

A typical nuclear power plant with an electric generating capacity of 1,000 megawatts is estimated to cost (without fuel) more than $300 million. The nuclear steam supply system is the largest single item of hardware, accounting for about 15 to 20 percent of total plant cost. Of course, the total cost of a nuclear plant increases with its size, but the incremental cost of each additional megawatt of plant capacity decreases as plant size increases. A 500-megawatt nuclear plant could cost about 15 percent more per kilowatt than a 1,000-megawatt plant. Moving further down the scale to even smaller reactors, the cost per kilowatt increases even more sharply. Thus, the major economy to be realized in building a nuclear power plant is economy of scale.

Where fossil fuels are available at reasonable cost, the minimum size of an economically competitive nuclear power reactor is generally considered to be in the 500- to 600-megawatt range. Thus, considerations of reliability and economy tend to limit the commercial use of nuclear power plants to geographic areas where a relatively large electric power grid already exists and a rapid increase in demand is anticipated.

*Mining and Milling.* Uranium ore contains uranium in concentrations of only a few kilograms per metric tonne.[4] Following its removal from a mine, the ore is concentrated by mechanical and chemical milling methods to 70 to 80 percent uranium—a product called "yellow-cake." Assured reserves of uranium ore appear adequate to meet worldwide demand. Little prospecting for uranium occurred from the early 1950s to the late 1960s because of the excess capacity of existing mines which were developed initially to meet military requirements on a crash basis. The rapid expansion of civilian nuclear power programs in the late 1960s led to a new round of exploration and drilling activity and a number of fresh discoveries. The price of uranium is not expected to increase substantially through the 1980s. By then, the breeder reactor is expected to reduce requirements for additional uranium.

*Conversion.* In order to produce enriched fuel, yellow-cake is converted into gaseous uranium fluoride, which is then fed into an enrichment plant. A typical conversion plant would cost about $25 million to build. Such a plant would have a capacity of about 5,000 tonnes of uranium per year and would be capable of servicing about 20,000 megawatts of nuclear power plant capacity. Conversion plant sizes vary from 1,500 to 15,000 tonnes, but even a relatively small conversion plant is capable of servicing a substantial nuclear power capacity. Consequently, only a few conversion plants will be needed to meet the world's requirements for feed material for enrichment plants during the 1970s.

*Enrichment.* Uranium enrichment is the most complex and by far the most costly step in the nuclear fuel cycle, accounting for roughly one-third of the fuel costs for a power reactor using slightly enriched fuel. Since isotopes of the same element have

---

[4] Throughout this book the metric system of weights is used. One metric tonne is roughly equivalent to 2,200 pounds or one long English ton.

identical chemical properties, there is no feasible chemical process to increase the content of uranium-235 occurring in natural uranium. Therefore, a physical process is required.

Diffusion of gaseous uranium fluoride through a large number of porous barriers is the only method for uranium enrichment currently in use on an industrial scale. When uranium fluoride gas is diffused through such a barrier, the uranium-235 molecules tend to move through the pores a little faster than the slightly heavier uranium-238 molecules. The amount of enrichment obtained with a single porous barrier is very small because the masses of the two isotopes are so close together. Continuous diffusion through thousands of stages is used to multiply the separative effect to useful proportions. A large number of compressors, driven by electric motors, are needed to compress the uranium fluoride gas so that it will flow through the tiny pores in the barriers.

Gaseous diffusion plants for uranium enrichment are among the largest and most technologically complex industrial facilities in the world. A typical plant would cover about 90 acres and use about 1,300 megawatts of continuous electric power to drive the compressors. In view of the large amount of electric power required, a diffusion plant should be located near a continuous supply of relatively cheap electricity.

A diffusion plant with a capacity of 6,000 to 8,000 tonnes separative work units (SWU)[5] per year may be considered typical for a commercial enrichment process. An 8,000-tonne SWU plant is estimated to cost about $1,200 million to build and $50 million per year to operate. Such a plant could provide enriched fuel for about 80,000 megawatts of nuclear power capacity. Small diffusion plants with capacities of about 400 tonnes have been built, but these plants are not large enough to be commercially competitive.

The gas centrifuge process is another way to enrich uranium.[6]

[5] Any separation job can be described in terms of the quantities of material fed to and withdrawn from the process and of the isotopic assay of each flow stream. This information can be appropriately combined into a single number which quantifies the job by a method of weighing the importance of each quantity and assay involved. The result is a measure of the isotopic separation effort involved and is, by definition, described in terms of separative work units or SWU.

[6] There are a large number of other isotope separation methods. The electromagnetic and jet nozzle methods have received the most attention. Neither of these appears likely to be used for commercial operations in the near future, although recent work on the jet nozzle has yielded some promising results.

The technology required to use this process on an industrial scale is not yet available, but it is under intensive development. In this method gaseous uranium fluoride is injected into a cylinder rotating at exceptionally high speeds. The centrifugal force resulting from the spinning causes the heavier uranium-238 molecules to accumulate farther from the axis of the cylinder than the lighter uranium-235 molecules. Enriched uranium is removed from the inside and depleted uranium from the outside of the spinning centrifuge.

The successful development of gas centrifuge technology would make it possible to meet future worldwide requirements for enriched reactor fuel by constructing a number of smaller enrichment plants instead of adding one or two large diffusion plants. Using the gas centrifuge process, commercial enrichment operations might be feasible in a plant with a capacity as little as 100 tonnes SWU per year. The capital cost of an economical centrifuge plant would be substantially less than the cost of a diffusion plant of economical size, although, of course, the output would also be less. Operating costs of a centrifuge plant would also be much less, primarily because the electric power required per unit output is only a fraction of that required for a diffusion plant. Hence proximity to a source of low-cost electricity need not be a decisive criterion in determining plant location, as in the case of a diffusion plant.

Although small compared with a diffusion plant, a centrifuge plant with a reasonably large output would, nevertheless, be a very complicated industrial facility. A prototype plant will have about 10,000 centrifuges. A total centrifuge capacity of 5,000 tonnes SWU per year, which might consist of several plants, would require somewhere between 500,000 and 5,000,000 centrifuges, depending on the size of each centrifuge. A very large manufacturing capability would be required to produce enough units at a low cost within a reasonable period of time. It would itself necessitate a large capital investment and would create strong economic incentives for the manufacturers to sell as many centrifuges as possible. Therefore, centrifuge technology might be rapidly adopted in a number of countries if it is fully developed. However, it remains to be seen whether the net cost of enrichment in a centrifuge plant will be more or less than in a diffusion plant.

*Fuel Fabrication.* Following enrichment, the next step in the nuclear fuel cycle is fuel element fabrication. Enriched uranium fluoride is converted into a uranium oxide powder. For natural uranium fuel, yellow-cake is converted into uranium oxide. In either case, the uranium oxide powder is pressed into pellets and loaded into thin-walled metal tubing. One purpose of the cladding is to contain the highly radioactive products formed when fissions occur. Fabricated fuel elements are transported to a reactor, loaded into the reactor core, and irradiated.

A typical fuel fabrication plant with a capability of handling 600 tonnes of fuel per year would cost about $25 million to build. Such a plant would be capable of fabricating fuel for about 17,000 megawatts of nuclear power capacity. There appear to be economies of scale in the fabrication process which could be realized by the construction of even larger plants.

*Chemical Reprocessing.* Nuclear fuel that has been used in a reactor is extremely radioactive. Therefore, following its removal from the reactor, fuel elements are stored, usually under water, at the reactor site for a period of several months, during which sufficient radioactive decay takes place to permit safe transportation and further processing. The spent fuel elements are shipped, in lead casks that weigh up to 150 tonnes each, to chemical reprocessing plants.

The final step in the nuclear fuel cycle is reprocessing the irradiated fuel. The fuel elements are chopped up, and the spent fuel pellets are mechanically released and chemically dissolved. Chemical processes are then used to separate and recover the residual uranium and produced plutonium. The remaining highly radioactive wastes are concentrated and stored. Because the level of radioactivity throughout chemical reprocessing is very high, the plant is heavily shielded, and most of the critical operations are conducted by remote control.

With respect to reprocessing, as elsewhere in the fuel cycle there are substantial economies to be realized in large-scale operations. A typical plant capable of reprocessing about 300 tonnes per year of irradiated nuclear fuels would cost about $35 million to build. A 1,500-tonne plant might be built for about $80 million. Thus, plant capacity might be increased by a factor of five with an increase in capital cost of less than a factor of three. A 300- and a 1,500-tonne plant would service about 10,000 and 50,000 megawatts, respectively, of nuclear power capacity.

*Plutonium.* The amount of plutonium produced in a nuclear power reactor will vary substantially with the type of reactor, the precise characteristics of the fuel, and the management of reactor and fuel together. Under commercial operating conditions, enriched reactors produce 200 to 300 kilograms of plutonium per year for every 1,000 megawatts of electric generating capacity. Natural uranium reactors typically produce plutonium at about twice this rate.

Plutonium has value for three major civilian purposes: as fuel blended with natural uranium and recycled in uranium reactors, in research and development work on fast breeder reactors, and, ultimately, as fuel for commercial fast breeders.[7] It has substantially more value as breeder reactor fuel than as fuel for the present generation of reactors. Therefore, it may prove profitable to store plutonium for a few years, but probably not for long periods of time because of carrying and storage charges.

The U.S. government purchase price for plutonium was $9.28 per gram until the end of 1970. Thereafter, the government stopped all purchases of plutonium produced in civilian power reactors, and the price is now determined in commercial sales. In any event, it is considered to be worth more than its weight in gold.

## INTERNATIONAL AND INTERNAL SECURITY IMPLICATIONS

Nuclear energy cannot be used to generate electric power without substantial international and internal or domestic security implications. Along several paths these implications may be traced to the

---

[7] Uranium recovered at a reprocessing plant from enriched fuel typically contains 0.7 to 0.9 percent uranium-235, which is still somewhat greater than the uranium-235 content of natural uranium. Recovered uranium can be recycled into the enriched uranium fuel cycle. On the other hand, uranium recovered in reprocessing natural uranium fuel contains less than 0.2 percent uranium-235. This is a lower concentration of uranium-235 than the depleted uranium in the tails of an enrichment plant. Ultimately, depleted uranium will be converted into plutonium in breeder reactors, but there is no present use for it.

fact that special fissionable material is the essential ingredient of nuclear explosives, as well as of nuclear reactor fuel.

## Manufacture of Explosives

Although detailed design information is still cloaked in secrecy, the manufacture of fission explosives is no longer considered a technically demanding or costly task if highly enriched uranium or plutonium is available. Moreover, the cost of explosives manufacture is small compared with any single step in the civilian nuclear fuel cycle. A weapons fabrication and assembly plant that can manufacture ten fission warheads per year has been estimated to cost only $8 million to build and $1 million per year to operate.[8]

Nuclear (fission) weapons can be made from enriched uranium or plutonium, or an alloy of both. A fission yield of 17 kilotons per kilogram of material is the theoretical upper limit on energy release, assuming 100 percent efficiency. An explosive yield in the 20-kiloton range, equivalent to the bombs used against Japan in World War II, might require 20 to 30 kilograms of uranium-235 or 5 to 10 kilograms of plutonium-239, using simple technology and relatively pure fissionable material.

Weapons-grade uranium generally contains above 90 percent uranium-235, although uranium containing less than that amount of the 235 isotope can be used in a lower performance explosive. It is not feasible to use directly in an explosive the slightly enriched uranium that is presently used in most commercial power reactors. However, the uranium fuel used in an HTGR or a breeder reactor is weapons-grade.

As previously mentioned, plutonium occurs in a number of

---

[8] It is important to note, however, that the total cost of warheads, including both production of special fissionable material and weapons manufacture, is small compared with the other essential component of a nuclear weapon capability—the delivery system. A small program to produce one 20-kiloton plutonium warhead per year for ten years has been estimated to cost $11 million per year. If the plutonium for such a program were obtained from a power reactor, the cost could be reduced to about $6 million per year. A moderate program to produce ten warheads per year for ten years would cost an estimated $19 million per year, indicating that the unit cost decreases substantially as the number of warheads produced increases. The cost of a modest nuclear weapon capability, including 30 to 50 jet bombers, 50 medium-range missiles in soft emplacements, and 100 plutonium warheads, has been estimated at $1.7 billion, or $170 million annually for ten years. Therefore, warhead costs would be slightly more than 10 percent of the total costs of a modest (and vulnerable) operational nuclear weapon capability. For comparison, up to 1969 the United Kingdom and France had each spent roughly $8.4 billion on their nuclear forces.

isotopes, 239 and 240 being the important ones for our present discussion. The plutonium produced during the normal commercial operation of a power reactor using slightly enriched or natural uranium fuel contains about 70 to 80 percent plutonium-239 and plutonium-241 and 20 to 30 percent plutonium-240. Plutonium-240 fissions spontaneously. The presence of this isotope in significant amounts in explosive material leads to "predetonation" effects which tend to reduce the reliability and efficiency of the weapon. The plutonium used in efficient weapons contains 95 percent or more plutonium-239. While the plutonium produced in the course of normal commercial operation of most types of power reactors is very difficult to use in an efficient explosive, it is relatively easy to use in a crude, inefficient explosive device. However, the plutonium that will be produced in the commercial operation of fast breeder reactors will be weapons-grade.

Assuming comparable quality, plutonium has a substantial advantage over uranium as the explosive ingredient for fission explosives because about half the weight of plutonium will produce an equivalent yield. However, it is toxic and more difficult to handle than uranium and also requires an implosion design for the explosive device, whereas either implosion or the simpler gun-type design will work with enriched uranium.

Thermonuclear (fusion) weapons are substantially more difficult to design and construct than fission weapons. Advanced thermonuclear weapons apparently use either uranium or plutonium as the fission trigger. Production of deuterium and tritium—the heavy hydrogen isotopes in which the fusion reaction occurs—is not especially difficult. The design of the weapons, however, is very sophisticated.

Having considered the explosive materials, a tour of the civilian nuclear fuel cycle, through which these materials flow, will serve to make explicit the international and internal security implications of each step. Because uranium-235 and plutonium offer distinct routes to nuclear weapons, they will be discussed separately.

## Uranium-235

With respect to the uranium-235 route to nuclear weapons, the enrichment plant has obvious strategic importance. Although a diffusion plant built solely to produce slightly enriched reactor fuel cannot be conveniently used for the production of fully enriched uranium, such a plant can be modified for this purpose by the addition of upper stages. Moreover, any new commercial diffusion plant that is built in the future is likely to include upper stages so that it will be capable of supplying fully enriched uranium for use as fuel in the thorium fuel cycle or in breeder reactors. A gas centrifuge plant would be more flexible than a diffusion plant and should be capable—with internal rearrangement, but without additions—of producing either reactor- or weapons-grade material.

Assuming the internal workings are flexible, the enrichment plant capacity required to supply the yearly enriched fuel requirements of 1,000 megawatts of nuclear power would, alternatively, be capable of producing over 500 kilograms of 90-percent-enriched uranium per year. Thus, the military potential of a plant intended to provide enrichment services on a commercial basis for peaceful nuclear power programs is very large, and the potential of even a small prototype gas centrifuge plant is significant.

A further military implication is raised by the possibility of clandestine construction and operation of small centrifuge plants. This problem does not arise with diffusion plants because their size and large electric power requirements make them impossible to conceal. Small centrifuge plants might be kept secret, however, either by construction at a remote site or by dispersing groups of centrifuges throughout an industrialized area.

Centrifuge technology, like the porous barrier technology associated with diffusion, is extremely sophisticated, and the details are still kept secret. In the 1970s and 1980s probably very few nations will possess the capability to manufacture their own centrifuges. However, given the incentives for large-scale mass production once the technology has been perfected, the operation of normal economic forces would tend to spread centrifuges widely, and the security problems associated with this aspect of civilian nuclear industry could increase correspondingly.

Considering the fact that slightly enriched power reactor fuel cannot be used directly in nuclear weapons, is such fuel without military significance? Most of the separative work required to produce weapons-grade uranium has already been accomplished in enriching uranium for reactor fuel. Therefore, if slightly enriched fuel were used as feed instead of natural uranium, even a small enrichment plant could produce large amounts of 90-percent-enriched uranium. It has been estimated that the enrichment plant capacity required to service 1,000 megawatts of nuclear power could, alternatively, produce over 2,500 kilograms of 90-percent-enriched uranium if slightly enriched uranium were used as feed, in contrast to the 500 kilograms referred to above using natural uranium. Slightly enriched uranium fuel for nuclear power reactors thus has considerable military potential.

## Plutonium

The enriched uranium fuel cycle is difficult to use for the production of almost pure plutonium-239. A reduction of fuel irradiation time to about one-fifth of that required for normal commercial operations is necessary to produce plutonium with the low plutonium-240 content desired for efficient weapons. Because fuel for most enriched uranium reactors cannot be changed without shutting the reactor down, shorter fuel irradiation would usually increase the period in which a power reactor is not producing electricity.[9] Furthermore, chemical reprocessing and fuel fabrication capacities to service the enriched reactors involved would have to be substantially increased in order to carry out the more frequent fuel processing required. Therefore, plutonium with the optimum quality for weapons could not be obtained from the enriched fuel cycle without disrupting the delicately balanced commercial operation of a nuclear power program and, consequently, paying an economic penalty.

The natural uranium fuel cycle is the preferred route to plutonium for weapons. Uranium enrichment, the most complex and costly step in the entire fuel cycle, is omitted. Furthermore, many natural uranium power reactors can be refueled without being shut down. This would permit short irradiation times for production of some almost pure plutonium-239 in natural uranium power reactors with relatively little disruption of electric power generation.

---

[9] In the large cores in nuclear power reactors, irradiated fuel is used in conjunction with fresh fuel in order to achieve maximum power production from each fuel element. Periodically part of the fuel is withdrawn, the remaining fuel is redistributed, and fresh fuel is loaded. A typical enriched fuel element is irradiated for three to four years before it is removed. However, some of the fuel elements are withdrawn and loaded annually.

Any nuclear reactor large enough to be used commercially to generate electric power produces plutonium in militarily significant quantities. This is true for reactors fueled with enriched as well as natural uranium, but the latter type produces substantially more plutonium. As a rough rule of thumb, one kilogram of plutonium can be produced per year for every three to five megawatts of enriched power reactors and for every two or three megawatts of natural uranium reactors. A nuclear power program of 1,000 megawatts will produce 200 to 300 kilograms of plutonium every year; a power program of 20,000 megawatts will produce 4,000 to 6,000 kilograms of plutonium.

However, the plutonium produced in nuclear power reactors is not available for any subsequent use until after reprocessing. Nothing can be done with it as long as it remains encased in irradiated fuel elements. The chemical reprocessing plant, therefore, has strategic importance. Although there are large economies of scale, a smaller plant can be built at the start and expanded as additional reprocessing capacity is needed to service a growing nuclear power program. If exclusively military purposes were to be served, a small plant could be built to reprocess enough fuel for a weapons program, and the remaining reactor fuel could be shipped to a large commercial facility for reprocessing. Like a small centrifuge plant, a small reprocessing plant might be secretly constructed and operated. Inasmuch as the technology is already widely understood and available, clandestine chemical reprocessing would seem to be a more likely possibility than clandestine enrichment using the more advanced centrifuge technology.

The fuel fabrication plant is a facility in the civilian nuclear fuel cycle that has a growing strategic significance with respect to both the enriched uranium and the plutonium routes to nuclear weapons. The recycling of plutonium in existing commercial power reactors will involve the handling of very large amounts of the ore in a fuel fabrication plant. Moreover, as previously noted, the high-temperature, gas-cooled reactor will exploit the thorium fuel cycle, and the fast breeder reactor will permit the energy potential in uranium to be much more fully exploited than in the existing uranium-fueled reactors. Both reactor types use fuel elements containing fully enriched or weapons-grade uranium. Each fuel load for a 1,000-megawatt HTGR or breeder reactor may contain more than 2,000 kilograms of fully enriched uranium. Fully enriched uranium or plutonium in a fuel fabrication plant will be in a form that makes it perhaps the least difficult to divert or steal of all material anywhere in the fuel cycle. Moreover, the fabrication processes result in scrap which can be difficult to account for precisely.

Finally, storage and transportation activities associated with the civilian nuclear fuel cycle have major security implications. Plutonium being shipped from chemical reprocessing plants to fuel fabrication plants and fuel elements containing fully enriched uranium or plutonium en route from fuel fabrication plants to reactors are more vulnerable to theft than elsewhere in the nuclear fuel cycle.

## NUCLEAR POWER CAPABILITIES

A nation that embarks on a civilian nuclear power program does not necessarily do so with a military intent, but the intentions of nations can change much more rapidly than their nuclear capabilities. The remaining task in this chapter is to depict the existing and projected pattern of national capabilities in each of the interrelated series of steps comprising the nuclear fuel cycle.

### Power Reactors

As of early 1971, nuclear power reactors were in operation in fifteen nations, under construction in six more, and planned in yet another six. Total nuclear power capacity in the world was less than 20,000 megawatts, but plants of a total capacity of 83,000 megawatts were under construction, and plants totaling 93,000 megawatts were planned (see Table 1). Of the nuclear plants in operation, the United States accounted for 8,000 megawatts, the United Kingdom 4,200 megawatts, the Soviet Union 1,500 megawatts, and France 1,600 megawatts. The bulk of the remaining operable nuclear power plants were scattered among Canada, the Federal Republic of Germany, India, Italy, Japan, Spain, and Switzerland. Of the countries with operable nuclear power plants, only India and possibly Spain may be considered in the less-developed category.

It is forecast that the world's nuclear power capacity will reach about 300,000 megawatts by 1980, of which 150,000 will be located in the United States. The United Kingdom, France, the

Table 1. World Nuclear Power Capacity (as of early 1972)

| Country | Operable | Under Construction or Planned | Total Megawatts |
|---|---|---|---|
| Japan | 1,255 | 14,043 | 15,298 |
| United Kingdom | 5,922 | 6,874 | 12,796 |
| Federal Republic of Germany | 1,118 | 11,291 | 12,409 |
| Soviet Union | 1,891 | 6,880 | 8,771 |
| France | 1,745 | 5,052 | 6,797 |
| Canada | 1,575 | 4,280 | 5,855 |
| Spain | 620 | 5,160 | 5,780 |
| Sweden | 612 | 4,651 | 5,263 |
| Switzerland | 372 | 3,984 | 4,356 |
| Belgium | 11 | 1,740 | 1,751 |
| Italy | 581 | 862 | 1,443 |
| India | 400 | 880 | 1,280 |
| Taiwan | | 1,272 | 1,272 |
| Czechoslovakia | 143 | 880 | 1,023 |
| Finland | | 880 | 880 |
| Hungary | | 880 | 880 |
| Argentina | | 840 | 840 |
| Bulgaria | | 800 | 800 |
| German Democratic Republic | 70 | 730 | 800 |
| Austria | | 724 | 724 |
| Brazil | | 600 | 600 |
| Mexico | | 600 | 600 |
| Portugal | | 600 | 600 |
| Korea | | 595 | 595 |
| Netherlands | 57 | 477 | 534 |
| Australia | | 500 | 500 |
| Ireland | | 500 | 500 |
| Israel | | 500 | 500 |
| Thailand | | 500 | 500 |
| Yugoslavia | | 500 | 500 |
| South Africa | | 400 | 400 |
| Pakistan | | 337 | 337 |
| United Arab Republic | | 150 | 150 |
| Subtotal | 16,372 | 78,962 | 95,334 |
| United States | 15,315 | 98,067 | 113,382 |
| Total | 31,687 | 177,029 | 208,716 |

Source: "Power Reactors 1972–Index," *Nuclear Engineering International* (April 1972), pp. 303-30.

Federal Republic of Germany, and Japan are expected to have nuclear power capacities of roughly 20,000 megawatts each. Less than 10 percent of the total world nuclear capacity will be located in less-developed nations. However, India plans to have 2,700 megawatts of nuclear power operational by 1980.

Virtually all nuclear power reactors built and planned in the United States and the Soviet Union will use enriched uranium fuel. Outside these two countries, it is anticipated that at least 80 percent of the total nuclear power capacity will be enriched uranium reactors by 1980, and no more than 20 percent will be reactors using natural uranium for fuel. Despite the uncertainty in these projections, it is clear that the spread of nuclear power is not confined to particular geographic regions, nor to specific political persuasions, nor to countries advanced in economic development.

## Uranium

Outside the Communist nations, roughly 80 percent of the proved reserves of uranium are located in three countries: Canada, South Africa, and the United States. France has indigenous deposits that are ample for its nuclear weapon program but probably not for its entire civilian nuclear power program as well. It is significant that the United Kingdom and the Federal Republic of Germany lack their own uranium. It is estimated that indigenous uranium reserves will cover only 20 percent of Western Europe's future needs and only a tiny percentage of Japan's.

Important uranium deposits are, however, being developed in a variety of countries scattered throughout the world, including Argentina, Australia, Gabon (which has close ties to France), and Spain. Brazil and India have substantial uranium and also the world's largest thorium reserves. Sweden has a very large amount of low-grade uranium ore which it has not been economical to exploit thus far. Of the Communist states, both the Soviet Union and China are believed to have adequate uranium reserves. The largest deposits in Eastern Europe are located in the German Democratic Republic (posing a trade possibly of strategic importance between the two halves of Germany), with smaller amounts in Czechoslovakia. As noted previously, at present uranium production capacity is substantially in excess of demand worldwide. Although no shortage of uranium exists and none is foreseen, the obvious imbalances in the locations of supply and demand will have strategic importance.

### Enrichment

Gaseous diffusion plants for enriching uranium are presently located only in the five nuclear-weapon states—China, France, the Soviet Union, the United Kingdom, and the United States. No non-nuclear-weapon state presently has a capability to enrich uranium on a substantial scale. The United States has three gaseous diffusion plants which represent a total investment of $2.3 billion and have a capacity of 17,100 tonnes SWU per year when operated at full power. Future government requirements for military purposes are expected to amount to only about 10 percent of existing plant capacity. U.S. enrichment plants are presently operating at partial capacity, but it is expected that full capacity will be reached in the mid-1970s.

The United States, with its large stake in the world's nuclear power industry, has given repeated assurances of the future availability of U.S. enrichment services to foreign countries on a long-term, non-discriminatory basis at attractive and stable prices. This "toll enrichment" policy is intended not only to aid the export of U.S. enriched reactor technology but also to minimize incentives for the construction of additional uranium enrichment plants outside the United States.

Three actions could be taken by the United States in order to meet future growth in domestic and foreign requirements for civilian enrichment services and to delay as much as possible the time when a new enrichment plant will be needed.[10] First, uranium could be enriched and stockpiled in advance of needs; second, a cascade improvement program, estimated to cost about $500 million, could expand total capacity from 17,100 to 22,000 tonnes SWU per year; and third, a $130 million power uprating program could further increase production capacity to over 26,000 tonnes. If all of these actions were taken in a timely manner, a new plant would not be needed to meet worldwide requirements for enriched uranium until the early 1980s. However, austere federal budgets, the unsettled question of future ownership (government or private) of the U.S. plants, and uncertainty concerning the relative efficiencies of diffusion and cen-

[10] Moreover, by increasing the tails assay, a higher volume of feed material can be processed and the output of the plants can be substantially increased.

trifugation have already delayed the cascade improvement program.

The British and French gaseous diffusion plants have a capacity of about 400 and 300 tonnes SWU per year, respectively. This is somewhat more than enough capacity to meet their respective military and civilian needs until the mid-1970s. However, these plants are not economically competitive with the larger and more efficient plants in the United States.

No precise information has been disclosed about the Soviet Union's gaseous diffusion plant capacity. In view of its recently expressed willingness to enrich uranium for foreign customers for civilian uses, however, the Soviet Union's capacity may be somewhat parallel to that of the United States. The Soviet Union first announced it would offer enrichment services to non-nuclear-weapon countries in 1968. The offer was rephrased in 1969 to apply to all parties to the NPT. The first commitment in principle under this new policy was made to Sweden in January 1970, and the second commitment was made to France. The Soviet Union is also reported to have offered its enrichment services to the Federal Republic of Germany even prior to the latter's formal adherence to the NPT, and to Japan at a price less than the U.S. price for toll enrichment.

Gas centrifuge technology is already under intensive joint development pursuant to a tripartite agreement among the Federal Republic of Germany, the Netherlands, and the United Kingdom. The agreement contemplates construction of two small demonstration plants, one in the Netherlands and the other in the United Kingdom, which will each have a capacity of 50 tonnes SWU per year by 1972 and a subsequent combined capacity of 350 tonnes. This initial program will be followed by the joint construction and operation of plants for the manufacture of centrifuges and commercial enrichment plants using the centrifuge process. The United States, France, Italy, Japan, and Australia also have substantial centrifuge research and development programs under way.

South Africa created an international stir when it announced in July 1970 that its scientists had developed a "unique" process for enriching uranium and that $70 million had been committed to construct a facility in order to exploit the "breakthrough." If true, this could be a development of major strategic importance in view of South Africa's large uranium reserves. At this writing, however, the claim remains unsubstantiated.

It is probable that an industrial-scale enrichment plant will be built on the territory of one or more non-nuclear-weapon nations in the future, although the enrichment method to be used and the arrangements for financial and political participation remain very uncertain. Because of the lead times involved, firm political decisions will be required in the early 1970s in order to meet the projected demands for enriched uranium fuel.

## Fuel Fabrication and Reprocessing

Fuel fabrication plants to supply the input and chemical reprocessing plants to recover the output of nuclear reactors are not yet as widely dispersed around the world as the reactors themselves. A number of factors account for the lag. Nuclear fuels are readily available in international commerce and, as noted previously, transportation costs are small in relation to the values involved. Furthermore, fuel fabrication and chemical reprocessing plants are not economical under present conditions unless they are large enough to service a civilian nuclear power capacity of 8,000 to 10,000 megawatts. In the future, however, it may be economically advantageous to locate smaller reprocessing and fuel fabrication facilities and very large nuclear power stations having three or four 1,000-megawatt reactors on one site.

Of course, the five nuclear-weapon nations already possess their own fuel fabrication and chemical reprocessing plants. Some now being used for commercial purposes were originally built for the production of plutonium for weapons. The United States presently has a commercial chemical reprocessing capability that substantially exceeds the requirements of its civilian nuclear power industry. If all announced plans are carried out, it will have a reprocessing capacity well above its forecast domestic needs throughout most of the 1970s.

Commercial fuel fabrication plants are also in operation or planned in Austria, Canada, Belgium, the Federal Republic of Germany, Italy, and Japan. Chemical reprocessing plants large enough to process industrial quantities of irradiated nuclear fuels are located in Belgium (the Eurochemic plant, which is under international ownership and operation) and India, and construction has begun or is planned in Canada, the Federal Republic of Germany, Italy, Japan, and Sweden.

## CONCLUSION

From the preceding analysis, we may assess the significance of the materials and facilities in the civilian fuel cycle from the viewpoint of safeguards against diversion of nuclear material. Since civilian nuclear technology is under intensive development, the points of principal concern will change with time.

Small quantities of plutonium can be used to make a nuclear explosive. Plutonium that is almost pure plutonium-239 is relatively easy to use in an efficient nuclear explosive. Plutonium containing a substantial amount of the isotope 240 is relatively easy to use in a crude, low-yield nuclear explosive but very difficult to use in an efficient explosive device. Large quantities of plutonium are produced in all types of nuclear power reactors (see Table 2) except the HTGR, which produces fissionable uranium-233 instead. Like plutonium, uranium-233 could be used to make a nuclear explosive, although this uranium isotope is not known to have been used for weapons so far.

The plutonium or uranium-233 produced in the fuel of a power reactor must be separated from the other constituents of irradiated nuclear fuel by complex chemical processes before it can be used in a nuclear explosive. Thus the chemical reprocessing plant, where plutonium or uranium-233 first becomes available in chemically pure form, is one facility of primary concern in the application of safeguards. The plutonium produced in uranium-fueled reactors and the uranium-233 produced in thorium-converter reactors will sooner or later be used as fuel in additional power reactors of various types. This is one reason why the fuel fabrication plant is also a primary safeguards concern.

A power reactor which uses natural uranium fuel produces more plutonium than a reactor of the same size which uses slightly enriched uranium. Moreover, a natural uranium reactor, in which fuel can be loaded and unloaded without reactor shutdown, can be used more easily to produce relatively pure plutonium-239 than an enriched reactor, since the isotopic composition of plutonium produced depends mainly on the fuel irradiation time in a reactor. The differences in the quantity and quality of plutonium pro-

### Table 2. Projections of Plutonium Production Capacities in Selected Non-Nuclear-Weapon Countries

| Country | Estimated Nuclear Power Capacity (megawatts) | | Estimated Plutonium Production Capacity* (kilograms per year) | |
|---|---|---|---|---|
| | 1975 | 1980 | 1975 | 1980 |
| Federal Republic of Germany | 5,000 | 20,000 | 1,000 | 4,000 |
| Japan | 5,000 | 25,000 | 1,000 | 5,000 |
| Canada | 2,500 | 6,000 | 600 | 1,500 |
| Sweden | 2,500 | 9,000 | 500 | 1,800 |
| Italy | 1,000 | 5,000 | 200 | 1,000 |
| Spain | 1,000 | 5,000 | 400 | 1,000 |
| Switzerland | 1,000 | 3,000 | 200 | 600 |
| India | 1,000 | 2,000 | 200 | 500 |
| Argentina | 300 | 1,000 | 100 | 300 |
| Israel | | 500 | 10 | 100 |
| Other | 3,000 | 15,000 | 3,000 | 3,000 |
| Rounded total for non-nuclear-weapon countries | 22,000 | 91,000 | 4,000 | 18,000 |
| United States (for comparison) | 50,000 | 150,000 | 10,000 | 30,000 |

* Using an approximate production rate of 0.2 kilogram plutonium per year per megawatt. Additional time, perhaps two years, must be allowed for extraction of plutonium in a form suitable for fabrication.

duced in natural and in slightly enriched uranium reactors are marginal from the safeguards viewpoint. A more important difference is that the fuel cycle for a natural uranium reactor omits the complex and costly enrichment step. This means that a country with a small nuclear power program can obtain nuclear independence without acquiring its own uranium enrichment capability.

Small quantities of uranium that is highly enriched in the isotope 235 can be used to make nuclear explosives. The slightly enriched uranium that is used as fuel in most power reactors presently in operation cannot be used directly in a nuclear explosive. However, most of the separative work required to produce highly enriched uranium has been done in producing slightly enriched uranium. The latter material thus has substantially more significance from a safeguards viewpoint than natural uranium.

Whether natural or slightly enriched uranium is diverted, further enrichment is required for use in nuclear explosives. For this reason, uranium enrichment facilities are a primary safeguards concern. For a variety of reasons, a gas centrifuge enrichment plant is easier to divert than a gaseous diffusion plant, especially one without the upper stages required to produce fully enriched uranium efficiently. In view of the future requirements for fully enriched uranium for a variety of civilian purposes, however, it is doubtful that a new gaseous diffusion plant would be built without upper stages.

Large quantities of highly enriched uranium, which could be used directly in nuclear explosives, are used as fuel for the HTGR and will be used initially for the fast breeder reactor. This is a further reason why fuel fabrication plants are a primary source of concern in the application of safeguards. Viewed narrowly from a safeguards perspective, the widespread use of the HTGR and the successful development and commercial use of the breeder reactor will complicate the problem of control of nuclear material. On the one hand, these reactor types will not only produce, but also consume as fuel, large quantities of material that can be used directly in nuclear explosives without further complicated processing. On the other hand, fuel fabrication and reprocessing facilities may be located on the same site as the fast breeder reactor, thus simplifying to some extent safeguards accountability and control measures.

Nuclear material that is being stored is easier to account for than material that is being actively processed in large amounts. However, it may be very vulnerable to diversion when it is in transit between nuclear facilities. Although the possibilities for, and significance of, diversion of nuclear material vary, the entire nuclear fuel cycle should be viewed as an integrated system. The safeguards applied to material that flows through the fuel cycle must be part of a system comprehensively applied to all stages in that cycle.

Our preceding analysis of the worldwide distribution of raw materials and operational facilities reveals that the United States, the Soviet Union, and Canada are the only nations that presently possess both large uranium reserves and a strong base in civilian nuclear technology. During the 1970s, most nations will of necessity remain dependent to an important extent on foreign sources of supply to develop and sustain their civilian nuclear industries. The United Kingdom, the Federal Republic of Germany, and Japan are making bids for leadership in civilian nuclear technology, in each case backed by a broad industrial capability and a firm commitment of governmental support, but each of these nations lacks a uranium supply of its own. France may lack adequate indigenous uranium to supply both its civilian and military needs and has decided to import enriched reactor technology for the near future. China, which probably has sufficient uranium to service both a military and a civilian program, has thus far focused its limited scientific and technical resources on the acquisition of a nuclear weapon capability. Although South Africa's large uranium reserves make that nation a major factor in the global nuclear context, its own power program is not far advanced. None of the other countries now establishing significant nuclear power programs—such as India, Spain, or Sweden—are likely to achieve self-sufficiency during the 1970s.

The important security issues arising out of the nuclear generation of electric power are derived both from the very large amount of plutonium that will be produced and accumulated in civilian industries and from the relatively small amount required for explosives. For example, it is estimated that 300,000 to 450,000 kilograms of plutonium will be accumulated worldwide in civilian nuclear industries by 1980, and this amount may reach into the millions of kilograms before the year 2000. Less than ten kilograms could destroy a medium-sized city. A small fraction of the plutonium output diverted from a modest nuclear power program could create grave new threats to international security and domestic tranquility. Thus the dimensions of the safeguards problem arising out of the use of nuclear energy to generate electricity will increase rapidly for the indefinite future.

# Part II

## Safeguards against Nuclear Diversion

# CHAPTER 4

# International Atomic Energy Agency Safeguards

## PAUL C. SZASZ

### INTRODUCTION

On the entry into force of the Treaty on the Non-Proliferation of Nuclear Weapons[1] (NPT) the experimental and troubled child-hood of international nuclear safeguards came to an end with the promise of a more unified and stable control system. Whether that system will prevail and whether it will succeed (two separate though interrelated questions) will depend in large part on certain extraneous political factors: can particular key states be per-suaded, through appropriate inducements and pressures applied either selectively or collectively, to renounce any residual nuclear ambitions and to submit to safeguards? But in part the durability and success of the new control system will depend on its own early successs: does it appear capable of inhibiting nuclear pro-liferation without unacceptable intrusions on legitimate activities?

---

[1] Annexed to UN General Assembly Resolution 2373 (XXII) (1968), reproduced in IAEA document INFCIRC/140, in *The United Nations and Disarmament 1945-1970,* Sales No. 70.IX.1 (New York: United Nations, 1970), Appendix IX, and in Allan D. McKnight, *Atomic Safeguards: A Study in International Verification,* UNITAR Series No. 5 (New York: UNITAR, 1971), Annex 7. See also the list of parties in Appendix D to this volume.

The new Treaty does not eliminate the controls based on earlier agreements. However, it seems likely, for reasons mentioned below, that the NPT safeguards implemented by the International Atomic Energy Agency (IAEA) will supersede the controls the Agency is currently administering as well as all other systems of international safeguards except those (notably those of Euratom) that are coordinated with or integrated into the IAEA's system. In any event, these earlier controls have already been sufficiently described and analyzed in the literature[2] and will be referred to here only to the extent that they provide instructive contrasts to safeguards under NPT or may survive in residual and perhaps eventually fossilized form.

## LEGAL BASIS

Lacking a world government, any system of controls to be applied within sovereign states must be based on their consent, primarily as expressed in treaties. The extraordinary sensitivity of nuclear non-proliferation controls, impinging simultaneously on crucial military, economic, and technical affairs, has resulted in a complicated construct involving several general treaties and a number of more detailed instruments of lower rank.

### The Statute of the IAEA

The Statute of the International Atomic Energy Agency is a treaty[3] to which, as of June 30, 1972, 102 states were parties.[4]

---

[2] See Paul C. Szasz, *The Law and Practices of the International Atomic Energy Agency*, IAEA Legal Series No. 7 (Vienna: IAEA, 1970), chap. 21, "Safeguards," and the references cited in n. 1 to that chapter. In addition to the items there cited, see *Atomic Safeguards* (the study cited above), recently published by the first Inspector General of the IAEA. See also *Safeguarding the Atom: A Soviet-American Exchange* (New York: UN Association of the USA, 1972).

[3] 276 U.N.T.S. 4, 8 U.S.T. 1093; amended 471 U.N.T.S. 334, 14 U.S.T. 135; reproduced in McKnight, *Atomic Safeguards*, Annex 4.

[4] For a list of members, see Appendix D to this volume or the latest revision of IAEA document INFCIRC/2 or INFCIRC/42. It should be noted that the membership does not comprise all parties to NPT, as some important ones such as the German Democratic Republic are still excluded; however, as pointed out below (see p. 80), the Agency can conclude safeguards agreements with non-members. A special problem is posed by China, whose Nationalist government became an initial member of the Agency and later also a party to NPT; following the change in representation in the United Nations decided by the General Assembly, the Board of Governors of the Agency on December 9, 1971, recognized the government of the People's Republic as the only one having the right to represent China in the IAEA; this left unclear both the continued membership of China

The Statute establishes the IAEA's principal organs: the General Conference, the Board of Governors, and the Director General/ Secretariat. It also establishes the safeguards functions of the Agency: primarily, the control of nuclear items held by the IAEA itself or supplied by it to its member states, and secondarily, the extension of these controls to other national nuclear activities at the request of the state or states concerned. The Statute specifies the main methods of control on which the Agency is to rely in carrying out safeguards but allows each of these methods to be applied only to the extent relevant, a delimitation that must be embodied in an agreement with the state concerned.[5] The financial provisions of the Statute give some indication of how the costs of safeguards are to be borne, but they stop short of establishing a clear, complete and binding fiscal regime for this purpose.

The IAEA Statute does not require any member of the Agency to submit to safeguards (except insofar as the state requests and receives nuclear assistance from or through the Agency), nor does it require that states make their international assistance or transfers subject to the recipient's acceptance of such controls. In short, the Statute merely creates a framework for controls within which member states can decide whether to submit and, if so, to what controls. In addition to providing specifically for the establishment of this somewhat circumscribed system of controls, the Statute also generally charges the Agency to cooperate with the United Nations in furthering any agreement for safeguarded worldwide disarmament.[6]

## The Non-Proliferation Treaty

The Non-Proliferation Treaty, unlike the Statute of the IAEA or several other similar instruments, does not establish a safeguards system or even a framework for one. Instead, the NPT builds on the system established by the IAEA:

1. The NPT requires all non-nuclear-weapon parties to submit to IAEA safeguards by means of agreements to be negotiated with

---

in the Agency and the implementation of the several safeguards agreements that had been concluded with the Nationalist government; in this connection it should also be noted that while the Nationalists (assuming they represent only Taiwan) acted for a non-nuclear-weapon state, the People's Republic is clearly a nuclear-weapon state.

[5] IAEA Statute, Articles II, III.A.5, III.B.2, XI.F.4, and XII.

[6] *Ibid.*, Article III.B.1.

the Agency by these states, either individually or collectively, within specified time limits.[7]

2. The NPT prohibits any party from supplying to any non-nuclear-weapon state (whether or not it is party to the Treaty) certain types of nuclear items for peaceful purposes, except subject to IAEA safeguards.[8]

The Treaty thus complements the IAEA Statute by supplying the two provisions indicated as lacking from that instrument: an obligation to submit to safeguards, and a requirement that most international transfers of nuclear material or equipment (except those to nuclear-weapon states) be subject to controls. However, NPT is even less specific than the Statute as to the control measures to be applied.

NPT also provides that safeguards implemented pursuant to it must permit peaceful research and development of nuclear energy in non-nuclear-weapon states; these controls must not hamper the economic or technological development of the parties or international cooperation in peaceful nuclear activities.[9] The Preamble also expresses support for research and development of safeguards techniques intended to make these controls less onerous and perhaps more effective.

### Instructions on Negotiating NPT Agreements

The IAEA is not a party to NPT, nor was it formally consulted on the formulation of that instrument. The Agency is thus under no legal obligation (except under its statutory charge to cooperate with United Nations disarmament efforts) to carry out any functions foreseen for it in that Treaty. Nevertheless, both the political and the administrative organs of the Agency were eager that it should do so, even though the functions assigned by the NPT to the Agency were not fully in accord with the control system it had already established or even with its Statute.

The NPT requires non-nuclear-weapon parties to commence negotiating safeguards agreements with the Agency within 180

[7] NPT, Article III.1,4.

[8] *Ibid.*, Article III.2. The restriction of this rule to material provided for peaceful purposes, thus in effect exempting those provided for "authorized" military activities, reflects a limitation in NPT the consequences of which are discussed on pp. 86-87 and 94-95 below.

[9] *Ibid.*, Article III.3.

days of the entry into force of the Treaty (or no later than upon ratification) and to conclude such agreements within eighteen months of the initiation of the negotiations.[10] Thus the Agency was faced with the simultaneous negotiation of a large number of safeguards agreements within a limited span of time. Moreover, though not required by either the Statute or the Treaty, it was highly desirable that these agreements be as uniform as possible— in fact, to avoid charges of discrimination and complications in implementation, they would have to be as nearly identical as was practical.

Prior to NPT, the Agency had negotiated numerous safeguards agreements over a period of years and had attempted to make them as uniform as possible considering their widely diverse legal bases (e.g., Agency projects, transfers of bilateral safeguards, unilateral submissions[11]). For this purpose the Board of Governors adopted a series of Safeguards Documents,[12] and the Secretariat used these Documents in negotiating individual safeguards agreements, as far as possible, by incorporating their provisions by reference. Though no formal "model" agreements were formulated, each successive agreement of a particular type followed closely the last previous agreement of the same type, so that one of the early texts in each series constituted an unofficial prototype.

The same somewhat unstructured technique could have been followed in respect of the NPT agreements, but their importance and sensitivity led to the adoption of a somewhat different approach. All members of the Agency were invited to participate in the ad hoc Safeguards Committee (1970), and some fifty sent representatives to the 82 Committee meetings between June 1970 and March 1971.[13] In effect, these meetings constituted the crucial phase of negotiating the NPT safeguards agreements. Practically all interested IAEA members were represented (including some that had not yet committed themselves to NPT, and might

10 *Ibid.,* Article III.4.

11 See Szasz, *Law and Practices,* sec. 21.5.2.

12 IAEA documents INFCIRC/26 (1961) and /Add.1 (1964); INFCIRC/66 (1965), /Rev.1 (1966) and /Rev. 2 (1968). The 1968 version is reproduced in McKnight, *Atomic Safeguards,* Annex 5.

13 The chairman of the Committee was Dr. Kurt Waldheim, who soon thereafter was elected Secretary-General of the United Nations.

not do so if they considered the Committee's report unacceptable): (1) the nuclear-weapon states, interested primarily in effective safeguards which should not, however, interfere with their
nuclear trade; (2) the advanced non-nuclear-weapon states, against
whom the controls would primarily be directed, interested in rules
that would not inhibit the development of their technology; (3)
the Euratom states, interested in a system that would permit the
preservation and utilization of as much as possible of the special
control system of their regional organization; (4) other non-
nuclear-weapon states, interested both in effectiveness and in
protecting their sovereignty against intrusions unwarranted by
their minor nuclear programs; (5) all states, interested in preventing the costs of the control system from burgeoning unduly; and
finally (6) the IAEA Secretariat, concerned that the instruments it
is to negotiate for the Agency be coherent and that the prescribed
limitations not be inconsistent with the implementation of the
responsibilities to be laid on the Agency.

The result of these extensive labors was a document, approved
by the IAEA Board in 1971, entitled "The Structure and Content
of Agreements between the Agency and States Required in Connection with the Treaty on the Non-Proliferation of Nuclear
Weapons"[14] (called hereafter the "Negotiating Instructions"). It
consists of 116 paragraphs, which, except for 19 definitions, are
almost all introduced with the words "The Agreement should
provide." Many of these provisions can readily be traced to paragraphs of the Agency's latest Safeguards Document, to standard
provisions of safeguards agreements previously concluded by the
Agency, or to the NPT itself. However, many provisions of the
earlier instruments were omitted and a number of important new
ones were added. As pointed out below, some of the omissions
resulted from the simplification that could be achieved by applying controls to substantially all nuclear materials in a state, instead
of only selectively on the basis of complex rules. Most of the new
provisions reflect either the novel view of the Agency as auditor of
national controls or newly developed technical understanding as to
where and how controls can be exercised most effectively. It is
also apparent throughout the Negotiating Instructions that a pur-

14 IAEA document INFCIRC/153.

poseful attempt was made to circumscribe the safeguards system more clearly than had been done in the past.[15]

## NPT Safeguards Submission Agreements with Non-Nuclear-Weapon States

Almost immediately after the IAEA Board had addressed the Negotiating Instructions to the Director General, the first two NPT Safeguards Agreements were negotiated and subsequently approved by the Board in June 1971.[16] Nineteen further, almost identical, agreements were approved by the end of February 1972 (the deadline for those non-nuclear-weapon parties that had ratified the NPT on or before its entry into force). These initial agreements follow the Board-approved document precisely. Most paragraphs of the Instructions are reproduced verbatim, only omitting the introductory words "The Agreement should provide" and appropriately modifying the remaining text; almost the only variations appear in a few paragraphs that explicitly require a choice among alternatives.

All five of the non-nuclear-weapon states that are Euratom members (Belgium, the Federal Republic of Germany, Italy, Luxembourg, and the Netherlands) have signed the NPT. However, none had ratified at this writing and thus are under no obligation to initiate formal negotiations. Nevertheless, from November 1971 to July 1972 these states, together with the Euratom Commission, negotiated with the IAEA an NPT Safeguards Agreement and a special Protocol thereto, to both of which the states as well as the two organizations are to become parties.[17] These instruments thus take advantage of the provision of the NPT permitting safeguards agreements to be concluded by non-nuclear-weapon states "together with other [such] States." Many non-nuclear-weapon states have no nuclear activities whatsoever. They too must conclude NPT Safeguards Agreements in the usual form, but with a special protocol providing for the suspension of those provisions that

15 The UN General Assembly noted "with satisfaction" the Agency's success in drawing up these detailed guidelines (Resolution 2825 A (XXVI)).

16 With Finland (IAEA Press Release PR 71/25 and document INFCIRC/155 and /Add.1) and Austria (PR 71/26 and INFCIRC/156).

17 The substantive provisions of these instruments are summarized on pp. 135-38 below.

depend on the presence of at least some nuclear materials (e.g., the conclusion of the Subsidiary Arrangements described below).[18]

Nothing in the IAEA Statute requires the Agency to restrict its safeguards to member states,[19] nor does NPT require its parties to join the Agency or exempt parties not IAEA members from the obligation to submit to Agency safeguards. Consequently, the Negotiating Instructions (which, of course, were formulated without the participation of non-members) explicitly foresee the conclusion of NPT Safeguards Agreements with non-members and only require that their fiscal provisions be somewhat different from those entered into by members.[20] In other respects non-members are to be treated on a par with members, though, despite their right to participate in Board debates of any safeguards questions raised by them,[21] they cannot exert direct political influence within the organs of the Agency.

The NPT cannot require non-parties to submit to Agency safeguards and to conclude agreements to that effect. However, it can and does prohibit parties to the NPT from transferring nuclear items for peaceful purposes to any non-nuclear-weapon state except under Agency safeguards.[22] It is likely there will be holdouts from NPT and that parties to the Treaty will desire to transfer nuclear items to them. Therefore, special safeguards agreements will have to be concluded to cover such items. These agreements will probably resemble more closely the pre-NPT safeguards agreements than the NPT versions, since the resultant partial rather than universal application of safeguards in a state is more nearly like the situation under the former type of agreement than under the latter. In fact, it is logical that non-NPT parties should not benefit from the relaxation of particular controls consequent on the safeguarding of all peaceful nuclear activities in NPT parties. Indeed, some states may be induced to become parties to the Treaty just in order to avoid the more rigid requirements of the safeguards system that pre-dated the NPT.

[18] For example, Protocol to the NPT Safeguards Agreement concluded with the Holy See (acting in the name and on behalf of the Vatican City State).

[19] See Szasz, *Law and Practices,* sec. 13.3.2. See also n. 4 above.

[20] IAEA document INFCIRC/153, par. 15(b).

[21] *Ibid.,* par. 21; see also Board Provisional Rule of Procedure 50 (IAEA document GOV/INF/60).

[22] NPT, Article III.2.

## Subsidiary Arrangements

As already indicated, the NPT Safeguards Agreements are almost entirely standard in form and thus do not reflect the particular nuclear energy activities of the non-nuclear-weapon state concerned. However, it is necessary for practical as well as for political and legal reasons to specify in some consensual instrument the specific control measures to be applied to actual materials and installations. The Agreements thus require the state and the Agency to conclude Subsidiary Arrangements in which these important details can be set forth.[23] A number of provisions of the Negotiating Instructions, and thus of the Agreements themselves, specify matters to be covered by these Arrangements.[24] This device has long been part of the Agency's safeguards practice.[25]

It is clear that the Subsidiary Arrangements are intended to be more flexible instruments than the NPT Safeguards Agreements themselves. In the light of this purpose and following past practice, the Arrangements will be concluded on an administrative level between the IAEA Director General or Inspector General and the state concerned, probably without prior or subsequent submission to the Board of Governors. Moreover, unlike the Agreements, which are issued as IAEA Information Circulars and are registered with and published by the United Nations, the Arrangements will most likely not be published at all. One reason for such reticence is that the Subsidiary Arrangements may contain or explicitly reflect information about national nuclear installations that the Agency is required by the Safeguards Agreements to keep confidential. In view of the international staff of the IAEA Department of Safeguards and Inspection, which is responsible for negotiating and implementing these Arrangements, it seems unlikely that this lack of publicity could be used either to discriminate significantly among similarly situated states or to weaken seriously the controls relating to particular states. The recent circulation to states of a "model text of a 'Subsidiary Arrangement' "[26] should further

[23] IAEA document INFCIRC/153, pars. 39-40. On July 20, 1970, the Director General submitted to the Safeguards Committee (1970) a tentative outline of the "Structure and Contents of Subsidiary Arrangements under [NPT Safeguards Agreements]."

[24] For example, *ibid.*, pars. 42, 46, 51, 60, 64(b), 65, 68(a, b), 75(d, e), 76(a, c).

[25] See Szasz, *Law and Practices*, sec. 21.5.7.3.

[26] Mentioned in IAEA Annual Report, July 1, 1971-June 30, 1972, GC(XVI)/480, par. 119(c).

serve to allay suspicions about these instruments. Finally, considering the substantial influence of the nuclear-weapon states throughout the Agency, it is also unlikely that a general relaxation with respect to all Subsidiary Arrangements would be permitted without substantial justification.

## Non-NPT Safeguards Agreements

As of June 30, 1972, some 49 non-NPT-IAEA safeguards agreements were in force.[27]  Eighteen of these were Project Agreements,[28] providing for the transfer through, or with the assistance of, the Agency of nuclear items (mostly nuclear materials and reactors) for specified approved "projects" in member states and subject to safeguards as provided in the Agreements. Twenty-five were trilateral Safeguards Transfer Agreements[29] by which it was agreed to substitute the Agency's safeguards for those previously exercised, pursuant to a bilateral agreement, by a supplying state in a receiving state—and sometimes, on a reciprocal basis, those exercised by the receiving state in the supplying state. Two were non-NPT Safeguards Submission Agreements, one with a non-nuclear-weapon state which agreed to accept safeguards on particular nuclear items and activities, because such submission was a condition of assistance received from other members of the Agency,[30] and the other Tlatelolco Safeguards Agreement with Mexico referred to below.

If states in which the Agency is exercising controls pursuant to any of these existing agreements (or similar ones that may be concluded in the future) enter into NPT Safeguards Agreements with the Agency, these will require (if the state concerned so desires) the suspension of safeguards exercised by the Agency

[27] *Ibid.,* table 21 (counting only the agreements then in force); see also the list in Appendix D to this volume.

[28] For example, Agreement between the IAEA and the Government of Pakistan for Assistance by the Agency to Pakistan in Connection with the Establishment of a Nuclear Power Reactor Project, 650 U.N.T.S. 243, reproduced in IAEA document INFCIRC/116, pt. 2.

[29] For example, Agreement between the IAEA, the Government of Israel and the Government of the United States of America for the Application of Safeguards, 573 U.N.T.S. 3, reproduced in IAEA document INFCIRC/84.

[30] Agreement between the IAEA and the Government of the Republic of China for the Application of Safeguards to the Taiwan Research Reactor Facility, 732 U.N.T.S., Reg. No. I-10517, reproduced in IAEA document INFCIRC/133.

under the other agreements.[31] However, the latter are not entirely superseded by the NPT Safeguards Agreements and thus may still restrain the use of nuclear materials for military purposes proscribed by the IAEA Statute or by a supplier, even though these military uses are not barred by the NPT or by the new Safeguards Agreements.[32] Though the Negotiating Instructions provide for the continuation of such residual restraints,[33] no provision in the Instructions appears to inhibit directly the international transfer of nuclear materials in violation of a safeguards agreement whose control provisions have been suspended by reason of an NPT Safeguards Agreement.[34] If such an Agreement is terminated (which is only possible if the state denounces the NPT itself[35]), all provisions of any suspended safeguards agreement automatically revive.

In addition to these residual effects of non-NPT safeguards agreements, the Agency may be expected to continue exercising non-NPT safeguards in certain situations.

1. Non-nuclear-weapon states that do not become parties to the NPT may be parties to agreements providing for Agency safeguards. In particular, nuclear items supplied to them by NPT parties must be subjected to controls at least as severe as under the NPT.

2. Nuclear-weapon states may be subject to IAEA safeguards, for example, under the reciprocal provisions of certain trilateral Safeguards Transfer Agreements.[36] In addition, the offers of the

[31] IAEA document INFCIRC/153, par. 24. Thus, for example, safeguards on a reactor and nuclear material supplied to Finland under a 1960 Agency project were suspended on the day the Finnish NPT Safeguards Agreement entered into force (IAEA document INFCIRC/24/Add.5). However, since many existing safeguards agreements are trilateral in form (the Safeguards Transfer Agreements), the other state party to that agreement must also consent to such suspension—as the United States did in respect to Austria in a somewhat ambiguously worded "Protocol of Suspension" (see INFCIRC/152/Mod.1).

[32] See pp. 86-87 below for a discussion of the differences between the assurances required under NPT and the IAEA Statute.

[33] IAEA document INFCIRC/153, par. 14(a)(i). See also pp. 86-87 below.

[34] In contrast, for instance, with the restriction in the latest Safeguards Document, INFCIRC/66/Rev. 2, par. 28(d).

[35] IAEA document INFCIRC/153, par. 26, NPT Article X.1, permits any party to withdraw from the Treaty "if it decides that extraordinary events, related to the subject matter of [NPT], have jeopardized [its] supreme interests," provided that it gives three months' notice to the other parties and to the UN Security Council, indicating its reasons.

[36] For example, the Safeguards Transfer Agreement referred to in n. 29 above.

United Kingdom and the United States to allow the application of IAEA safeguards on certain peaceful nuclear activities as soon as NPT controls are sufficiently widely accepted may lead to an important set of arrangements under which safeguards will be applied in at least two nuclear-weapon states. These arrangements, which have not yet been negotiated,[37] will not purport to impose meaningful restraints on these countries (which have extensive military programs entirely separate from their civilian activities) but will be designed to place enterprises in these nuclear-weapon states on a basis of parity with similar enterprises in non-nuclear-weapon states that might otherwise consider themselves unfairly disadvantaged, economically or technically. Since the purpose is to mitigate discrimination, it is likely that the actual controls to be provided for nuclear-weapon states will correspond to those applied in non-nuclear-weapon states; however, as safeguarding nuclear-weapon states will serve no genuine purpose as far as non-proliferation is concerned, it is likely that to conserve financial and other resources (e.g., trained inspectors), only representative facilities in these states will be subject to full controls.

### Tlatelolco Safeguards

A special type of Safeguards Submission Agreement is called for by the 1967 Treaty for the Prohibition of Nuclear Weapons in Latin America (the Tlatelolco Treaty).[38] The requirements of Article 13 of that instrument resemble closely those of Articles III.1 and III.4 of the NPT, which were indeed modeled on that earlier instrument. In brief, each party to the Tlatelolco Treaty must, within periods identical to those specified in NPT, enter into negotiations with the IAEA and conclude with it a safeguards agreement. Under such an agreement, the Agency is to apply

---

[37] On April 20, 1971, the Board of Governors of the IAEA authorized the Director General to enter into consultations with the American and British governments as to the desirable contents of the required agreements (IAEA document GC (XV)/455, par. 5), and discussions actually started in December 1971. These governments had already previously submitted to temporary Agency safeguards certain facilities—see, e.g., the Agreement between the IAEA and the Government of the United Kingdom of Great Britain and Northern Ireland for the Application of Safeguards with Regard to the Bradwell Nuclear Power Station, 588 U.N.T.S. 269, reproduced in IAEA document INFCIRC/86, pt. 1.

[38] 634 U.N.T.S. 281, reproduced in *The United Nations and Disarmament 1945-1970*, Appendix VIII, and in McKnight, *Atomic Safeguards*, Annex 8. See also the list of parties in Appendix D to this volume.

safeguards to the state's nuclear activities for the purpose of verifying compliance with the Treaty obligation to "use exclusively for peaceful purposes the nuclear material and facilities which are under [its] jurisdiction" and to avoid any direct or indirect dealings with nuclear weapons. Up to now only Mexico, the first state to ratify the Tlatelolco Treaty, has entered into an appropriate safeguards agreement with the Agency,[39] but by June 30, 1972 some 18 other Latin American states had become parties to Tlatelolco, and the time limits for most of them to enter into similar agreements had expired or were fast expiring.[40]

The basic requirements for IAEA safeguards under both the Tlatelolco and Non-Proliferation treaties are similar, although they differ with respect to non-weapon military nuclear activities and peaceful nuclear explosives. Therefore, various possibilities would in principle be open to states parties to both treaties: (1) a type of safeguards agreement could be formulated to cover both treaties, with only minimal modifications of the NPT Safeguards Agreements;[41] (2) separate safeguards agreements could be negotiated for each treaty, but the Tlatelolco-related safeguards could be suspended as long as those relating to NPT remained in force; (3) a standard NPT Safeguards Agreement could be concluded and supplemented by a protocol specifying that the safeguards thereunder also apply to the Tlatelolco obligations;[42] (4) the Tlatelolco

[39] Agreement between IAEA and Mexico for the Application of Safeguards under the Treaty for the Prohibition of Nuclear Weapons in Latin America, 650 U.N.T.S. 311, reproduced in IAEA document INFCIRC/118 and in McKnight, *Atomic Safeguards,* Annex 9. This 1968 instrument was still based on the latest IAEA Safeguards Document (INFCIRC/66/Rev. 2), rather than on the NPT Negotiating Instructions, which had not yet been formulated. On September 27, 1972, Mexico and the IAEA signed a new Safeguards Agreement nominally applying equally to the Non-Proliferation and Tlatelolco treaties and providing for the suspension, *inter alia,* of the earlier Tlatelolco Safeguards Agreement; in fact, the new instrument is an entirely standard NPT Safeguards Agreement with merely preambular references to the Tlatelolco obligations.

[40] The General Conference of the Agency for the Prohibition of Nuclear Weapons in Latin America (OPANAL) therefore urged its members to initiate and conclude negotiations with the IAEA as soon as possible (Resolution 31(II), adopted on September 9, 1971, reproduced in UN document A/8653, Annex, chap. 2).

[41] The Board of Governors indicated in its 1971 Report to the General Conference that the Tlatelolco Safeguards Agreements were expected to be "essentially similar" to the NPT Safeguards Agreements (GC(XV)/455, par. 7). However, in its 1972 Report the Board stated that "safeguards will be applied under a single set of comprehensive arrangements which will satisfy the requirements of both Treaties" (GC(XVI)/480, par. 6); see also nn. 39 (final sentence) and 42.

[42] This was the solution actually adopted in concluding the first NPT agreement with a Tlatelolco party (Uruguay) after the approval of the Negotiating Instructions (IAEA document INFCIRC/160).

parties could agree among each other to suspend the Tlatelolco obligation to enter into safeguards agreements for states that enter into a NPT-type Safeguards Agreement with the IAEA.[43]

## SAFEGUARDS OBJECTIVES

### Types of Activities Proscribed

In the IAEA Statute, the objective of safeguards is repeatedly declared to be to ensure that nuclear material and certain other nuclear items "are not used in such a way as to further any military purpose."[44]  In related contexts, this clause is replaced by the obverse: to ensure that such items "are used only for peaceful purposes."[45]  Though neither "military" nor "peaceful" are defined, it is clear that all activities of the former nature are to be proscribed, while all of the latter are to be allowed, if not encouraged.[46]  On the other hand, the NPT proscribes for non-nuclear-weapon states "nuclear weapons or other nuclear explosive devices."[47]

The discrepancy between these two instruments is evident. For example, under the Statute nuclear-propelled military vessels are prohibited, and Agency safeguards would seek to prevent such use of nuclear material, but there is no such ban under the NPT or the Negotiating Instructions. However, peaceful nuclear explosives probably do not fall under the IAEA ban, though they do explicitly come under the prohibition of the NPT, which recognizes that there is no practical way of distinguishing between a nuclear weapon and a peaceful explosive device—except in their intended or actual use.

The NPT takes account of the statutory difficulty the Agency would have in safeguarding non-weapon military activities, by requiring merely that these controls extend to peaceful activities.[48]  Therefore, the NPT Safeguards Agreements permit a state

[43] This solution was evidently rejected by OPANAL in the resolution cited in n. 40 above.

[44] For example, IAEA Statute, Articles II, III.A.5, XI.F.4(a), XII.A.1.

[45] For example, *ibid.*, Article III.B.2.

[46] See Szasz, *Law and Practices,* sec. 15.1.2.

[47] NPT, Article II.

[48] *Ibid.,* Article III.1 (final sentence).

to remove from IAEA control nuclear material it intends to use for an "authorized" military purpose—provided such material is not under some independent legal constraint, such as supply through the Agency or a "peaceful uses" guarantee in a bilateral supply agreement, which would bar any military use.[49] But no corresponding provision of the NPT frees the Agency from applying its controls to prevent the "diversion" of nuclear material to the manufacture of peaceful explosive devices.

The exercise of safeguards in accordance with the NPT will thus lead to a distortion of the original statutory purpose of Agency safeguards, as narrowly construed. But before such a construction is urged, it should be recalled that Article III.B.1 of the Statute specifically charges the Agency to "conduct its activities . . . in conformity with policies of the United Nations furthering the establishment of safeguarded world-wide disarmament and in conformity with any international agreements entered into pursuant to such policies." In view of the UN General Assembly's sponsorship of the NPT, the Agency's assistance in its implementation falls clearly within this general statutory mandate. In any event, most, if not all, members of the Agency have accepted this interpretation, and none has raised a formal objection.

## Inhibition of Proscribed Activities

The IAEA Statute states as one of its objectives to "ensure, so far as it is able," that assistance supplied by or through it or otherwise subject to its control not be used to further any military purpose.[50] It also outlines the tools for achieving this limited objective.

1. For the most part, the IAEA is merely to gather information (through records, reports, and inspections) about the nuclear items and activities under its control. From this information the Agency should be able to determine whether or not any proscribed activities are being carried out.[51]

2. The Agency may approve the design of each nuclear facility under its control, *inter alia,* "from the viewpoint of assuring that it

[49] IAEA document INFCIRC/153, par. 14.
[50] IAEA Statute, Article II.
[51] *Ibid.,* Article XII.A.3,4, and 6.

will not further any military purpose"—a technically almost meaningless provision.[52]

3. The Agency may require the deposit with it of any special fissionable material in excess of the immediate needs of each state subject to safeguards. For this purpose the Agency may establish geographically scattered depots to be protected by IAEA guards.[53]

4. The Agency may impose sanctions on detecting any violations, consisting of: (i) reports to member states and to UN organs; (ii) a call on the offending state to return nuclear items supplied to it; (iii) a call on other member states to curtail or suspend assistance to the offending state.[54] Even in the earlier safeguards practice of the Agency, the power to veto designs had been almost abandoned, and the requirement that nuclear material be stored with the Agency (which through dispersion and international guarding might offer some physical security against forcible diversion) had not been implemented. In practice, therefore, the control system at most enables the Agency to detect violations and to report them to the world community—in the hope that Agency members and perhaps other NPT parties would observe any boycott declared, thereby inhibiting the nuclear activities of the delinquent state.

This limitation on the Agency's safeguards system is fully recognized by the NPT, which merely requires the Agency to verify compliance with the principal prohibitions laid on non-nuclear-weapon states by the Treaty. No system of physical security is provided. Consequently, the Negotiating Instructions and the NPT Safeguards Agreements themselves specify the objectives of safeguards as "the timely detection of diversion of significant quantities of nuclear material . . . and deterrence of such diversion by the risk of early detection."[55] The Agency cannot directly prevent diversion by means of its safeguards, especially as these will be applied to implement the NPT. However, the threat of exposure of violations may be an indirect deterrent. In any event, the Agency must attempt to detect any violation promptly and with certainty and to sound the alarm in the world community.

52 *Ibid.*, Article XII.A.1.
53 *Ibid.*, Article XII.A.5.
54 *Ibid.*, Article XII.A.7, XII.C.
55 IAEA document INFCIRC/153, par. 28.

Any consequent reactions are left to Agency members, to the parties to the NPT, and to the competent UN organs.

Consistent with this understanding of the functions of Agency safeguards is the rule permitting a state to escape them entirely by denouncing the NPT. A state may do so if it decides that "extraordinary events, related to the subject matter of [the NPT], have jeopardized the supreme interests of its country" and notifies the other parties and the Security Council. Three months later, both the NPT and any Safeguards Agreements contracted pursuant to it terminate.[56] Except insofar as other safeguards agreements are automatically revived, the country then holds its nuclear material free of any restrictions or controls. All the Agency can do in such an event is to notify the world community of the types, forms, and amounts of nuclear material thus released from restraint.

## SCOPE OF IAEA/NPT SAFEGUARDS

### General Rule

The NPT requires the Agency to control all "source" and "special fissionable" material in non-nuclear-weapon states except for those used in legitimate non-peaceful activities (i.e., military activities other than weapons manufacture). This basic coverage, modified by certain further exceptions, is also reflected in the NPT Safeguards Agreements.[57] This simple rule contrasts sharply with non-NPT safeguards, in which a number of complex attribution formulas determine whether particular materials are both dangerous enough and closely enough associated with nuclear items under safeguards (e.g., plutonium produced in a safeguarded reactor) to become subject to control themselves. Moreover, elaborate substitution rules in effect permit a state to juggle materials subject and not subject to safeguards, as long as the latter category does not increase at the expense of former.[58] Obviously, no such rules are necessary or even possible when, under NPT, all nuclear material in a given jurisdiction is automatically subject to controls.

The non-NPT rules cannot, however, be entirely disregarded, for they still continue to apply: (1) in nuclear-weapon states and

[56] See n. 35 above.
[57] IAEA document INFCIRC/153, par. 2.
[58] IAEA document INFCIRC/66/Rev. 2, pars. 19-20, 24-25, 26(d).

in non-nuclear-weapon states not parties to the NPT in which the Agency for any reason exercises safeguards; (2) in determining what material, generally under NPT controls, is also subject to more stringent restrictions—such as a prohibition of use for any military purpose;[59]   (3) in sorting out, if an NPT Safeguards Agreement should be terminated, material which is then completely free of safeguards from material which continues under IAEA safeguards pursuant to other agreements that had been suspended by the NPT Agreement. However, under normal NPT safeguards administration, it should be possible to ignore these vestigial effects. The result will be a dramatic simplification not only of the NPT Safeguards Agreements and the Subsidiary Arrangements but also of the records, reports and inventories the controlled states or the Agency must keep or make, and the performance of physical inventories and other inspection measures.

The terms "source" and "special fissionable material" are not defined in the NPT. The Treaty thus implicitly relies on the definitions of these terms in the IAEA Statute,[60] which are also incorporated into both the Safeguards Documents[61] and the Negotiating Instructions,[62] and hence into both non-NPT and NPT safeguards agreements. Special fissionable material includes Pu-239 and uranium having a higher than "natural" ratio of fissionable isotopes (U-233 and U-235) to U-238. Source material includes all other uranium (natural or depleted) and thorium, in the form of metal, alloy, chemical compound, or concentrate. Though the Board of Governors is specifically authorized by the Statute to expand these definitions, any such extension does not apply to NPT Safeguards Agreements without the consent of the state concerned.[63]

## Exceptions

Despite the basic coverage of all nuclear material, NPT Safeguards Agreements contain a number of explicit or implicit exceptions from safeguards. Some exceptions were agreed to because the

---

59 IAEA document INFCIRC/153, par. 14(a)(i).
60 IAEA Statute, Article XX.
61 IAEA document INFCIRC/66/Rev. 2, par. 77.
62 IAEA document INFCIRC/153, par. 112.
63 *Ibid.*

material in question is considered genuinely irrelevant in determining the capacity of a country to produce nuclear weapons or explosives. Others were accepted for irresistible practical or political reasons, and these exceptions may constitute significant limitations on the control system.

*Ores.* Materials "in mining or ore processing activities" are specifically exempted from safeguards.[64] In a sense, this exemption merely serves to clarify somewhat (though by no means completely) IAEA's statutory definition of "source material," which requires the material in question to be at least somewhat beyond the "ore" stage.[65] Though no safeguards are applied to ores, states exporting or importing any material not yet "of a composition and purity suitable for fuel fabrication or for being isotopically enriched" should notify the Agency. Such notice is not required, however, if the material is destined for specific non-nuclear purposes (discussed below).[66]

The basic reason for this exemption is that unconcentrated nuclear material requires elaborate processing in complicated and conspicuous facilities before it can be converted into a threatening form. Thus, controls would be premature at a stage so distant from any weapons use. On the other hand, the Agency should be aware of the movements of significant quantities of even such material, to make it less likely that these will disappear into clandestine nuclear plants and to facilitate the application of safeguards when such material enters the controlled parts of the nuclear fuel cycle.

*Irrecoverable Materials.* The provision relating to ores regulates the threshold for the initiation of safeguards. Two conceptually analogous provisions permit the termination of safeguards as to material transformed in the course of use so that it is no longer useful for any nuclear activity. Such transformations may occur either due to changes resulting from nuclear activities or by application to certain non-nuclear purposes, such as the produc-

---

[64] *Ibid.,* par. 33; see also par. 112.
[65] IAEA Statute, Article XX.3.
[66] IAEA document INFCIRC/153, par. 34(a), (b).

tion of ceramics or alloys, involving the massive dilution of any uranium used.[67]

If changes are due to nuclear activities, it is up to the Agency to determine whether the material has been sufficiently diluted or otherwise transformed so as to be practically irrecoverable. Though no standards are set for such a determination, the Agency will no doubt take into account all relevant circumstances, including the type of material and the ability of the state to process it effectively and clandestinely. If the material is in such a condition that the state no longer desires to use it but the Agency is unwilling to relinquish all controls (e.g., if reprocessing would be feasible, though expensive), special control measures may be agreed.[68]

In respect to material applied to non-nuclear purposes, the state and the Agency must agree on the circumstances of termination, if it is considered irrecoverable, and of exemption (almost indistinguishable from termination) even if it is recoverable.[69] Presumably such agreement, to be included in the Subsidiary Arrangements, will call for some controls as long as the material is still in a form usable for nuclear purposes, including tests from time to time to indicate how much of it has been "consumed" non-nuclearly. One gap in the system should be noted. As mentioned above, the international transfer of unprocessed nuclear ores need not be reported if destined for non-nuclear purposes. Thus, the Agency will not necessarily even be aware of all such material transferred to a state for ostensibly non-nuclear purposes.

*Minimal Quantities.* Safeguards may also be lifted in respect of minimal quantities of special fissionable material used in instruments and in respect of plutonium consisting substantially of non-fissionable isotopes.[70] In addition, some "free" exemptions are provided up to specified quantitative limits, ranging from 1 kilogram of plutonium (or its "equivalent" in the form of enriched uranium) to 20 tons of considerably depleted uranium or of thorium.[71] The assumption is that the prescribed quantities of

67 *Ibid.,* pars. 11, 13.
68 *Ibid.,* par. 35.
69 *Ibid.,* pars. 13, 35, 36(b).
70 *Ibid.,* par. 36(a), (c).
71 *Ibid.,* par. 37.

material, even if taken together with other material escaping controls on other grounds, will not significantly advance any country's nuclear weapon potential. Moreover, the possibility of using small amounts of nuclear material free of controls can save both the state and the Agency much bookkeeping and trouble.

*Material in Transit.* Material in transit presents, in addition to special and as yet unresolved problems of physical security, the question of assigning responsibility to a particular state. This is important because the IAEA's authority to exercise controls derives entirely from its safeguards agreements with individual states (pending the eventual recognition of some implied authority arising out of still undeveloped universal regulatory principles). Thus, safeguards cannot extend beyond the jurisdiction (or at least the effective control[72]) of the states that have concluded such agreements.

The rules regarding international transfers must be considered in this light. Basically, safeguards responsibility passes from an exporting to an importing country not at the boundaries of their respective jurisdictions (which will rarely adjoin), but at a point agreed by them. In any event, this transfer of responsibility must occur no later than when nuclear material reaches its final destination. No state is responsible for material merely because it is in transit through its territory or is on a ship or plane under its flag.[73] This means that an exporting or an importing state may be responsible, vis-à-vis the Agency, for nuclear material actually within the jurisdiction of a third state; in turn, the third state may have no responsibility towards the Agency and need not permit it to exercise any controls.

Normally these lacunae will be brief. If they become extended under suspicious circumstances, the Agency could issue an alarm, similar to that applicable to any frustration of safeguards, leaving the world community to deal with the states concerned on the basis of the information the Agency can supply about the nature and likely location of the missing material. As a preventive mea-

---

[72] NPT Article III.1 requires the application of safeguards to "all source or special fissionable material in all peaceful nuclear activities within the territory of [a non-nuclear-weapon] state, under its jurisdiction, or carried out under its control anywhere."

[73] IAEA document INFCIRC/153, par. 91. This appears at best as a very narrow construction of the NPT provision quoted in the previous note.

sure, the Agency might try to insist that material subject to safeguards be transported under the flag of either the exporting or the importing state, or of some other state willing to assume responsibility vis-à-vis the Agency.

*Non-Proscribed Military Uses.* In the course of the NPT negotiations it became apparent that the non-nuclear-weapon states were not willing to eschew all military nuclear activities—only those that involved nuclear weapons or explosives. And, while these states might be willing to permit some outside authority to control their peaceful nuclear material to verify that none was being clandestinely diverted to weapons, they were not willing to permit similar controls over any military activities that were not proscribed by the Treaty. Furthermore, even if states allowed such military activities to be controlled by the IAEA, the organization's Statute might be interpreted to bar any Agency involvement with such activities even if it were only to safeguard them against diversion for worse ends.[74]

Therefore, the NPT only requires non-nuclear-weapon states to submit their peaceful nuclear activities to Agency controls. The Negotiating Instructions consequently provide that safeguards shall extend solely to such activities. The Instructions also outline a procedure whereby nuclear material may be released from safeguards under arrangements agreed between the Agency and the state concerned. These arrangements must identify, to the extent possible and without revealing any classified information to the Agency, the period of time or circumstances under which safeguards will not apply.[75] However, no material may be released if it is subject to some other undertaking (e.g., through an IAEA Project Agreement or a bilateral nuclear assistance agreement) prescribing solely peaceful uses.[76]

Though this may appear to be a huge and fatal loophole, in practice it is unlikely to damage seriously the effectiveness and

[74] See Szasz, *Law and Practices*, sec. 15.1.2.2(c).

[75] IAEA document INFCIRC/153, par. 14.

[76] Consistent with this principle, the United States, in agreeing to the suspension of IAEA safeguards under the Safeguards Transfer Agreement with Austria, obtained the right to assure itself that any material released from safeguards under Austria's NPT Safeguards Agreement is not subject to bilateral guarantees to the United States (see Protocol of Suspension of September 21, 1971 [IAEA document INFCIRC/152/Mod. 1], par. 2).

credibility of the IAEA/NPT system of safeguards. First, the state must persuade the Agency that a "legitimate" military activity will actually be undertaken—that suspension of safeguards will not merely constitute a cover for diversion. Second, the suspension of safeguards is to be limited strictly to what appears necessary to avoid Agency intrusion on sensitive military areas. In relation to both these limitations, it may be expected that the IAEA will adopt a tougher attitude than the Euratom Commission, which, in implementing its somewhat similar obligation to confine controls to peaceful activities (and to allow any military activity—including the production of weapons—not prohibited by some international agreement),[77] has in effect given France *carte blanche* in deciding which activities may be controlled and which ones (e.g., reactors producing plutonium for weapons) may not. Finally, it appears unlikely that important non-weapons military uses will be found for nuclear material, except for nuclear propulsion of submarines and surface warships. Such programs would have to be so massive that it is hard to conceive of them as merely covers for the diversion of some nuclear material to weapons uses.

*Unreported Materials.* The most serious limitation on the IAEA's safeguards is that they apply only to registered material, that is, to material of which the Agency is cognizant. These include material reported in an initial inventory or imported (possibly notified by both the exporter and the importer) or produced in registered and thus safeguarded facilities.[78] No matter how thorough and effective the Agency's controls of these materials are, it is in principle possible for a state to have an unregistered domestic source of nuclear material (i.e., a uranium mine) and clandestine production facilities. It is also possible for a state to receive unregistered material from non-parties to the NPT either for immediate use in weapons or for prior processing in clandestine facilities.

Again, this apparently massive loophole turns out to be more hypothetical than realistic. Most nuclear facilities are so large and use or release so much energy that it is not easy to conceal them even in a large country. The same is true of shipments of necessar-

[77] Treaty Establishing the European Atomic Energy Community, 298 U.N.T.S. 167 (reproduced in *Multilateral Agreements,* IAEA Legal Series No. 1 [Vienna: IAEA, 1959], p. 79), Article 77.

[78] IAEA document INFCIRC/153, pars. 12, 62-67, 92, 95.

ily large quantities of nuclear raw material. Furthermore, though
Agency inspectors normally will have access only to the location
of officially registered material,[79] there are circumstances (described below) under which the Agency may demand the right to
inspect other locations where clandestine material or activities are
suspected.[80]

## IAEA/NPT SAFEGUARDS PROCEDURES

### General Approach

*Audit of National Controls.*  Agency safeguards agreements pursuant to NPT require the controlled states to "establish and
maintain a system of accounting for and control of all nuclear
material subject to safeguards." This is a signal departure from
previous safeguards agreements, which took no explicit account of
any domestic safeguards. The NPT Safeguards Agreements further
specify certain of the procedures to be followed by the national
system so as to assure compatibility with the controls to be
exercised by the Agency.[81]

The reason for these requirements is that the Agency intends
to rely, as far as possible, on such national controls in order to
execute its own responsibilities. Thus, the Agency is to have the
right to verify the findings of the state's own control system.
Though it also retains the right to make independent measurements and observations, these should not duplicate the national
accounts and controls unnecessarily.

*Method of Control.* The method of control explicitly set out in
the Negotiating Instructions is to divide each state into one or
more "material balance areas," some of which might comprise one
or more nuclear facilities, while others might consist of only a
fraction of one facility.[82] Strict inventory controls must be instituted for each area. Starting from an initial inventory, established
and verified as far as appropriate, every change in the quantity or

[79] See pp. 103-6 below.
[80] *Ibid.* and pp. 114-15 below.
[81] IAEA document INFCIRC/153, pars. 7, 32.
[82] *Ibid.,* pars. 6(a), 110.

form of nuclear material within the area must be taken into account, whether it is the result of transfer from or to other areas (or foreign countries), production, nuclear transformation, consumption, or other losses. Thus from time to time new inventories are calculated, and these in turn are subject to physical and other checks.[83] This "material accountancy" is considered the fundamental control measure, with containment and inspection as important secondary ones. The NPT Safeguards Agreements provide that "the technical conclusions of the Agency's verification activities shall be a statement, in respect of each material balance area, of the amount of material unaccounted for over a specified period, giving the limits of accuracy of the amounts stated."[84] The Agency's sole concern with the design and operation of nuclear facilities therefore relates to the possibility of establishing accurately the quantities of nuclear material consumed by, contained in, or produced by these facilities.

The NPT emphasizes the importance of developing control measures that use "instruments and other techniques at certain strategic points"[85] to minimize the need for direct human intrusion. This objective is restated in the Negotiating Instructions, which require the Agency (1) to "ensure optimum cost-effectiveness . . . by the use of instruments and other techniques" applied at "certain strategic points"; (2) to use means such as "statistical techniques and random sampling"; and (3) to concentrate its "verification procedures on those stages in the nuclear fuel cycle involving . . . nuclear material from which nuclear weapons or other nuclear explosive devices could readily be made."[86] The Agency has conducted and sponsored research in safeguards techniques ever since it was established. However, this effort was put into high gear only after the adoption of the NPT, and may now be expected to continue until new instruments and techniques are actually developed and sufficiently tested.[87]

[83] *Ibid.*, pars. 56, 63-67.

[84] *Ibid.*, par. 30.

[85] NPT, Preamble, fifth paragraph.

[86] IAEA document INFCIRC/153, par. 6.

[87] IAEA Annual Report, July 1, 1971-June 30, 1972, GC (XVI)/480, pars. 128-37 and table 23. The annual rate of expenditures for outside research is running at about $200,000, to which should be added $50,000 expended in the Agency's laboratory and the value of any free research performed in member states—see The Agency's Budget for 1973 (IAEA document GC (XVI)/485), table V.13.1 and pars. V.7.14-17, V.7.20-23, and V.13.23-66.

*Physical Security.* The most hotly contested provision in negotiating the IAEA Statute was one authorizing the Agency to
require the storage, in its own custody, of excess special fissionable material accumulated by member states from safeguarded
activities, to be released by the Agency only when the state that
owned it needed it immediately in another safeguarded facility. [88]
Other provisions of the Statute call for the employment of
"guards" and for the establishment of geographically scattered
depots for material within the Agency's custody.[89] However,
since the establishment of the Agency, no steps have been taken to
implement any of these provisions. The status quo is implicitly
recognized by the NPT, which foresees that the Agency will
merely verify, rather than ensure, that safeguarded material is not
diverted. Consequently, the Negotiating Instructions equally avoid
any suggestion that the Agency might itself physically control any
nuclear material.

Furthermore, nothing in the NPT Safeguards Agreements specifically requires a state to take any particular measures to assure
the physical security of safeguarded material, whether during use,
in storage, or even in the vulnerable stage of transport. While the
Instructions include several provisions about "containment," [90]
these are merely meant to facilitate accounting. Of course, if any
nuclear material were seized while under national safeguards, the
state concerned would have to convince the Agency that no
diversion to a weapons or other prohibited use would result.
Otherwise, the Agency might raise an international hue and cry
about the purloined material.

## Principal Procedures

Each of the principal safeguards procedures called for by the
Negotiating Instructions is, to some extent, based on one of the
procedures set forth in Article XII.A of the Agency's Statute,
though several have suffered change and diminution in the decade
and half since the Statute was unanimously adopted.

*Design Information.* The Statute foresees that, as part of its

---

88 IAEA Statute, Article XII.A.5.
89 *Ibid.,* Articles VII.G and IX.H-I.
90 See p. 101 below.

safeguards, the Agency will examine the designs of safeguarded facilities and approve these in order to assure that they will not further any military purpose and will permit the effective application of safeguards.[91] Only a pale shadow of this potentially powerful, but therefore politically unacceptable, authority remains in the NPT Safeguards Agreements. The idea of reviewing designs to assure that facilities will only be used peacefully was abandoned years ago, when it was concluded that such a check was technically meaningless. No feature of the design of a facility (such as a reactor) could guarantee its future use for peaceful purposes.[92] However, the principle was maintained that the Agency would review designs, if possible in advance, to determine whether they permitted the facile application of safeguards.[93] This power to "approve" designs might be used by the Agency to induce an operator of a facility to incorporate in the design instruments and other features that would ease the application of controls, either by increasing the certainty of measurements or by diminishing the need for inspections.

The NPT Safeguards Agreements no longer authorize the Agency to approve or even to "review" designs. The Agency is merely to be informed of the design of the facilities it is to safeguard so that it can determine what control measures are required and can incorporate these in the Subsidiary Arrangements. Moreover, the Agency may request only the minimum information needed to carry out its functions, and the Arrangements must spell out in some detail what types of data are required for this purpose. Where information is particularly sensitive (i.e., from a commercial point of view), it need not be physically transmitted to the Agency itself if it is made available for examination in the state concerned.[94] The Agency may, however, take the safeguards-related features of the design into account in determining the actual intensity of its inspections.[95]

---

[91] IAEA Statute, Article XII.A.1.

[92] There still might be cause for suspicion if a reactor, ostensibly installed to produce power, should be designed to be more efficient as a producer of plutonium than of electricity, and in particular if it is foreseen that due to low excess reactivity the fuel would receive only an inefficiently low burnup so that the plutonium produced would of necessity be of high bomb-grade quality (i.e., be low in Pu-240 and 242).

[93] IAEA document INFCIRC/66/Rev. 2, pars. 30-32.

[94] IAEA document INFCIRC/153, pars. 8, 42, 43, 46.

[95] *Ibid.*, par. 81(c).

The possibility of less frequent inspections may reinforce Agency suggestions that certain features be adopted.

*Records.*   The NPT Safeguards Agreements require states, as part of their national safeguards systems, to maintain records for each material balance area. These must be subdivided into accounting and operational records. The Negotiating Instructions specify certain requirements, such as the period of retention and the standards of the system of measurements to be used, but the specific details are to be included in the Subsidiary Arrangements.[96]

For a number of reasons, the records system is crucial to the scheme of IAEA safeguards. The Agency's control system is based on accounting, which in effect means record-keeping. Each state's records are the basis of the reports required to be submitted to the Agency, from which the Agency's own safeguards records are to be derived. Finally, an important feature of the inspections will be an examination of the state's records for consistency within themselves, with the reports filed, with the available information about nuclear facilities, and with data obtained in other ways.[97]

*Reports.*   Unlike records, the reports required to be made to the Agency are not expected to be a part of a state's own safeguards system. In other words, ordinarily they need not be the ones prepared for some domestic purpose. However, they must be based on the records. The general rules relating to the reports are set forth in the Negotiating Instructions and thus in the Safeguards Agreements, while specific details will be included in the Subsidiary Arrangements.[98]

Corresponding to the accounting records, accounting reports must be submitted for each material balance area, at regular intervals (monthly or less frequently, down to annually) or ad hoc (for reports relating, for example, to the results of a physical inventory). Special reports must be submitted without delay if material losses in excess of limits specified in the applicable Subsidiary Arrangement may have occurred or if the "containment" of some material has been breached in violation of

96 *Ibid.,* pars. 51-58.
97 *Ibid.,* pars. 61, 72(a), 74(a).
98 *Ibid.,* pars. 59-67.

rules agreed upon with the Agency.[99] When significant quantities of nuclear material are transferred into or out of a state, special advance reports are required; in some instances, subsequent reports are also required indicating the due receipt of the material. States must amplify or clarify any reports, at IAEA request. [100]

*Containment.* As noted previously, the IAEA Statute foresees that physical storage of excess fissionable material by the Agency should be an important safeguards measure. [101] The Negotiating Instructions make no provision whatsoever for Agency custody of nuclear material. They do, however, foresee the use of "containment" as a safeguards device, but only as a "means of defining material balance areas for accounting purposes." [102] In other words, the purpose is not to assure the physical security of the material, but merely to help the Agency keep track of it.

Once a batch of material has been inventoried (potentially an elaborate process) under the supervision of Agency inspectors, it can be stored in a container to which the inspectors affix a seal. [103] As long as the seal is not broken, as ascertained by periodic but simple inspections, the inventory need not be repeated. When it becomes necessary to remove some of the material, the Agency is notified so that an inspector can be present when the seal is broken.

*Inspection.* While the efficacy of IAEA safeguards rests primarily on the records that must be maintained about all peaceful nuclear material, facilities, and operations in non-nuclear-weapon states, the credibility of these controls depends almost entirely on the fact that the Agency may and does carry out inspections to determine the extent to which the records correspond to reality. However, while this right and the measures taken pursuant to it are crucial to any credible control system, they are also the most manifest intrusion upon the sovereignty of the controlled states. Consequently, the inspection procedures are politically delicate and controversial. They must be most precisely delineated in the

99 *Ibid.,* par. 68.

100 *Ibid.,* pars. 69, 92, 95.

101 IAEA Statute, Article XII.A.5.

102 IAEA document INFCIRC/153, par. 6(a).

103 *Ibid.,* par. 75(e); see also par. 68(b).

NPT Safeguards Agreements and are substantially hedged about with limitations and constraints.

Designation of Inspectors.    The procedure for "designating" the Agency officials who will be authorized to carry out inspections within a state is detailed in its NPT Safeguards Agreements. The Director General must inform the state concerned of the name, qualifications, nationality, grade, and other relevant particulars of any official he proposes to use as an inspector. The state must indicate within thirty days whether it accepts this proposal, and if it does so, the Director General may make the designation, informing the state thereof. [104]

Two preliminary protective measures exist to make it unlikely that the Director General will propose unacceptable persons to a state. In the first place, the appointment of each inspector, unlike that of other staff, must be specifically approved by the Board of Governors. [105]   Although this requirement is primarily designed to permit the Board to supervise the geographical (political) spread of the entire corps of inspectors, it also reduces the possibility that clearly unqualified or "difficult" persons will be included in that group. Furthermore, the Director General has declared to the Board that he will informally consult the government concerned before formally proposing to it the name of any inspector. This procedure, reminiscent of that preceding the formal request for an *agrément* for a diplomatic envoy, can be used by a state to inform the Agency, with minimum embarrassment, of the unacceptability of a given individual or of certain groups (i.e., the nationals of particular states).

The state need give no reason for refusing to accept a nomination. Furthermore, even a designation which has been accepted must be withdrawn if the state so requests—again no reason need be given. [106]   It should be recognized that the right of a state to demand an inspector's withdrawal could be used as a means of pressuring an unduly inquisitive inspector, and even of promptly banishing him should he be close to some discovery embarrassing to the host state.

---

[104] *Ibid.,* pars. 9, 85.
[105] IAEA document GC(V)/INF/39, par. 2.
[106] IAEA document INFCIRC/153, par. 85(d).

In the event of such an objection, the Director General may propose alternative designations. Only if the repeated refusal of a state to accept proposed designations impedes the inspections to be conducted under the NPT Safeguards Agreement may the Director General refer the matter to the Board "with a view to appropriate action." [107] What Board action may be taken is not specified. Presumably, such a situation might be considered a dispute regarding the application of safeguards, to which the procedures described below under that heading would apply.

The debates preceding the adoption of these provisions (and their predecessors in the Agency's "Inspectors Document"), [108] together with the Agency's prior practice, suggest the types of differences that might arise in the course of designating inspectors. The IAEA Secretariat has always conceived the state's veto as permitting a "selection out," whereby officials who are for some narrowly circumscribed reason unacceptable to a state may be eliminated from the list of its inspectors. Although this may inconvenience the Agency by preventing optimum staff utilization, it is a political price that must be paid for the system to be accepted. [109] However, some states have argued that they should have the right to choose inspectors acceptable to them from the Agency's entire panel. This claim has never been allowed, but a practically unlimited right to reject proposed designations could be used to the same effect unless the Director General, backed by the Board, takes a strong stand.

Visits by Inspectors. Inspections are classified by the Negotiating Instructions as ad hoc, routine, or special. Different rules regarding frequency or rationale, notice, and access apply to each category.

One type of ad hoc inspection may be carried out primarily at the inception of safeguards in order to verify and update information received in the initial reports. Inspectors may also be sent to verify the design information received on facilities. At least a week's notice must be given, and inspectors are to have access to

---

107 *Ibid.,* par. 9.

108 IAEA document GC(V)/INF/39, Annex; reproduced in McKnight, *Atomic Safeguards,* Annex 6.

109 The importance of this right to challenge inspectors was emphasized in par. 2(c) of Resolution F of the Conference of Non-Nuclear-Weapon States, reproduced in UN document A/7277, par. 17.

all locations where the initial report, or the inspection itself, indicates the presence of nuclear materials. [110] Another type of ad hoc inspection may be made of nuclear materials before they are transferred out of one state and as they are received in another. Only twenty-four hours' notice is required, and access is limited to the location specified in the earlier notification of transfer. [111]

Routine inspections are to be carried out to verify the consistency of a state's reports with its records, to verify the location, identity, quantity, and composition of all nuclear materials subject to safeguards, and to obtain information on possible causes of materials unaccounted for or of various uncertainties in records. [112] Special formulas establish the maximum frequency and/or intensity (in terms of duration and of number of inspectors) of inspections of specified categories of facilities or of other locations of nuclear material. The formulas are used to determine either the number of inspections per year or the number of man-days of inspection per year on the basis of the quantity of nuclear material within or passing through such locations. [113] There is no explicit provision for the stationing of "resident" inspectors, but the number of man-days of inspection technically necessary per year for large facilities is usually great enough to make such arrangements a practical requirement.

The NPT Safeguards Agreements also provide that the actual number, intensity, and duration of inspections must be kept to a minimum consistent with the Agency's responsibilities. In particular, the Agency is required to take account of the form of nuclear material under control, the effectiveness and reliability of the Agency's controls, the characteristics of each state's nuclear fuel cycle, and its international interdependence (i.e., the extent to which its nuclear activities are interrelated with those of other states). [114]

Ordinarily, at least twenty-four hours' notice must be given for routine inspections relating to plutonium or to uranium enriched to at least 5 percent and one week for other nuclear material. However, a certain number of routine inspections may be carried

110 IAEA document INFCIRC/153, pars. 48, 71(a), 76(a), 83(a).

111 *Ibid.*, pars. 71(c), 76(b), 83(a), 93, 96.

112 *Ibid.*, par. 72.

113 *Ibid.*, pars. 78-80.

114 *Ibid.*, par. 81.

out unannounced; such surprise inspections are to be randomly scheduled, though the state should be informed of the projected general pattern of announced and unannounced inspections. On any routine inspection, access is limited to certain "strategic points" identified in the Subsidiary Arrangements, as well as to all required records. [115]

One type of special inspection may be carried out to verify the information contained in special reports, i.e., reports of unusual incidents or unexpected changes in the containment of nuclear material. Such inspections require prior consultation with the state, during which the notice to be given and presumably the scope of access will be determined. [116]

If the Agency considers that the information made available by the state, including that obtained from routine inspections, "is not adequate for the Agency to fulfill its responsibilities," then additional inspections may be carried out, for which access may be had to locations other than those open to ad hoc or to routine inspections. [117] However, use of this extraordinary measure requires prior consultation with the state concerned and agreement upon any additional locations to be inspected.

The IAEA Statute foresees, perhaps naively, that Agency inspectors are to "have access at all times to all places and data . . . as required to account for [nuclear] materials . . . and to determine whether there is compliance with . . . any . . . conditions prescribed in the [safeguards] agreement." [118] The paragraphs above indicate the extent to which the broad powers foreseen in the Statute are, characteristically, whittled down by the Negotiating Instructions. Ad hoc, routine, and most special inspections may reach only narrowly circumscribed locations, and even the extraordinary special inspections may extend only to places agreed by the state. Moreover, a state may, though only under "unusual circumstances," further limit access, subject to

---

[115] *Ibid.*, pars. 76(c), 83(c), 84.

[116] *Ibid.*, pars. 73(a) (read together with par. 68), 77, 83(b).

[117] *Ibid.*, pars. 73(b), 77, 83(b).

[118] IAEA Statute, Article XII.A.6. These rights were in effect maintained by par. 9 of the Inspectors Document (see n. 108 above), which has been (and presumably will continue to be) incorporated into all non-NPT safeguards agreements; the NPT Safeguards Agreements do not incorporate the Inspectors Document, since they set out all the essential terms directly.

special arrangements with the Agency. [119] These restrictions will, except as indicated below, preclude inspectors from roaming around in an attempt either to locate materials missing under suspicious circumstances or to detect any clandestine material or activities.

Activities of Inspectors.   Regardless of the extent of the Agency's inspection efforts, and even without the restrictions described, it is most unlikely that an inspector would ever be able to observe diversion or misuse of nuclear material. The constant presence of inspectors may sometimes have a deterrent effect on illegal activities, but even these instances will probably be rare. Instead, inspectors will primarily have the more prosaic task of ascertaining the truthfulness of the records that show where nuclear materials are being kept and how they are being used. The measures inspectors will be permitted to take are prescribed in the NPT Safeguards Agreements, in considerably greater detail than in any previous safeguards agreements. The principal activities of Agency inspectors are to (1) examine the domestic records; (2) observe the sampling of nuclear material, obtain duplicate samples (to be sent to the Agency for direct analysis), and make other independent measurements; (3) verify the functioning and calibration of instruments and of other measuring and control equipment, observe calibration procedures, use their own equipment for independent measurements, and, if allowed by the Subsidiary Arrangements, install such equipment at facilities; (4) use appropriate surveillance and containment measures, such as the application of seals and other tamperproof identifying devices, if allowed by the Subsidiary Arrangements; and (5) use other "objective" methods demonstrated to be feasible. [120]

It should be noted that nothing is said about the human contacts of the inspectors. No doubt these might be "professionally" important, especially for a resident inspector, which is perhaps the real reason why resident inspection has often been firmly resisted. Over the years, an inspector is likely to become well acquainted with a substantial number of members of the relevant scientific community in a state to which he is assigned, and he

119 IAEA document INFCIRC/153, par. 76(d).
120 *Ibid.,* pars. 74-75.

may be able to suspect significant clandestine activity merely by observing the movements of his acquaintances. Moreover, no state can rely on all its scientists and technicians being uniformly discreet, content, and loyal solely to national objectives; if an inspector's ear is available, it may hear tales.

Rights of Inspectors. The NPT Safeguards Agreements provide either for the application to Agency inspectors of the appropriate provisions of the Agreement on the Privileges and Immunities of the IAEA [121] or for the grant of substantially equivalent rights designed to enable inspectors to discharge their functions effectively and formulated so as not to place the state concerned in a more favorable position (vis-à-vis the Agency) than those that are parties to the standard Immunities Agreement. [122]

Inspectors thus enjoy the normal immunities of international officials, such as freedom from arrest or other legal process for anything they do in their official capacity (unless the Agency should itself waive this protection). In addition, they have the rights attributed to "experts on mission" for the Agency: absolute immunity from arrest and detention and from seizure of baggage (including the right to diplomatic facilities for the handling of even personal items), inviolability of papers, and the right to communicate with the Agency through codes, couriers, and sealed bags. [123]

Unlike diplomats, inspectors cannot be declared *persona non grata* and may be expelled only after a formal procedure in which the Director General may intervene. [124] However, this technicality may be of little use, in view of a state's right to demand at any time the immediate withdrawal of the designation on which rests the inspector's right to enter and stay in its territory.

Limitations on and Duties of Inspectors. In addition to certain general constraints on the Agency in carrying out its control measures and the strict circumscriptions on the activities of inspectors, several specific limitations are imposed on their conduct:

[121] 374 U.N.T.S. 147, reproduced in IAEA document INFCIRC/9/Rev.2.
[122] IAEA document INFCIRC/153, par. 10.
[123] See n. 121 above, secs. 18(b) and 23.
[124] *Ibid.*, sec. 27(b).

1. Inspectors must avoid hampering or delaying the construction or operation of facilities or affecting their safety. [125]

2. Inspectors may not themselves operate any nuclear facility or direct its staff to carry out any operations. They may only request the facility operator to arrange to have particular operations carried out. [126]

3. Inspectors must comply with the health and safety procedures of the facilities inspected. This requirement might well be used to discourage snooping. [127]

4. The state may, as provided in the IAEA Statute, arrange to have inspectors accompanied by its own representatives, provided that the inspection process is not thereby delayed or impeded. [128]

### Constraints on the IAEA

The Negotiating Instructions provide for the inclusion in the NPT Safeguards Agreements of a formidable list of limitations on the Agency. Some of these can be traced to the Agency's successive Safeguards Documents, in which an ever longer list of such constraints appeared. Some were included in the NPT, while still others were first proposed by the 1968 Conference of Non-Nuclear-Weapon States. [129]

Reflecting the principal concern of the states to be controlled, the Agency must avoid hampering economic and technical development and international cooperation in the field of nuclear energy, including the export of nuclear material. [130] This charge is repeated several times in the provisions for inspections, which are to be arranged so as to reduce to a minimum any inconvenience and disturbance to states and activities inspected; thus even unannounced inspections are to be scheduled so as to minimize any practical difficulties for the facility operator and the state. Safeguards must, moreover, be implemented in a manner "designed to be consistent with prudent management practices required for the economic and safe conduct of nuclear activities." [131]

125 IAEA document INFCIRC/153, par. 87.
126 *Ibid.*
127 *Ibid.*, par. 44 (final sentence).
128 *Ibid.*, par. 89; cf. IAEA Statute, Article XII.A.6.
129 The report of which was published as UN document A/7277.
130 IAEA document INFCIRC/153, par. 4(a), based on NPT, Article III.3.
131 *Ibid.*, pars. 4(c), 9, 78, 79, 84.

Echoing NPT, the Agency is also required to take full account of technological developments in the field of safeguards and to make every effort to ensure optimum cost-effectiveness. [132]

Responding to another old concern, the NPT Safeguards Agreements charge the Agency to take every precaution to protect commercial and industrial secrets and any other confidential information coming to its knowledge in the implementation of safeguards. For that purpose, even the distribution of such information within the Agency must be restricted. As a further guarantee, the Agency may require from the state only the "minimum amount of information and data consistent with carrying out its responsibilities." This limitation applies particularly to operating and design information about facilities, and to the extent that a state considers the latter to be particularly sensitive, the Agency must arrange to examine it *in situ* rather than at its headquarters. [133]

## Obligations of States

The NPT Safeguards Agreements also place certain general responsibilities on the controlled state. The principal one is to cooperate with the Agency to facilitate the implementation of safeguards. The state must take the necessary steps to ensure that Agency inspectors can effectively discharge their functions, specifically by facilitating the examination of records (especially if not kept in English, French, Russian, or Spanish) and by procuring services and equipment required by the inspectors. [134]

Unlike other safeguards agreements, the NPT Agreements do not specifically require the state to inform inspectors of the location of all nuclear material and to give them access thereto. [135] However, inspectors should be able to establish this information from the reports the state is obliged to make. To the extent they are unable to do so, the disputes and sanctions procedures discussed below may become applicable.

The NPT Safeguards Agreements express, more clearly than previous safeguards agreements, that a reduction in the number

---

[132] *Ibid.*, par. 6, based on NPT, Preamble, fifth paragraph.

[133] *Ibid.*, pars. 5, 8.

[134] *Ibid.*, pars. 3, 52, 88.

[135] A requirement formerly set out in the provision cited in n. 118 above.

and intensity of inspections actually carried out is to be the *quid pro quo* for effective cooperation by a state with the Agency (e.g., by permitting the installation of measuring instruments supplied by the Agency). [136]

## DISPUTES, VIOLATIONS, AND SANCTIONS

### Failure To Conclude Safeguards Agreements or Subsidiary Arrangements

No state is obliged to become a party to the NPT, although a state that has signed the Treaty may be under some constraint to give it formal consideration and to take no action meanwhile that would preclude a favorable decision. [137] Aside from extraneous pressures, the only leverage that parties to the NPT may have in persuading others to join would be a boycott of nuclear assistance, but up to now no leading nuclear state has shown any inclination to institute such an embargo, either alone or in cooperation with others. Of course, any nuclear assistance now granted by an NPT party to a non-party non-nuclear-weapon state must be subjected to Agency safeguards, and the Agency is not required to ease the application of such controls, except to the extent required by NPT itself. [138]

Non-nuclear-weapon states that become parties to NPT are obligated to initiate negotiations with the Agency and to conclude NPT Safeguards Agreements within a limited period of time. The maximum is about two years for states that ratified the NPT on or before its initial entry into force on March 5, 1970. Thus some fifty-seven states should have concluded these agreements by the beginning of 1972 and still more should have done so shortly

---

136 IAEA document INFCIRC/153, par. 81(b).

137 Vienna Convention on the Law of Treaties (UN document A/CONF.39/27), Article 18(a). Though not yet in force, this provision is one recognized as merely restating an existing legal principle.

138 Thus the principles of NPT Article III.3 are clearly applicable to such controls, but other provisions of the Negotiating Instructions need not necessarily be—and indeed it would be illogical to permit non-party states to benefit from those features of the Instructions that permit certain controls to be relaxed only because all nuclear activities in NPT non-nuclear-weapon states are to be controlled. On the other hand, IAEA Statute Articles III.C, III.D, and IV.C would seem to preclude the Agency from using an unreasonably tough implementation of NPT Article III.2 controls to induce non-party states to become parties to the Treaty.

thereafter. [139] The failure to conclude such an Agreement either within the time limit or at all is a violation of the NPT. Though no sanction is prescribed, NPT parties may only give nuclear assistance to a delinquent state (as to a non-party) if the assistance is subject to safeguards. [140] Failure to conclude a Safeguards Agreement is not a violation of any obligation due the Agency, since the latter is not a party to the NPT.

It seems unlikely that any non-nuclear-weapon party to the NPT would flatly refuse to conclude a Safeguards Agreement with the Agency, for this would make its participation in the Treaty worse than meaningless. If a state has serious reservations about the Agreement, it will presumably clarify these before ratifying the Treaty. However, a state might refuse to conclude an Agreement on the terms foreseen in the Board's Negotiating Instructions to the Director General. Should the difference be a minor one, the Board might agree to a deviation if controls could still be effectively carried out and other states were not disadvantaged. Indeed, if the Board failed to agree, the Agency might be faulted for being too inflexible and the state concerned might thus be absolved of its default under the Treaty. However, if the difference were major, going to an essential part of the safeguards system, then the Board might be disinclined to yield, so as to avoid accepting responsibilities that the Agency might not be able to carry out and to prevent the establishment of unfortunate precedents.

After a Safeguards Agreement is concluded, the initial Subsidiary Arrangements under it must be negotiated and enter into force within ninety days. This deadline can be extended only by agreement with the Agency. [141] Failure to meet this timetable might make it difficult, or even impossible, for the Agency to carry out its responsibilities under the Safeguards Agreement. In that event,

---

[139] As indicated in the list in Appendix D to this volume, as of June 30, 1972, twenty-seven of these negotiations had been completed and sixteen of these agreements had already entered into force. In addition, negotiations were proceeding with thirty-one further non-nuclear-weapon states, including the five non-nuclear-weapon members of Euratom (none of which were yet NPT parties), with which agreement was reached a few weeks later.

[140] The United States decided not to cut off the supply of nuclear material to the Euratom non-nuclear-weapon states (or even to require the imposition of the IAEA controls required by NPT Article III.2) because it considered that these states were negotiating their NPT Safeguards Agreements with the Agency "in good faith," though already two years after the entry into force of NPT (*New York Times*, March 17, 1972).

[141] IAEA document INFCIRC/153, par. 40.

presumably the measures described in the following section would apply.

## Disputes about the Application of Safeguards

The NPT Safeguards Agreements provide for the Agency and the state concerned to consult about any question arising out of their interpretation or application. In particular, consultations are required if the state considers that the Agency is unduly concentrating inspections on particular facilities. If these consultations, which presumably will take place with the Director General, the Inspector General, and their staff, do not resolve the issue, the state concerned may refer the matter to the Board, which must invite the state to participate in the debates on the matter. [142]

Generally speaking, if any dispute about the interpretation or application of a Safeguards Agreement cannot be settled by consultation with the IAEA Secretariat or by the Agency's Board, it may be submitted by either party to an ad hoc three-member arbitral tribunal, the majority decision of which is binding on both parties. [143] The only question that may not be referred to such a forum is a dispute relating to a Board finding of a violation or a consequent Board decision to impose sanctions (see below)—the Agency's decisions in such matters are thus not open to any challenge. [144]

Although the Board's Safeguards Committee briefly considered the establishment of a standing "safeguards tribunal," [145] the idea was dropped. The lack of such a tribunal might be considered a significant flaw in the Agency's safeguards system. Questions of major significance relating to the implementation of NPT Safeguards Agreements are to be decided by ad hoc and consequently basically inexperienced arbitrators possibly desirous of finding

---

142 *Ibid.*, pars. 20, 21, 82.

143 *Ibid.*, par. 22. In negotiating NPT Safeguards Agreements with some of the Eastern European states (e.g., Romania), the Agency agreed to a significantly weaker provision for the contingency that no agreement can be reached for the appointment of the neutral chairman.

144 For this reason this exception was strongly controverted in the Safeguards Committee (1970).

145 Such as exists for ENEA under the Convention on the Establishment of a Security Control in the Field of Nuclear Energy (*Multilateral Agreements*, p. 187), pt. 3 and annexed Protocol (*ibid.*, p. 197).

some middle ground between the conflicting claims of the Agency and the controlled state, rather than by a specially chosen standing body conscious of its status and responsibilities as an organ established to further the effective functioning of a control system of worldwide importance.

Unlike many of the arbitral tribunals for which provision is made in all non-NPT safeguards agreements, [146] those established under the NPT Safeguards Agreements will not have the power to make interim, provisional decisions binding on the parties. Instead, if the Board decides, upon a report of the Director General, that certain safeguards measures are essential and urgent to ensure verification of non-diversion, it may call on the state to take the required action without delay whether or not procedures for the settlement of the dispute have been invoked. [147] In principle, this power is very broad and might apply to a variety of situations:

1. If a facility operator fails to carry out certain operations or to take measurements requested by an inspector, and the inspector persuades the Director General and the Board that such measures are essential to the effective implementation of controls, the Board might invoke its power to issue directives.

2. If a state delays or declines to enter into Subsidiary Arrangements, it might be required by the Board to enter into these Arrangements or to permit the provisional exercise of controls as if it had done so.

3. If a state repeatedly turns down proposed designations of inspectors or unnecessarily withdraws its consent to existing ones, the Board might require the acceptance of at least some qualified inspectors. [148]

4. If the Agency decides it is necessary to carry out special inspections, at places or at times not open to ad hoc or routine inspections, [149] the Board might issue an authorizing directive. In the long run, however, the Board's decisions pursuant to these interim powers might be reversed by an arbitral tribunal convened with regard to the same matter.

---

[146] See Szasz, *Law and Practices*, secs. 21.10 and 27.2.2.2.1.
[147] IAEA document INFCIRC/153, par. 18.
[148] *Ibid.*, par. 9.
[149] *Ibid.*, par. 77 (final clause).

## Suspected Violations

The system of IAEA safeguards in relation to NPT is built on the assumption that states agreeing to such controls intend to comply with their fundamental obligations and will, more or less graciously, cooperate with the Agency in enabling it to verify such compliance with an acceptable degree of certainty. The substantial restraints imposed on the Agency in exercising its controls can only be justified on that assumption. Nevertheless, the safeguards system must, by its very nature, take account of the contingency that a state may indeed attempt to carry out undetected illicit activities.

The Agency has secured one potent device to counter these threats: it can request, and if necessary require, a state to afford Agency inspectors access beyond that available for ad hoc, routine, or "normal" special inspections. [150] Exercise of this right would be useful in two types of situations.

1. If the Agency suspects diversion but cannot either prove or disprove the suspicion through its circumscribed routine inspections, it might need access to parts of a nuclear facility or material balance area normally closed to it. Such a situation might result from unexpected technical advances in the activities under control, or from Subsidiary Arrangements containing technically faulty definitions of the material balance areas or of the "strategic points" to which Agency inspectors have normal access.

2. If the Agency learns from unofficial sources, such as informers in the state concerned or the intelligence services of other states, about otherwise undetected diversion or about unregistered material and activities, it will need special inspections to establish the facts. However, if the Agency merely wishes to trace material inexplicably missing, the right to demand extended access would probably not be of much use. Inspectors cannot hope to detect, without special leads, missing nuclear material located somewhere outside a narrowly circumscribed area.

As noted previously, the right to carry out an extended inspection is the vestige of the "access to all places and data and to all persons" foreseen in the IAEA Statute. [151] It is by no means an unlimited license to search, for the places or data that may thus be

150 *Ibid.*, pars. 73 and 77.
151 Article XII.A.6.

investigated must still be defined more or less precisely, either in agreement with the state concerned or by direction of the Board of Governors, which is not likely to act without the presentation of a convincing case by the Director General. Thus, states are protected against any unreasonable use of the right to carry out special inspections.

## Sanctions

It appears most unlikely that Agency inspectors will, in the normal course of their visits, ever be permitted to detect any illicit nuclear activities. Except where a state has decided to defy the Agency and the NPT openly, any violation or suspected violation of the Treaty is therefore likely to come to the Agency's attention in one of the following ways:

1. Through open defiance of the NPT and the Safeguards Agreement by a state prepared to convert quickly into nuclear weapons the stocks of peaceful nuclear material available to it and unwilling to await the three-month denunciation period required by the Treaty. [152] In this situation the Agency's role would be to force an earlier disclosure of the state's military nuclear intentions than would occur without the exercise of controls.

2. Records, verified by inspections, may indicate that substantial quantities of nuclear material cannot be accounted for. The material may not be recorded at all, or the records pertaining to it may be false, or the explanation given for its consumption or disappearance may not be plausible. As pointed out in the previous section, even the right to make special inspections would probably not suffice to satisfy the Agency of the state's innocence unless the latter were able and chose to lead inspectors to the location of incontrovertible proof.

3. A state, without plausible cause, may impede the access of inspectors to locations or data necessary to verify the existence and proper use of nuclear material. Such interference might occur during either normal, ad hoc, or routine inspections, leading to a suspicion that the state is diverting controlled nuclear material. More probably it would relate to a special inspection aimed at detecting unregistered nuclear material or clandestine activities. Of course, it is possible that frustration of inspections might not

152 NPT Article X.1.

stem from an effort by the state to conceal guilt but from a desire to hide some embarrassing event, such as a substantial loss of nuclear material as a result of careless handling or a loss inexplicable to the state's own authorities.

When the Agency either knows of or strongly suspects a violation and is unable to dissipate such suspicion, it can only take the limited steps foreseen for this eventuality in its Statute, the relevant provisions of which are incorporated by reference into the NPT Safeguards Agreements. [153]

1. It may call on the state concerned to "return" any nuclear material made available to it—a measure clearly requiring the voluntary compliance of the state. [154]

2. It may call on all its members (whether or not they are parties to the Treaty), and presumably also on all other parties to the Treaty, to curtail or suspend any nuclear assistance they are giving the state concerned. Even if this call is obeyed, it can only be effective if that state is substantially dependent on such foreign assistance.

3. The Agency may report the violation to its own members and to the UN Security Council and General Assembly—and thus, in effect, to all NPT parties. The UN organs can thereupon take whatever measures are available to them under the Charter, presumably including a Security Council finding of a threat to the peace and a call by it for collective measures under Chapter VII of the Charter. The NPT parties have no executive organ, though individually or collectively they can take whatever action appears called for: denunciation of the Treaty by the non-nuclear-weapon states that consider themselves immediately threatened or threats or actual intervention by the nuclear-weapon states that were the principal sponsors of the Treaty or by other parties to it.

## ADMINISTRATION OF SAFEGUARDS

The sections above describe the legal and to some extent the technical parameters determining the potential efficacy of IAEA

[153] IAEA document INFCIRC/153, par. 19, which refers to IAEA Statute Article XII.C; the sanctions provided in that Article also cover those specified in Article XII.A.7.

[154] As pointed out in Szasz, *Law and Practices*, sec. 21.7.2.4, pars. v and vi, the statutory language and meaning are by no means clear: does this section refer only to material supplied by or through the Agency, and, if not, is the original supplier obliged to accept such a return?

safeguards. However, the actual effectiveness of these controls, and above all their credibility, will depend on how conscientiously the various organs responsible for implementing the control system operate in practice. Will they toughmindedly check out any reasonable suspicion, or will they tend to yield to political exigencies and to avoid challenging any state determined not to be inconvenienced (whether for innocent or for improper reasons) by international controls? It is therefore necessary to examine all these organs in turn, to determine what motives and constraints each may have for either strict or lax enforcement. Such factors may be internal to a particular organ or they may relate to its interaction with another. They may be directly connected with NPT concerns or in substance be extraneous to them.

## The IAEA Secretariat

*The Inspectors.* The inspectors, inevitably, constitute the cutting edge of the safeguards system, not only because of the nature of their functions but also because the IAEA Statute foresees that diversion or "non-compliance" will be detected by inspectors who then set into motion the machinery for calling the state concerned to account. [155] In fact, violations are more likely to be signaled by a refusal to grant access to inspectors. Such revealing confrontations are, however, more likely when the inspectors are acute, knowledgeable, and honest than when they are careless or venal.

The number of inspectors will inevitably have to grow as more and more states join the Treaty and as their peaceful nuclear activities gradually increase. This increase in the size of the corps of inspectors may well change its character. Inspectors are Agency officials, chosen by the Director General (presumably on the advice of the Inspector General) and specifically approved by the Board of Governors. [156] The Board is concerned primarily with the geographically and politically representative nature of the inspector corps, but this concern may itself be a source of difficulty. If geographic diversity is pushed too far, and the recruitment of inspectors from countries having no nuclear programs or only rudimentary ones is required, these candidates will not have the proficiency necessary for a truly elite corps. On the other hand,

[155] IAEA Statute, Article XII.C (second sentence).
[156] IAEA document GC(V)/INF/39, par. 2.

wide geographic distribution will ensure that no weakness in the control system, detected by the Secretariat but not revealed to the public or even to the Agency's political organs, can be concealed for long. Thus, a variety of nationalities tends to guarantee to all nations that the controls are really working to protect them all. [157]

Since the establishment of the IAEA, there has been debate over whether its inspectors should generally be tenured officials with "permanent" appointments or should serve the Agency for only a term. [158] Most other professional-grade staff members of the Agency, especially in the technical departments, are appointed for fixed terms, but as far as inspectors are concerned the issue has not yet been resolved. A few officials with permanent appointments have become inspectors, but the great majority only have fixed-term contracts. In 1968 the Director General announced that, after satisfactory completion of two years of probation, inspectors could expect to receive a series of five-year contracts (the maximum length of fixed-term arrangements allowed by the Agency's Staff Regulations). The principal argument favoring long-term or permanent contracts is that they serve to ensure that inspectors are subject to the Agency's discipline and reasonably independent of outside blandishments. This is essential if the Agency is to protect industrial secrets. On the other hand, it can be argued that an inspector without career prospects in the Agency is less likely to succumb to pressures that might be exerted within the organization against overzealous personnel.

The sense in which the above questions are resolved will define the types of pressures determining whether Agency inspectors will tend to be lax or strict. Probably these pressures will be mainly in the direction of leniency. An inspector is unlikely to be disciplined for failing to detect a diversion, since the same clues must also have escaped a number of other inspectors. On the other hand, each inspector is likely to be conscious of a potential personal responsibility for any false alarm. A tough inspector is likely to

157 On June 30, 1972, the Division of Operations of the Department of Safeguards and Inspection (to which most of the inspectors are assigned, though the Director General has authority to use specified officials from other divisions and departments for this purpose) had thirty-seven professional members, from twenty-eight states (IAEA document INFCIRC/22/Rev. 12).

158 See Szasz, *Law and Practices*, sec. 21.8.1.1.

engender friction with states, which may not be reluctant to express displeasure to his superiors. Indeed, an inspector with a reputation for zealousness may find countries reluctant to accept his designation (thus reducing his usefulness to the Agency). He may also feel exposed to a substantial risk that his designation may be withdrawn while he is carrying out inquiries uncomfortable to the host country. Finally, it is not impossible that some inspectors, even though well paid by most standards, will succumb to bribes. On the other hand, threats of criminal or civil sanctions should normally be ineffective, in view of the immunities protecting inspectors.

To the extent that the Agency is conscious of these dangers, it may be expected to combat them. It is attempting to create a strong *esprit de corps,* which might be easier with permanent than with temporary staff. It may also rotate inspection assignments, even at some cost in nominal efficiency. However, for this device to work, it will be necessary to designate a number of "excess" inspectors for each state, which means, in effect, that the states cannot be permitted to choose their inspection teams.

*Inspector General and Director General.* Most practical decisions in implementing safeguards must be made by the Director General or the Inspector General, who is the head of the Department of Safeguards and Inspection within the Secretariat. These decisions include the terms of the Subsidiary Arrangements; the determination of the actual schedule of inspections; the instructions to inspectors; and the questions of whether to seek extended access in the course of special inspections and of whether to inform the Board that a violation is suspected. The character of these two officials and the pressures operating on them will thus shape the nature and success of safeguards.

The Director General is appointed for a renewable four-year term by the Board of Governors with the approval of the General Conference. [159] Though no procedure exists for dismissal during a term, in view of the predominant influence of the Board within the Agency a Director General who lost the confidence of a majority of the Governors might, in effect, be forced out. The Board could make it extremely difficult for an unpopular Director

159 IAEA Statute, Article VII.A.

General to conduct the affairs of the Agency, whether in relation to safeguards or to other matters, and might even reassume powers previously delegated to the Director General.

The Inspector General is appointed by the Director General, though only with the explicit approval of the Board. [160] The appointment is for a fixed term, not exceeding five years, and is subject to extension for similar maximum periods. [161] Again, though dismissal for subjective, political reasons (rather than for any objective misbehavior) is formally difficult, an Inspector General who had lost the confidence of the Director General or of a majority of the Board would find it almost impossible to maintain his position, and his authority, in any event, could be circumvented.

In administering safeguards, these two officials have to perform a delicate balancing act. On the one hand, most states subject to safeguards are likely to exert pressure for a light-handed administration. On the other, certain states (in particular the nuclear-weapon states that sponsored the NPT) are likely to urge that no compromise be made where international security is at issue and that no chances be taken. Certain states may present special problems: for example, a majority of the IAEA membership might desire that controls be carried out with special thoroughness in Portugal and South Africa.

### Political Organs of the IAEA

The Board of Governors of the Agency has a number of important functions in connection with the administration of safeguards.

1. The Board approves NPT Safeguards Agreements negotiated by the Secretariat with individual states. [162] In view of its dual nature as an organ of the Agency but composed of the representatives of states, the Board is in a position to resolve differences that arise between the negotiators.

2. The Board appoints the Director General [163] and approves

---

160 IAEA document GC(V)/INF/39, par. 2.

161 IAEA Staff Regulation 3.03(b) (INFCIRC/6/Rev.2).

162 This is nowhere provided for explicitly but derives from the Board's general authority, under the IAEA Statute, Article VI.F, "to carry out the functions of the Agency."

163 IAEA Statute, Article VII.A.

the appointment of the Inspector General and the assignment of Agency officials as inspectors. [164]

3. The Board may decide that particular safeguards measures are essential and urgent and may call on the state concerned to take the required action (e.g., the admission of inspectors to areas not normally open to them) without delay and irrespective of any pending dispute settlement proceeding. [165]

4. The Board decides when the Agency is unable to verify the non-diversion of nuclear material and is responsible for issuing the required reports to states and UN organs and for initiating other appropriate sanctions. [166]

5. The Board will have to decide when, on the basis of . technological changes, existing control measures should be eased, tightened, or otherwise changed. [167]

6. The Board proposes the budget, including the appropriation for safeguards, to the General Conference—which cannot change it without Board concurrence. [168]

At present, the Board consists of the representatives of twenty-five member states, selected according to intricate formulas. Just over half the Board is coopted by the outgoing Board, the rest being chosen by the General Conference. North America and Western Europe hold a total of eight seats, Australia, Japan, and South Africa three, Eastern Europe three, and Latin America and the rest of Africa and Asia eleven. Almost all significant producers of uranium are regularly represented on the Board. [169]

At the 1968 Conference of Non-Nuclear-Weapon States, which followed the adoption of NPT, the Board was severely criticized as improperly composed to supervise NPT safeguards. Furthermore, the Conference urged that if the Agency were chosen as the instrument to carry out NPT Articles IV and V (relating to promotional functions in the nuclear energy field), the composition of its governing body should be democratized. [170] After the

[164] IAEA document GC(V)/INF/39, par. 2.

[165] IAEA document INFCIRC/153, pars. 18, 77.

[166] *Ibid.*, par. 19, and IAEA Statute, Article XII.C.

[167] This too flows from the Board's general authority, cited in n. 162.

[168] IAEA Statute, Articles XIV.A and V.E.5.

[169] *Ibid.*, Article VI.A.1-3. See Szasz, *Law and Practices*, sec. 8.2 and table 8C.

[170] Conference of Non-Nuclear-Weapon States Resolutions F (third paragraph of preamble and par. 1), H (seventh paragraph of preamble and Part V), and K, all reproduced in UN document A/7277, par. 17.

UN General Assembly also showed interest in the matter, [171] the IAEA General Conference proposed an amendment to the Statute which will result in a considerably altered Board when ratified by two-thirds of the IAEA membership. Under the amendment the outgoing Board will select only twelve of a total Board membership of about thirty-four. The Board will probably include ten governors from North America and Western Europe, three from Australia, Japan and South Africa, four from Eastern Europe, and seventeen from Latin America and the rest of Africa and Asia. [172] The overall effect of the amendment will be to increase the representation of less developed states and also to make the Board more responsive to the General Conference. Furthermore, two additional states technically able to choose the nuclear-weapon option, West Germany and Italy, will practically be assured of permanent seats on the Board. With certain exceptions not relevant here, all decisions of the Board can be taken by a simple majority of the members voting. [173] No state or small group can exert a veto or constitute a blocking minority.

Though in principle the Board is organized to function continuously, [174] in practice it is convened for only two major sessions a year, with two more short sessions immediately preceding and following the annual General Conference. This may not suffice when the Agency is applying safeguards in dozens of states, all of which are entitled to convene the Board on seventy-two hours' notice on any matters arising out of any inspection. [175] Rather than change its pattern of meetings at that time, the Board might constitute a committee to supervise the administration of safeguards. To such a committee might be delegated certain of the Board's safeguards functions, perhaps even some that by default are now exercised by the Director General. [176]

In contrast to the Board, the General Conference of the Agency, in which all member states are represented, has no direct

---

[171] UN General Assembly Resolutions 2456 A (XXIII), pars. 3-4, and 2457(XXIII), pars. 2-3.

[172] IAEA General Conference Resolution GC(XIV)/RES/272.

[173] IAEA Statute, Article VI.E.

[174] Board of Governors Rule of Procedure 11 (IAEA document GOV/INF/60).

[175] *Ibid.*, Rule 11(c).

[176] This has not been done up to now. The several Safeguards Committees created from time to time have merely been charged with advising the Board on the formulation of the Safeguards Documents and more recently of the Negotiating Instructions.

functions in relation to safeguards. The Conference passes on the Board's appointee for the post of Director General, elects twelve of the twenty-five members of the Board (and will elect twenty-two out of thirty-four under the amendment proposed), and approves the Board-formulated budget (including the safeguards item). Despite its lack of formal authority regarding safeguards, the Conference functions as a general sounding board where states not entitled to choose a Governor can express their views on any Agency function. The Board, though not bound to do so, has always been responsive to views shared by a significant fraction of the membership. Should a substantial majority strongly favor easing safeguards (or, what is less likely, tightening them), it may be expected that the Board will pay close heed.

Finally, it should be recalled that the Agency, under its Statute and indirectly under Articles IV and V of the NPT, has important promotional functions with respect to peaceful nuclear development. Though there need not be and should not be any real contradiction between the promotional and the control functions, there will almost certainly be instances where such a conflict is asserted and the Agency is asked to ease certain actual or proposed safeguards measures so as not to hamper the development of a nuclear enterprise. The cost of safeguards, no matter how it is borne, will exert pressure in the same direction. Thus, the international community will have to develop and maintain constant interest in and vigilance concerning non-proliferation lest the Agency, like many national institutions established to control particular industries, find itself, when public concern has waned, the political captive of the enterprises it was meant to control.

## Political Organs of the United Nations

By reason of its Statute and its Relationship Agreement with the United Nations, the Agency is bound to consider resolutions relating to it adopted by the General Assembly or by any of the UN councils. [177] In practice, a General Assembly recommendation on the subject of safeguards is apt to have a similar and perhaps even stronger influence on the IAEA Board than a resolution

---

[177] IAEA Statute, Article XVI.B.2, and Article V of the Agreement Governing the Relationship between the UN and the IAEA, 281 U.N.T.S. 369, reproduced in IAEA document INFCIRC/11, pt. I.A.

emanating from the Agency's General Conference (whose composition is substantially the same as the UN Assembly's, but whose
international authority naturally is less).

The only direct function of either the General Assembly or the
Security Council in relation to safeguards would take place if the
IAEA Board should impose sanctions on a controlled state and
make the consequent reports required by the Statute [178] and the
Relationship Agreement. [179] The General Assembly could consider the matter under Article 11 of the UN Charter and could
address recommendations to the IAEA or its members or to the
Security Council. The Council, which would probably be able to
act more promptly, could consider the matter under either Chapter VI or VII of the Charter and, if acting on the latter basis, could
take decisions binding on UN members—perhaps requiring the
imposition of a nuclear or a general embargo, or (subject to
Charter Article 43) even the use of armed force. Of course, any
such decision would be subject to the veto of any permanent
member of the Council. If a party to NPT denounced the
Treaty [180] the Security Council would also have to be notified and
might take appropriate action.

### The NPT Parties

Except for a conference to review the NPT to be convened in
1975 and potentially at five-year intervals thereafter, [181] the
parties to NPT are not structured into any organ. Consequently,
their reaction to an event relating to the Treaty or to the safeguards exercised under it would have to be individual rather than
collective. NPT parties would be concerned with the following
matters: (1) the refusal of states to become parties to the Treaty,
or the withdrawal of parties from it; (2) the refusal of a non-nuclear-weapon state party to the Treaty to enter into a Safeguards
Agreement with the IAEA; (3) a report from the Agency that it is
unable to verify compliance with the Treaty by a non-nuclear-
weapon state; (4) information that any party to the Treaty is
violating the provision against the unsafeguarded supply of nuclear
assistance to a non-nuclear-weapon state.

[178] IAEA Statute, Articles III.B.4, XII.C, XVI.B.1.
[179] IAEA Statute, Article III.1(b) and III.2.
[180] NPT Article X.1.
[181] NPT Article VIII.3.

To any of these events, the parties to the Treaty can only give a limited range of reactions within the context of that instrument: (1) they may refuse to transfer nuclear items to a state that does not accept and comply with adequate Agency safeguards; (2) they may refuse assistance to such a state under NPT Articles IV and V (even if such a state were willing to accept Agency safeguards with respect to such assistance); (3) they may denounce the Treaty on the ground that a refusal of some other state to comply with the NPT restraints jeopardizes the "supreme interests" of the withdrawing state; (4) they may amend the Treaty—but no amendment can bind a party without its consent. [182]

## FINANCING IAEA/NPT SAFEGUARDS

The financing of safeguards has been a divisive question ever since the first detailed plans for a nuclear-control organization were formulated. One issue is the incidence of the financing: should it rest primarily on the states or enterprises under control, on the ground that it is their potentially dangerous activities that make safeguards necessary? Or should it rest on the supplying states, on the ground that, in the absence of international measures, they would be responsible for controlling the use of the items they have supplied? Or should the costs of safeguards be borne by the world community as a whole, on the ground that the benefits of nonproliferation extend to all? A second issue is the total weight of the financial burden, regardless of who bears it. Not surprisingly, those who must pay these costs are apt to opt for easing the load, even if controls must be weakened as a consequence.

### Estimated Costs

Over the years numerous estimates of safeguards costs have been made. It is difficult to reconcile these estimates because of differences in the assumptions about the scope and volume of controls, assumptions which depend, respectively, on estimates of political developments and of the use of nuclear power. However, the trend of the estimates is downward, reflecting in part developments in the technology of controls, in part lower demands put on the control system, and, finally, recognition that the fate of the

[182] NPT Article VIII.2.

safeguards system depends on keeping its costs within reasonable limits.

The specter of 60,000 inspectors, which was raised in early projections of international nuclear controls, was abandoned long ago as totally unrealistic. The world community is not willing to bear such a financial burden for the sake of the limited assurance that even the most perfect safeguards can provide, and states and nuclear operators within them cannot reasonably be expected to accept such massive intrusions; finally, a reasonable and technologically sophisticated control program evidently should not require the presence of full shifts of resident inspectors at all facilities in an effort to prevent diversion by their constant presence.

Considerably lower estimates were presented in 1968 to the Foreign Relations Committee of the U.S. Senate when it was considering the ratification of the NPT: for 1975, alternate estimates of 993 to 1,295 inspectors, at an annual cost of $40 million to $91 million, and for 1990, 12,290 to 16,725 inspectors at a cost of $518 million to $1,171 million. [183] In 1970 the Brookhaven National Laboratory presented figures to the Joint Congressional Committee on Atomic Energy of 755 inspectors at a cost of $36 million for 1975 and 2,162 inspectors at a cost of $170 million for 1990. [184] Responding to requests of the Safeguards Committee (1970), the IAEA Director General in November 1970 (at a time when the inspection portions of the Negotiating Instructions were not yet agreed) estimated requirements for 1975 at 167 inspectors costing a total of $4.6 million. Both these figures were within sight of the 1971 budget, which authorized 45 inspectors at a cost of $1.1 million. The Director General refused to make longer projections on the ground that forecasts of nuclear energy development beyond that date were completely uncertain. In a later paper, he estimated that from 1971 to 1980 the cost of safeguards might increase by a factor of two to four, which makes

[183] *Hearings on the Treaty on the Non-Proliferation of Nuclear Weapons, before the Senate Committee on Foreign Relations,* 90th Cong., 2d sess. (Washington, D.C.: U.S. Government Printing Office, 1968), pp. 277-88.

[184] "IAEA Safeguards Costs and Manpower Requirements under the Non-Proliferation Treaty," *Hearings on AEC Authorizing Legislation for Fiscal Year 1970 before the Joint Committee on Atomic Energy,* 91st Cong., 1st sess. (Washington, D.C.: U.S. Government Printing Office, 1969), pp. 2115-36.

his estimates about one-tenth of the maximum figures considered by the Senate Committee in 1968. [185]

## Dividing Costs between IAEA and Controlled States

As a result of a compromise achieved at a relatively late stage of negotiating the IAEA Statute, that instrument has two provisions relating to the financing of safeguards. The general rule is that these costs are considered "administrative" and thus are to be borne by all member states in accordance with a scale to be fixed by the General Conference "guided by the principles adopted by the United Nations in assessing contributions of Member States to the regular budget of the United Nations." It is, however, also provided that from the costs of safeguards there should be deducted "such amounts as are recoverable under agreements regarding the application of safeguards between the Agency and parties to bilateral or multilateral arrangements." [186]

The Soviet Union and its allies have repeatedly argued that the latter provision *requires* the inclusion in safeguards agreements (except those which relate to Agency-assisted projects) of a rule according to which the Agency shall be reimbursed for expenditures incurred. The majority of the Board has, however, consistently rejected this interpretation. The pre-NPT safeguards agreements indeed provide that the Agency will bear all costs (whether incurred by it or by the controlled state or facility) except if an expense is occasioned by the failure of a party to live up to its obligations (e.g., the cost of a special inspection necessitated by a misleading report from a state). [187] This rather onesided rule is somewhat weakened in the related subsidiary arrangements, which generally provide that the Agency is not to be charged for certain national outlays, such as those incurred in preparing routine reports or in exercising a state's right to have Agency inspectors accompanied by national officials. [188]

As a result of extensive debates the Negotiating Instructions as

[185] These several estimates all appeared in restricted documents prepared for the Board's Safeguards Committee (1970).

[186] IAEA Statute, Articles XIV.B.1(b), XIV.C, and XIV.D.

[187] See, e.g., sec. 27 of the Safeguards Transfer Agreement cited in n. 29 above.

[188] An abbreviated provision of this type appears in sec. 24(b) of the Mexican Tlatelolco Safeguards Submission Agreement cited in n. 39 above.

approved require each party (i.e., the Agency and the state) to bear the expenses incurred in carrying out its responsibilities under NPT Safeguards Agreements. However, the Agency must bear the expenses of any special measurements and sampling requested by inspectors, as well as other extraordinary expenses incurred at the request of the Agency. Obviously, the Agency must also bear the cost of any special measuring equipment installed at its request. [189] In effect, the Negotiating Instructions do not substantially alter the practice that had evolved in pre-NPT agreements, but the more complete statement may avoid disputes. If the state concerned is not a member of the Agency, then the NPT Safeguards Agreement requires it to reimburse to the Agency the safeguards expenses incurred by the latter under the Agreement; however, somewhat contradictorily in this context, any extraordinary expenses incurred at the specific request of the Agency must be reimbursed to the state. [190]

### Distributing Costs within the IAEA

Since the NPT Safeguards Agreements provide that in most instances the Agency is to bear the predominant share of all safeguards expenses, it is clear that these costs will constitute a rapidly increasing portion of the IAEA budget, even if one accepts the conservative estimates of the Director General. Under some of the less restrained projections, safeguards costs will soon exceed all other budgetary items. Under ordinary circumstances, the Agency's safeguards expenses, like its other "administrative" expenses, would be shared by all member states according to a scale derived from the UN scale of contributions, adapted to take account of the difference in the membership of the organizations. Accordingly, some 35 of the 102 members would each pay only 0.04 percent, while other states would pay increasing amounts, according to their ability, up to the roughly 31.5 percent shouldered by the United States. [191]

189 IAEA document INFCIRC/153, pars. 15(a), 75(d).

190 *Ibid.*, par. 15(b).

191 See, e.g., IAEA document GC(XV)/463, Annex, pars. 1-3 and table 1, for the calculations applicable to 1972. In this connection it should be noted that, presumably because of the Agency's safeguards responsibilities, the U.S. Congress specifically exempted the IAEA from the 25 percent limitation on U.S. contributions to be applied to the United Nations and its other affiliated agencies (P.L. 92-844, 86 Stat. 1109, at 1110); however, this indulgence may be largely frustrated by Article XIV.D of the IAEA

Many developing states object strenuously to the prospect of paying increasing sums for the implementation of safeguards from which they see themselves as deriving scant benefits. This is especially true of those IAEA members that have chosen not to participate in the NPT. The Safeguards Committee (1970) therefore considered various proposals that safeguards costs be borne only by NPT parties. These were rejected, in part so as not to inhibit participation in the NPT. In addition, there was doubt about the legality of having only certain members charged for particular administrative costs (as safeguards expenditures are classified), but this formal objection could have been overcome by having the NPT parties agree among themselves on the distribution of the relevant costs and making special contributions to the Agency accordingly. [192]

A compromise was finally recommended by the Committee to the Board of Governors and was later adopted by the IAEA General Conference. The member states with a per capita net national product of less than one-third that of the ten members having the highest per capita product will bear only one-half of their normal share of all safeguards costs or 16.9 percent (the 1971 ratio of safeguards to non-safeguards expenses in the Agency's budget) of their contributions to the non-safeguards budget, whichever is the less, but an amount at least as great as their share of the 1971 (the last pre-NPT year) safeguards expenses. The rest of the safeguards expenditures will be divided among the remaining states in proportion to their normal assessment ratios. [193] The result is to relieve about 70 percent of the membership from most NPT-related safeguards costs.

Again, legal objections were raised against this formula on the ground that in effect it established two contribution scales, [194] one for the administrative budget but excluding safeguards and one for safeguards, in violation of Article XIV.D of the Statute,

---

statute, which requires the Agency to be guided by the UN scale of contributions in establishing its own.

[192] On April 16, 1971, the Director General communicated to the Board the texts of letters he had exchanged with the Governor for Belgium in which the latter had asked and had been assured that such a fiscal device would be compatible with the IAEA Statute.

[193] IAEA document GC(XV)/RES/283, the implementation of which is calculated for 1972 in GC(XV)/463, Annex, pars. 4-7 and tables 2-4.

[194] Though the terminology used carefully refrains from referring to two scales.

which appears to allow only a single scale. Additionally, it was objected that the special safeguards scale, which would relieve some states and burden others, would be an impermissible departure from "the principles adopted by the United Nations" in establishing a contribution scale, by which the General Conference must be guided. These objections were answered by reference to the carefully qualified language of the Statute, which does not bind the Agency rigidly to the UN scale, and to provisions that charge the Agency to bear in mind "the special needs of the underdeveloped areas of the world." It was argued that carrying out its NPT responsibilities was undoubtedly a legitimate Agency function for which appropriate means of financing should be permissible, unless directly contrary to the Statute.

### Liability

A constant, almost obsessive, concern of those faced with safeguards has been the possibility that the inspectors sent by the Agency will, through carelessness or malice, cause major damage to complicated and expensive nuclear facilities and even to their surroundings. In addition, it is feared that these inspectors, to whom many technical details will have to be revealed, might disclose to others data of commerical value. These concerns elicited two types of provisions: those that reduce the likelihood of events resulting in significant loss or damage and those that specify how any loss or damage that may occur should be borne.

The Agency's Secretariat has repeatedly attempted to allay fears of massive nuclear damage caused by inspectors by pointing out that inspectors have only strictly circumscribed functions, that they can be accompanied by national officials, and that they will be strictly instructed and carefully trained to avoid dangerous activities. In particular, the NPT Safeguards Agreements require inspectors to comply with national and facility health and safety procedures communicated to the Agency and prohibit them from operating any facility themselves or directing its staff to carry out any operation. [195]

The NPT Safeguards Agreements also provide (as most safeguards agreements have for some years) that the Agency and its officials should be covered by any available protection against

---

[195] IAEA document INFCIRC/153, pars. 5, 9, 44, and 87.

third-party liability for nuclear damage. [196] Aside from insurance, such protection in many states includes legislative and treaty provisions which channel all liability arising out of a nuclear "incident" to the operator of the facility, who is to be considered absolutely liable without the possibility of recourse against others (except under particularly flagrant circumstances). This liability is, however, limited in amount and must be entirely covered by liquid assets, insurance, and governmental or international guarantees. [197] Thus, an inspector involved in a nuclear incident would ordinarily be exempt from third-party liability even if he contributed to the accident, and he and the Agency would be financially covered for any damage they might suffer.

With respect to any other damage, for example, as a result of conventional accidents or because of the disclosure of confidential data, the NPT Safeguards Agreements provide that claims "be settled in accordance with international law." [198] No special forum for settling such claims is prescribed. Consequently, any disputes would fall within the competence of the ad hoc arbitral tribunal provided under each Safeguards Agreement. [199]

To avoid leaks of valuable commercial or technical data, [200] numerous precautions are taken, some of which have already been described. In addition, the Agency reminds inspectors (and other officials having access to safeguards information) about the statutory prohibition against disclosing "any industrial secret or other confidential information coming to their knowledge by reason of their official duties for the Agency." [201] The Agency also instructs inspectors not to reveal unnecessarily any information (even if not confidential) coming to their attention and not to seek to obtain any confidential information not necessary for the efficient per-

---

[196] *Ibid.,* par. 16.

[197] As provided in the Vienna Convention on Civil Liability for Nuclear Damage, 1963 (for the text see *International Conventions on Civil Liability for Nuclear Damage,* IAEA Legal Series No. 4 [Vienna: IAEA, 1966], p. 3) and in the [Paris] Convention on Third Party Liability in the Field of Nuclear Energy, 1960 (for the amended text see *ibid.,* p. 21), supplemented by the [Brussels] Convention Supplementary to the Paris Convention, 1963 (for the amended text see *ibid.,* p. 47).

[198] IAEA document INFCIRC/153, par. 17.

[199] *Ibid.,* par. 22.

[200] See pp. 108-9 above.

[201] IAEA Statute, Article VII.F. This caution is repeated in expanded form in IAEA Staff Regulation 1.06 (INFCIRC/6/Rev. 2).

formance of their duties. [202] Moreover, disciplinary and fiscal penalties may be imposed on inspectors by the Agency if, through their misbehavior, they cause any damage, [203] and the Agency may waive their immunity against prosecution in national courts. [204] It is, of course, recognized that these strictures are likely to be more of a deterrent to permanent staff than to inspectors attached to the Agency for merely a fixed term of years, after which they may return to a national nuclear energy authority or accept employment with some interested nuclear enterprise.

## INTERACTION WITH OTHER SAFEGUARDS

One complicating factor in the administration of NPT safeguards by the IAEA is the existence of several other control systems with which, ideally, the Agency's efforts should be coordinated and with which, in any event, they must coexist. This interaction can take several forms, depending on how the relationship among the various control systems is perceived: (1) as complementary, in that the other controls fill gaps in the Agency's system by performing checks that the Agency does not make; (2) as supplementary, in that those who operate the other controls basically rely on the Agency's safeguards but may carry out checks relating to nuclear items or activities that are for some reason outside the Agency's ken; (3) as duplicative, in that both systems attempt to perform basically the same task, so that repetition of checks may, on the one hand, make diversion even less likely but, on the other, may permit gaps as each system implicitly but unjustifiably relies on the other for certain control measures; or (4) as competitive, in that the systems contain some incompatible features (e.g., an obligation to store the same excess nuclear material with two different organizations) or the organs carrying out one set of controls attempt to exclude those who are to carry out others.

202 "Administrative and General Instructions for Safeguards Inspectors."

203 IAEA Staff Rule 13.03.4 enables the Agency to require a staff member to reimburse it "for any financial loss suffered by the Agency as a result of his negligence or of his having violated any regulation, rule or administrative instruction" (Administrative Manual, pt. AM.II/1).

204 As it may be required to do pursuant to secs. 21 or 25 of the Agreement on the Privileges and Immunities of the IAEA (see n. 121 above).

## Domestic Controls

The principal reason why the IAEA expects to be able to carry out its responsibilities under the NPT Safeguards Agreements with a corps of inspectors and a budget amounting to only a fraction of that estimated by several knowledgeable outside observers is that it intends to rely largely on control measures to be instituted by each safeguarded state with regard to all nuclear material within its territory. [205] These "national" systems are to encompass both accounting for and control of safeguarded material. Even without this control requirement, it is clear that the Agency would hold a state responsible before the world community for any unexplained loss of nuclear material. Though not stated as an explicit requirement, the provision of at least some physical security as part of a domestic control system is therefore expected.

Domestic controls are thus meant to be essentially complementary to Agency safeguards. This relationship is underlined by a provision in the Negotiating Instructions whereby the actual number, intensity, duration, timing, and mode of routine inspections of facilities is to depend, *inter alia,* on the effectiveness of the state's accounting and control system as tested against a number of specified criteria. [206] The state may also use its controls to achieve supplementary purposes, such as fiscal accountability or compliance with safety regulations. No competition need or should exist between the IAEA and domestic systems. Duplication should occur only insofar as it is necessary for the Agency to verify, through random sampling or otherwise, the reliability of data yielded by the domestic controls.

## Foreign Controls

Before the Agency was established and during its early years, most of the principal suppliers of nuclear material applied formal controls (e.g., the United States) or informal controls (e.g., France and the Soviet Union) to nuclear assistance provided by them to other states. As discussed in Chapter 2, the formal "bilateral safeguards" have during the past several years mostly been trans-

---

[205] See pp. 96-98 above.
[206] IAEA document INFCIRC/153, par. 81(b).

ferred or delegated to the Agency [207] and will now largely be superseded by NPT safeguards. [208] In any event, it is unlikely that many non-nuclear-weapon states will tolerate continued controls by their suppliers after the Agency has started implementing its NPT controls on the same items. Thus, formal bilateral safeguards will not constitute a system with which the Agency will have to coordinate its NPT controls.

However, supplying states and possibly other nations on occasion carry out informal or secret checks within or concerning countries whose nuclear development interests them. Such clandestine checks, though never officially recognized or referred to in connection with the Agency's controls, may still have an important complementary role to play. If a state determines by these means, whether they are legitimate (e.g., through satellite observations) or otherwise, that another state is carrying out illicit nuclear activities, it may publicly accuse the violator, thus bringing the matter to the attention of the Agency. Alternatively, it could confidentially inform the Inspector General where and how it might be profitable to conduct a special inspection.

As noted previously, the Agency is not equipped, either technically or legally, to search out unregistered material or facilities entirely on its own initiative and without any clues. However, once given a convincing lead, it can request, and, with the Board's support, indeed insist on, the right to carry out special inspections outside the areas ordinarily open to inspectors. [209] Such an inspection should enable the Agency either to absolve from suspicion an area or activity previously suspected or to detect actual violations (which need not involve the manufacture of nuclear weapons but may be merely the operation of an unregistered but otherwise innocent nuclear enterprise). Though, in practice, a guilty state would almost certainly forestall such a discovery by prohibiting the inspection, it would thus provoke the imposition of sanctions on the basis of suspicious non-cooperation rather than of established violation.

Such informal collaboration between national intelligence

207 See Stephen Gorove, "Transferring U.S. Bilateral Safeguards to the International Atomic Energy Agency: The 'Umbrella' Agreements," *Duquesne University Law Review* 6 (1967):1-14.

208 IAEA document INFCIRC/153, par. 24.

209 See pp. 103-6 and 114-15 above.

systems and the Agency's controls would therefore be a complementary one. The former would supply information that the Agency cannot otherwise get, and the latter would use these data and its right to make special inspections to prove or disprove the accusation in the public eye—an important result that secret services alone may not be able to achieve.

It should be noted that under NPT or the related Agency controls there is no formal way that one state may bring charges to the IAEA against another. Such a device does exist under the Tlatelolco Treaty, [210] however, and to the extent that parties to that instrument also consent to NPT safeguards, the IAEA could indirectly but openly take account of charges made by one Latin American state against another.

## International Controls

*Euratom.* The stubborn issue that first delayed the conclusion of the NPT and later its entry into force for a number of signficant states was whether the five non-nuclear-weapon states that are members of Euratom [211] should continue to be subject to its controls while also accepting IAEA safeguards or whether one of these organizations should yield to the other by formally or informally delegating its responsibilities. The Euratom Commission and some of the Euratom states clearly preferred a transfer to their own control organ of the Agency's safeguards functions under NPT and were unwilling to consider either a reversal of these roles or the implementation of substantially identical control measures by both organizations. [212] However, states outside this regional group objected to any assumption by Euratom of the

210 Article 16(1)(b) of the Treaty (n. 38 above).

211 Belgium, Federal Republic of Germany, Italy, Luxembourg, and the Netherlands; the sixth Euratom member, France, is a nuclear-weapon state and has declined to become an NPT party, though stating that it is prepared to behave as one. In addition, two of the three states that have agreed to join Euratom in the expansion of the European Communities are non-nuclear-weapon states. Norway, another non-nuclear-weapon state that had planned to join Euratom, in negotiating an NPT Safeguards Agreement with the IAEA also agreed on a protocol according to which its separate Agreement was to be replaced by the one to which Euratom and all the Euratom non-nuclear-weapon states are to be parties.

212 This question is discussed by Allan D. McKnight, *Nuclear Non-Proliferation: IAEA and Euratom,* Carnegie Endowment for International Peace, Occasional Paper No. 7 (New York: Carnegie Endowment for International Peace, 1970), and by Lawrence Scheinman, "EURATOM and the IAEA," in *Nuclear Proliferation: Prospects for Control* (New York: Dunellen, 1970), pp. 63-79.

Agency's control functions under the NPT, asserting that such responsibility must not be entrusted to a narrow, regional group whose members might collude to produce nuclear weapons under the benevolent gaze of their own inspectors.

The resolution of this conflict proceeded in several stages. In the first, it was merely agreed, using deliberately vague compromise language, that the NPT should include a provision permitting non-nuclear-weapon states to fulfill their obligation to conclude Safeguards Agreements with the Agency "either individually or together with other States." [213] In other words, the non-nuclear-weapon members of Euratom could enter into separate agreements with the Agency, or the Euratom Commission could conclude a single agreement in all their names. But nothing was indicated in the Treaty about whether a Safeguards Agreement concluded collectively might differ in substance from one concluded individually—for example, by providing that Euratom would replace, in whole or in part, the IAEA as the authority responsible for the administration of safeguards. This question was not answered by the Negotiating Instructions, which were ostensibly directed to the conclusion of individual agreements. However, the Euratom states did participate actively in the Board's Safeguards Committee (1970), and as a result the Instructions were formulated so as to require only minor modifications to adjust them to various possible models of cooperation with Euratom.

After the Council of Ministers of the European Communities in September 1971 authorized the Euratom Commission to enter into negotiations, the five non-nuclear-weapon Euratom members, the Commission, and the IAEA met from November 1971 to July 1972. [214] An apparently acceptable solution was found, which was embodied in a Safeguards Agreement and a Protocol, to both of which the five states (as well as any other non-nuclear-weapon states that join Euratom later) and the two organizations are to become parties. [215] These instruments are, as usual, to be supplemented by Subsidiary Arrangements, which, however, the Agency

---

[213] NPT, Article III.4.

[214] IAEA document GC(XVI)/480, pars. 4 and 121.

[215] This solution may have been necessitated in part by the circumstance that a number of the facilities to be controlled are Euratom enterprises, and thus not fully under the authority of the host state—though it may be questioned whether such a state could plead diminished responsibility vis-à-vis other non-Euratom states or the Agency.

is to conclude primarily with Euratom, while the states concerned will at most become ancillary parties.

The Safeguards Agreement itself is almost entirely standard in form—that is, it follows the Negotiating Instructions closely. A few provisions have been substantively modified to specify a special role for Euratom, but in others the latter has merely been included as an additional party with a posture vis-à-vis the Agency similar to that of a safeguarded state; in the majority of the provisions Euratom has been substituted for the state as the party with which the Agency is to deal in exercising its controls. The special features of the arrangement are set out in the Protocol, which deals exclusively with the distribution of various control functions between the Agency and Euratom. How this apportionment is to work in practice will be specified in the Subsidiary Arrangements, the general part of which was agreed to, together with the principal instruments, while the portions relating to each facility are to be negotiated in a continuing process. These negotiations, as well as the practical arrangements reached in the day-to-day implementation of the Safeguards Agreement, will constitute further and, it may be hoped, increasingly easy stages in achieving an effective accommodation between the organizations. To assist this process a Liaison Committee of their representatives is to be established, to meet at least annually, with special and lower-level technical meetings to be convened as necessary.

These arrangements clearly constitute a mixed solution to the original rivalry: Euratom is to act in part as agent of its member states, in part as an instrument of the Agency, in part as an independent actor carrying out its peculiar responsibilities, and in most respects as a buffer between the Agency and the Euratom states. How this is to work in practice can only be understood in the context of the principal safeguards procedures.

1. Design information about facilities is to be provided by Euratom to the Agency, is to be examined jointly by the two organizations, and is to be verified by the Agency in cooperation with Euratom.

2. Euratom, rather than its member states, is to arrange for the keeping of the necessary records.

3. The reports that would normally be submitted by states to the Agency are to be made by Euratom, to which any Agency reactions with respect to this information will be addressed.

4. The most delicate and crucial compromises had to be made in respect to inspections. The Agency will not ordinarily carry out routine inspections itself but is to content itself with observing the inspection activities of Euratom. Any direct inspections by the Agency are generally to be carried out simultaneously with Euratom inspections. Foreseeable exceptions to these general rules must be spelled out in the Subsidiary Arrangements relating to particular facilities, but the Agency has reserved the right to carry out some additional direct inspections if they are "essential and urgent" and the circumstances could not have been foreseen. In return for this forbearance, the Agency will be entitled to participate in the scheduling and planning of Euratom inspections and in any event is to receive full information about these operations and the data secured by them.

5. Since Euratom constitutes a nuclear free-trade area, no special measures (special reports or inspections) need be observed in transferring nuclear material among its members.

6. The authority of the IAEA Board to impose sanctions and to make certain other decisions unilaterally and definitively is substantially the same as in conventional Safeguards Agreements.

To fulfill its functions under the Agreement and Protocol, Euratom will to some extent have to modify its current regulations and procedures for collecting and evaluating information, in particular by adopting the accounting techniques specified in the Agency's Negotiating Instructions. The Agency's own adjustments will be somewhat easier and to some extent mostly psychological: in respect to the Euratom area its safeguards functions (in particular inspections) will definitely be less than for other non-nuclear-weapon states, and it will have to rely to a considerable extent on the results of Euratom's control activities. However, once it has developed adequate techniques for supervising rather than performing inspections, there is little reason why it and the world community should not feel confident about these jointly exercised controls.

*The European Nuclear Energy Agency.* The safeguards to be carried out by the European Nuclear Energy Agency (ENEA) of the Organisation for Economic Co-operation and Development (OECD, formerly OEEC) pursuant to the European Security Control Convention [216] are basically similar to the IAEA's statutory system. However, unlike the control system of Euratom, which was actually developed and set into operation simultaneously and perhaps even somewhat in advance of that of the IAEA, ENEA safeguards have been implemented in only a rudimentary way because the principal precondition for their application never arose: the transfer of nuclear assistance from one ENEA member to another, either through the organization or directly but subject to its controls. Consequently, ENEA safeguards have up to now been applied only to the several "joint enterprises" of the European Agency: the Halden reactor in Norway, the Dragon reactor in England, and, in principle, the Eurochemic reprocessing plant in Belgium. However, since the Eurochemic plant is within the territory of a Euratom member, that organization actually safeguards it. [217]

No agreement has been concluded between ENEA and IAEA, as foreseen by the Security Control Convention, [218] under which the latter would take over safeguards responsibilities from the former. However, unlike Euratom safeguards, the preservation of ENEA controls never became an issue in the NPT negotiations. It thus seems likely that ENEA safeguards will quietly fade away, with or without a formal agreement concerning control over the joint enterprises.

*The Latin American Agency.* The Tlatelolco Treaty basically provides that the controls it requires will be carried out by the IAEA, pursuant to safeguards agreements concluded individually between the IAEA and each party to the Treaty. However, the Treaty also establishes the Agency for the Prohibition of Nuclear Weapons in Latin America to supervise the execution of these controls. [219]

[216] See n. 145 above.

[217] This has occurred in the absence of a formal agreement under which ENEA is to delegate its control functions and responsibilities to Euratom with respect to joint enterprises located within the latter's jurisdiction. Such an agreement is foreseen in Article 16(a) of the European Security Control Convention (see n. 145 above).

[218] *Ibid.,* Article 16(b). However, a general Co-operation Agreement has long been in force between the two organizations (see 396 U.N.T.S. 273 or IAEA document INFCIRC/25, pt. 1).

[219] Article 7 of the Treaty (see n. 38 above).

The Latin American Agency thus has certain safeguards tasks. In particular, it is to receive copies of safeguards reports submitted to the IAEA by parties to the Treaty. [220] More important, any party to the Treaty may, within the Council of the Latin American Agency, accuse another party of a violation. The Council may thereupon arrange for a special inspection to check the truth of the allegation (at the cost of the accuser, if the charge turns out to be unjustified). [221] Though not specified in the Treaty, special inspections might be assigned to and carried out by the IAEA. Indeed, this would be the natural solution, since it is not foreseen that the Latin American Agency will establish its own corps of inspectors. But whether or not special inspections are assigned to the IAEA, the mechanism of accusation will, in respect to Latin America, effectively formalize the interaction with foreign intelligence services discussed above.

As already noted, the provisions of the Tlatelolco Safeguards Agreements to be entered into with the IAEA have not yet been precisely formulated, though it has been stated that they will be similar to the NPT Agreements, [222] nor has the special agreement between the Latin American Agency and the IAEA (foreseen by the Tlatelolco Treaty [223] and permissible under the IAEA Statute [224] ) been concluded. [225] Thus the nature of the collaboration between these two institutions cannot yet be foreseen. Nevertheless, it appears clear that no duplication of controls will occur. Whatever safeguards the Latin American Agency exercises will complement those of the IAEA, and most likely will indeed be delegated to it.

## CONCLUSION

The assumption by the IAEA of the control functions foreseen for it in the NPT marks a signal advance in the development of its

[220] *Ibid.,* Article 14(2).

[221] *Ibid.,* Article 16(1)(b), (2)-(6).

[222] See nn. 41-42 above.

[223] Article 19(1) of the Treaty (see n. 38 above).

[224] IAEA Statute, Article XVI.A.

[225] During 1972 a general Co-operation Agreement was negotiated between the IAEA and OPANAL (IAEA document GC(XVI)/481), but that instrument does not purport to relate to the specific collaboration on safeguards foreseen by the Tlatelolco Treaty.

safeguards system. These new responsibilities will not only require a considerable expansion of this type of work but also have already resulted in qualitative changes in the existing system. These are due in part to the comprehensive rather than merely selective safeguards to be exercised in the non-nuclear-weapon parties to the NPT and in part to the potential universality of that Treaty, bringing under controls many advanced states that had previously escaped significant international controls because of the relative self-sufficiency of their nuclear industry.

The fact that substantial agreement has been reached on all essential details of the new system augurs well for its success. In any event, it demonstrates the possibility of significant accords on a technical level, achieved within a technical organization, even when major related political questions continue to defy solution in other forums. The understanding concerning the means and techniques by which the Agency is to carry out its NPT functions was made possible by the confidence earned by the Agency and its staff in a dozen years of undramatic operation and by the habits of collaboration developed by the representatives to the organization during that time.

Whether the difficult and long-term task of implementing the agreement now reached will be accomplished as successfully as have the initial steps will depend on many factors, by no means all under the control of the Agency. One crucial element will be the sustained, positive interest of all types of states not only in the controls that they themselves may be subject to but in the effective maintenance of safeguards throughout the world. It may be hoped that the Agency itself—the political representatives as well as the international staff—will demonstrate the ability and stamina to carry out its essential but unglamorous task fairly, efficiently, and, above all, reliably.

# CHAPTER 5

# National Safeguards

## EDWIN M. KINDERMAN

### INTRODUCTION

This chapter discusses the U.S. national safeguards system as it has evolved from its beginnings in 1943 and suggests modes for its future operation. The initial objectives of the system were the management of small quantities of valuable material to ensure its effective use and protection against theft (or diversion) by or for a foreign nation. At present, the U.S. system is undergoing substantial modifications to reflect the rapid growth of the nuclear power industry. These modifications are being made with due regard to the offer by the U.S. government to permit the application of IAEA safeguards on all peaceful nuclear activities in the United States. Most of these actions strongly reflect the continuing needs of national security as well.

The regulatory changes being made by the U.S. Atomic Energy Commission appear intended to provide the basis for what is described as "deterrent type action against diversion by petty thieves, organized criminal groups, disgruntled plant employees and politically motivated individuals bent on assisting a foreign power to acquire a nuclear weapons capability."[1] Organizational changes are also under way at this writing (May 1972).

---

[1] D. L. Crowson, "Progress and Prospects for Nuclear Material Safeguards," *Safeguards Techniques, Proceedings of a Symposium, Karlsruhe, 6-10 July 1970* (Vienna: IAEA, 1970), 1:23-24.

## EVOLUTION OF THE U.S. SAFEGUARDS SYSTEM

Significant quantities of nuclear materials were first produced, processed, and used during World War II under military control and conditions of extreme secrecy in the Manhattan Project. The purpose of the Project was, of course, the development of the atomic bomb. The first small samples of enriched uranium and plutonium were jealously guarded. They were passed from hand to hand by scientists who were eager to extract every bit of information about the chemical and physical properties of the priceless materials.[2] As the knowledge developed by this early laboratory research was translated into full-scale production plants and operations, careful control was maintained over each gram of product material.

These precautions were taken not only to protect our military secrets but also because all possible material was needed to fabricate the first weapons. Plant managers and their military supervisors were kept currently informed of the status of the material and its use. Material balances were important primarily in order to improve and control the processes involved and to ensure that all available materials were converted to the intended end use. Plant inventory information was accumulated. However, no formal material control over the entire operation had been instituted by the end of 1946, when the Manhattan Engineering District operations were transferred to the AEC.

In 1947 the Source and Fissionable Materials Accountability Branch of the Production Division of the AEC was formed. From its inception, the functions of this small group were accountancy and control against loss. The Branch established an overall reporting and records system that summarized the quantities of each material, its location, and its physical form. It also encouraged improved measurements and systems within each operating component of the AEC weapons manufacturing complex. In 1949 the functions of record-keeping and audit were completely divorced from such operating functions as inventory management. Thus nuclear material control was separated from the main stream of

---

[2] The author worked in an analytical laboratory supporting Calutron development in 1943-1944. More than once when a sample of isotopically enriched uranium was spilled, concrete flooring was scraped up and the "mess" was subjected to elaborate chemical procedures to retrieve a few milligrams of material.

AEC action. The number of AEC operations and quantities of material increased greatly in the following decade, but the general direction of the Branch and its successors did not change until the mid-1960s. During this period the material balance, which is the backbone of a modern safeguards system, generally was not closed by a complete series of measurements: "Materials balance areas existed but measurements were dependent on the willingness of production managers to make them. Then, as now, many production managers did not see the need for measurements on scrap materials. In some very important cases, the measurement procedures did not exist."[3]

While the nuclear material control function did not gain all the authority and influence it needed to become fully effective, it was upgraded to divisional status at AEC headquarters, and the function became a part of each field office and contractor operation. Even though control through the Division of Nuclear Materials Management was not complete and the Division had little to do with policy making, the overall security against loss was high. The AEC had multiple avenues for protection against loss. To achieve the necessary control, it depended on responsible management furnished by its operating contractors, on loyal employees, and on physical protection measures as much as on accountancy. With these measures in effect, transfers between plants or operations were considered transfers between friends. Separate measurements by shipper and receiver were infrequent, and, if the measurements taken indicated that a discrepancy existed, it was frequently negotiated away.

The Atoms for Peace program announced by President Eisenhower in 1953 and implemented by Congress in the Atomic Energy Act of 1954 had an important impact on the U.S. nuclear material control program. It authorized the transfer of special fissionable material to foreign countries and also permitted the private ownership of production facilities, subject to AEC licensing. Commercial power reactors producing significant quantities of special fissionable material were thus authorized. The establishment of the necessary commercial and licensed supply facilities were also encouraged by the 1954 Act.

---

[3] James E. Lovatt, *Nuclear Materials Management and Control* (New York: Gordon & Breach, 1972).

While special fissionable material in private hands under license still belonged to the United States, it was loaned under favorable terms to domestic companies and to foreign nations. U.S. agreements for nuclear cooperation required material supplied by the United States to foreign countries to be carefully accounted for. U.S. AEC personnel conducted inspections of foreign installations to assure that the transferred material was in its proper place and applied to the intended use.

The people in charge of the activities of commercial nuclear facilities originally came from AEC-directed operations, and much the same attitudes toward material control prevailed in private as in government installations. Some persons did recognize that commercial operations did not take the same measures for physical protection and that their employees' background had not necessarily been investigated for security purposes to the same degree as that of personnel in the AEC-directed weapons-production complex. However, many people assumed that special fissionable material would be well guarded because of its intrinsic high unit cost. The AEC endorsed this position,[4] as did, apparently, the members of the Joint Committee on Atomic Energy of the Congress. During the late 1950s and early 1960s, most operating personnel in the AEC and commercial operations thought of safeguards as directed against a surreptitious national effort to develop weapons under the cover of a nuclear power program. They believed that since the United States already possessed nuclear weapons, U.S. nuclear operations would not require safeguards. The possibilities of diversion and successful use by non-governmental groups or of black markets in nuclear material, discussed in Chapter 7 below, were not seriously considered by most of the officials concerned. Two beliefs later proved incorrect were also commonly held. The first was that plutonium with a high content of the 240 isotope, the type produced in "economic" nuclear power operations, was unsuitable for explosives.[5] The second was that a "nuclear weapon

[4] Remarks of Ralph Lumb at the Atomic Industrial Forum, Conference on Nuclear Fuels—1972, Dallas, Texas, reported in *Nuclear Industry* 19 (February, 1972):19-20.

[5] See, for example, the following statement contained in "Study by Edison Electric Institute on Status and Potential of Plutonium as a Power Reactor Fuel, Plutonium Survey—1963":

By way of definition, plutonium is generally classified as weapons or reactor grade depending upon its isotopic composition. That grade of plutonium which is

program" was beyond the technical and economic capabilities of all but the major industrial powers.[6]

The idea of strategic value, as distinct from economic value, was advanced by several people at this time,[7] but it was not explicitly a part of AEC regulation or operation. This concept places a special value on highly enriched uranium, plutonium, or other material essential for nuclear explosives because of the presumed severe effects of misuse of nuclear weapons. For example, a large explosion, say from 5,000 tons of TNT, would cost over $3 million for the explosive plus a substantial amount for transportation and emplacement. This explosion could be duplicated with 5 to 10 kilograms of plutonium. On this basis, the plutonium would be worth $300,000 to $600,000 per kilogram, without regard to the advantages of the smaller size of the nuclear explosive. Thus far, the concept of strategic quantity, i.e., a quantity large enough to be inimical to national interests, had not been explicitly formulated. However, it has been implicit in the *"de minimis"* quantities cited in various government regulations.

Some differences existed between the material control procedures applied by the AEC to the nuclear weapon program and those applied to the civilian power program. These differences, while annoying and sometimes confusing, were not significant, and

---

produced (and recoverable) from commercial power reactors is referred to herein as reactor grade, recycle or fuel grade plutonium. In practice, the isotopic composition of this material covers a wide range depending upon its exposure and the reactor design and operations characteristics. For purposes of this report it is assumed to contain about 75 to 80 percent of the fissile isotopes Pu-239 and Pu-241. Weapons grade plutonium is assumed to be nearly 100 percent Pu-239.

This was published, among other places, as appendix 6 of "Private Ownership of Special Nuclear Materials," *Hearings before the Subcommittee of Legislation of the Joint Committee on Atomic Energy, July 30, 31 and August 1, 1963* (Washington, D.C.: U.S. Government Printing Office, 1963). According to testimony presented in those hearings, the report was reviewed by the AEC staff prior to publication. The author pleads guilty to accepting and propagating this belief in the early 1960s.

[6] One example of many studies which emphasize this belief was the Report of the Secretary General of the United Nations, "On the Effects of the Possible Use of Nuclear Weapons and on the Security and Economic Implications for States on the Acquisition and Further Development of These Weapons," UN General Assembly Document A/6858, October 10, 1957. Senior experts from several nuclear weapon powers, including the United States, participated in preparing this report.

[7] Ralph Lumb, *Report to the Atomic Energy Commission by the Ad Hoc Advisory Panel on Safeguarding Nuclear Material, March 10, 1967*, p. 28, refers to a classified "Study of Strategic Importance of Nuclear Materials" dated December 5, 1966. The author advanced the concept of strategic quantity in the early 1960s.

the controls applied were not onerous. In the early 1960s plant operations in both civilian and weapons programs were not shut down or senior management alarms sounded if, after the closing of a formal material balance, substantial quantities of nuclear material were unaccounted for. The weapons production facilities were run by "friends," and the fledgling nuclear power industry was to be encouraged rather than hampered by "stringent" controls. In fact, during this period the AEC decided not to impose on licensees all the requirements applicable to those operating government facilities under cost-type contracts. The Commission noted, however, that the adoption of the policy did not imply that the AEC was not concerned with safeguarding the material. If its policy proved inadequate, other means of assuring adequate protection would be adopted.[8] Formal AEC policy thus encouraged independent operations, and smaller companies gained entry into the developing nuclear industry, specifically in hexafluoride conversion, fuel preparation, and scrap recovery.

By the mid-1960s it became apparent that reliance on financial responsibility alone was unsatisfactory. A review of the situation by an independent panel in 1967[9] was followed by administrative action.[10] The responsibilities for the material control aspects of the weapons production program and overall nuclear materials management policy was assigned to the newly established Office of Safeguards and Nuclear Materials Management, which was, in effect, the direct successor of the Division of Nuclear Materials Management. Responsibility for licensee programs, the civilian nuclear power industry, and ancillary activities was assigned to the Director of Regulation as a separate Division of Nuclear Materials Safeguards.

These administrative changes were accompanied by new attitudes in the AEC and elsewhere. It was slowly recognized that nations of moderate size and technical skills could afford nuclear weapons if they so wished and that all nations did not need the

[8] J. V. Vinciguerra, "Safeguards—Past, Present and Future," Address to the Institute of Nuclear Materials Management, June 19, 1967, AEC Press Release IN-798. See also Lovatt, *Nuclear Materials Management.*

[9] See n. 7 above.

[10] J. V. Vinciguerra, "Organizational Changes with the AEC Affecting Safeguards," *Proceedings of the Symposium on Safeguards Research and Development, June 26, 27, 1967,* WASH 1076 (Washington, D.C.: AEC, 1967), pp. 35-43.

kind of weapons program supported by the United States or the Soviet Union.[11] Somewhat later the possibility was recognized that non-national groups could make nuclear explosives of tremendous force, effect, and influence.[12] This substantially changed the attitudes of experts in material control. A safeguards system which must guard against thefts for sale in a potential black market or for subversive use is different from one which only guards against governmental diversion to establish a national nuclear weapon capability. Protection against loss of material which would reveal to a foreign country that the United States could manufacture certain classes of weapons requires a still different system. These systems can also be different from an international system which attempts to detect national diversion. The experts did not always agree on the objective of the material control program.

## THE CURRENT NATIONAL SYSTEM

Even though the current safeguards system established in the United States is in transition, some elements are clearly established and not likely to change. The United States as a nuclear weapon power whose peaceful facilities and activities have been offered to IAEA inspection must have a records and inspection system which clearly distinguishes between peaceful and military uses. The United States, while wishing to prevent diversion for any reason, must also exclude other countries from programs dealing with weapons and military capabilities. The distinction is recognized by a clear separation of the overall material control system into two operating organizations reporting to the Director of Regulation and the General Manager of the AEC, respectively.

The material control system used for military production is based on measurement, inventory control, record-keeping, and audit functions performed by the industrial contractors who oper-

---

11 Several authors have expressed this view. Among them are Leonard Beaton, *Must the Bomb Spread?* (Harmondsworth: Penguin Books, 1966); W. R. VanCleave, "Nuclear Proliferation. The Interaction of Politics and Technology," Ph.D. diss., Claremont Graduate School, 1967; R. W. Lawrence et al., "Nth Country Threat Analysis: West Germany, Sweden, Canada, Israel, and Selected Other Nations," Stanford Research Institute Technical Report 5025-32, Contract DA 79-092, ARO-10.

12 T. B. Taylor, "International Safeguards of Nonmilitary Nuclear Technology," *Nuclear Journal* 1 (June 1969):1-2.

ate the government-owned plants. This is supplemented by further record-keeping and audits performed by units in each AEC field office and by record-keeping functions performed by the Division of Nuclear Materials Security, which is the successor to the Office of Safeguards and Nuclear Materials Management. This division reports to the Assistant General Manager for National Security. Management functions of this Division include the supervision of a safeguards research and development program and a review of the performance of field office material management operations.

The part of the national safeguards system open to IAEA verification is under the control of the Director of Regulation. Organizational changes begun in April 1972 have resulted in the dispersal of functions which since 1967 had been centered in the Division of Nuclear Materials Safeguards. Functions formerly in that Division were assigned to the Directorate of Licensing and the Directorate of Regulatory Operations. Thus, nuclear materials licensing and audit functions are now being treated in the same manner organizationally as is all other licensing of radioisotopes under AEC control.

The U.S. national safeguards system applicable to peaceful nuclear activities depends, in the first instance, on process, inventory control, and shipment and receipt measurements common to well-ordered commercial activities. Company audits and government inspections, which may include independent sampling and/or measurement, review the effectiveness of the material control system. A system of records which contains information about all shipments, receipts, and discards to waste, as well as materials on hand, is maintained by the government.

The U.S. system operates through two legal methods of control, contracts and licenses. Contracts between the AEC and private industrial organizations specify the operations, procedures, and other material control activities for safeguarding special fissionable material used, produced, or processed in government-owned or government-controlled facilities. These are operated by contractors to AEC who are usually exempt from the licensing requirements.[13] Contracts are also used at times to supplement regulatory control over suppliers of services required by the government that deal with special fissionable material. These suppliers

---

[13] 10 Code of Federal Regulations 70.11.

must be government licensees. Contracts between a licensee and the AEC may be written to include requirements beyond those specified in most licenses.

Current federal regulations pertaining to licenses are broadly written. The regulations restrict the privileges of the license to the specific license conditions, absolve the United States from responsibility for damages resulting from use of licensed special fissionable material, prohibit the licensee from making nuclear explosives, and permit the United States to reclaim the special fissionable material. Beyond these requirements:

The Commission may incorporate in any license such additional conditions and requirements with respect to the licensee's ownership, receipt, possession, use, transfer, import and export of special nuclear material as it deems appropriate or necessary in order to:
(1) Promote the common defense and security;
(2) Protect health or to minimize danger to life or property;
(3) Protect Restricted Data;
(4) Guard against the loss or diversion of special nuclear material;
(5) Require such reports and the keeping of such records, and to provide for such inspections, of activities under the license as may be necessary or appropriate to effectuate the purposes of the Act and regulations thereunder.[14]

This section gives the AEC great latitude. It has led to requirements for physical protection and establishment of pro formas for inventory-taking. It may lead to requirements for prior approval of new construction or of alteration of facilities. There are many who believe the license requirements imposed on individual licensees under this section should be made the subject of specific and uniformly applicable regulations,[15] if they are to be imposed at all.

## DIMENSIONS OF THE NATIONAL SAFEGUARDS PROBLEM

As described previously, the U.S. national system for controlling nuclear material is in a state of flux. In the remainder of this chapter, therefore, the dimensions of the problem that the nation-

[14] 10 Code of Federal Regulations 70.32.b.

[15] Ralph J. Jones, Address to the Atomic Industrial Forum, Annual Conference, Miami Beach, Florida, October 17-21, 1971, reported in *Nuclear Industry* 18 (October-November 1971):41.

al material control system must meet will be described briefly and the form I believe the system should take will be suggested.

## Sources of Special Fissionable Material

*The Nuclear Weapon Program.* The weapons-oriented safeguards system in the United States currently has larger quantities and more varieties of materials to control than do the civilian-oriented activities subject to IAEA review. The U.S. inventory of special fissionable material in its weapons program has an announced value which exceeds $12 billion.[16] Included in this weapons manufacturing inventory are weapons components and plutonium and highly enriched uranium metal readily transformable into weapons components. The saboteur would probably prefer the "clean" weapons materials which are available in some weapons production facilities. Moreover, the material and components present in these facilities are of special interest to the espionage agent who seeks information about the composition and geometry of explosive devices.

*Civilian Nuclear Industry.* Although the nuclear materials and quantities most attractive to the thief are found at present in the U.S. weapons manufacturing complex, before long the quantities of special fissionable material available in industrial facilities will far exceed those in the weapons program. This is especially true of plutonium inventories. The production rate of 15 tonnes per year for plutonium predicted for 1980[17] is much larger than plutonium production rates achieved in the past by weapons programs. Thus plutonium produced in electric power plants must represent an attractive target for the potential thief, whatever his motive. A program to manufacture ten nuclear weapons per year could be supplied by diverting less than 1 percent of the projected 1980 plutonium production in the United States. Therefore, controls will be required that limit diversion to extremely small percentages of the throughput of a nuclear facility in order to prevent theft of

[16] D. E. George, "The United States Atomic Energy Commission Program of Nuclear Materials Management," *Nuclear Materials Management, Proceedings of the Symposium held by the International Atomic Energy Agency, Vienna, 1965* (Vienna: IAEA, 1966), p. 615.

[17] J. Mommsen, "The Market for Uranium and Plutonium," *Nuclear News* 15 (May 1972):40.

a significant amount of material that is capable of being used in a nuclear explosive.

## Methods of Acquiring Special Fissionable Material Illegally

*Clandestine Diversion.* Diversion from a single plant is more likely than diversion from all plants simultaneously, since it requires technical skill and access to material measurements and records. Diversion can be successful only if the material control system is so lax that small-scale theft, i.e., theft less than the limit of error in the material unaccounted for, goes undetected (see also Chapter 8). Thus a diverter must be at the proper place at the proper time. Since a loyal, honest work force is generally the best protection against any type of theft or sabotage, the best guard against diversion is selection and assignment of employees; the next is a proper control system with high performance standards.

Two types of diversion can be envisioned. A single employee or a small group of employees might act without the knowledge of plant management. The diversion group would have to evade company surveillance and control actions, as well as the national safeguards system. A second type of diversion would involve the collusion of plant management. The most likely sources of detection in these circumstances will be companies dealing with the plant where the diversion is occurring and the national safeguards system.

In the absence of effective safeguards, a 5 percent diversion rate might be maintained for two to three years before corrective action were taken. In a single plant with a throughput of 2 tonnes per year of plutonium, diversion on this scale could represent the equivalent of ten or more nuclear weapons. Stringent material control and safeguards could limit the potential undetected diversion rate to less than 0.5 percent and the detection time to one year. This would restrict the potential loss in the plant to about the equivalent of one explosive device. A weapons program could not be based on such a diversion, but a single sabotage attempt could.

*Direct Theft.* Direct theft requires skills different from those required for diversion. Furthermore, the thief or thieves need not be employees of the organization plundered, although inside information about location, security precautions, routes, and cargo is undoubtedly helpful.

The transportation portion of the nuclear industry is the most fragmented and also most vulnerable to physical assault and theft. A few members of the industry most closely aligned with transport of special fissionable material have acquired trucks and cabs specially designed for the purpose. Some have also taken special care to screen employees.[18] However, the carriers of nuclear material generally have taken little action on their own initiative. Moreover, the U.S. government, while requiring hand receipts and prompt notifications of disappearance of materials in transit,[19] has taken no action to supply armed guards or to require the protection they afford.

*Recovery of Stolen Material.* Theft or diversion of special fissionable material causes an immediate financial loss to the industrial organization responsible. Damage to the nation's defense, health, and safety may come later, after the criminal has transferred the stolen material to other hands or has attempted to make a nuclear device. It is important to the nation that the stolen material be recovered before it can be misused. Use of nuclear material for explosives is so complicated that thieves must spend days or weeks fabricating an explosive device. Any plan for recovery of the material during this crucial period must take two factors into account. First, it may be quickly exported from the United States to be used elsewhere or reimported in finished form at a later date. Second, it is well recognized that quick action is most effective in apprehending thieves and recovering any kind of stolen goods.[20]

The recovery of stolen material and the conduct of recovery operations are likely to be primarily the responsibility of the Federal Bureau of Investigation and local law enforcement offi-

---

[18] The concerns of this group are represented in working papers of the Atomic Industrial Forum; see "Transportation Subcommittee Position Report on Safeguards of Strategic Material during Transportation," March 1972 (draft).

[19] 10 Code of Federal Regulations 73.31.42.

[20] Peter W. Greenwood, "An Analysis of the Apprehension Activities of the New York City Police Department," R-529-NYC (New York: RAND Institute, 1970). See also President's Commission on Law Enforcement and Administration of Justice, *The Challenge of Crime in a Free Society* (Washington, D.C.: U.S. Government Printing Office, 1967).

cials, rather than the AEC. Recently proposed license provisions require plans for notifying local law enforcement officials of disappearance of materials as a licensing condition.[21]

## GENERAL REQUIREMENTS OF THE NATIONAL SAFEGUARDS SYSTEM

The U.S. national safeguards system must accommodate two subsystems, one directed to activities of a military (weapons) orientation, the other directed to civilian nuclear industry. Both must prevent or detect diversion and theft and act to recover promptly all stolen material. The civilian subsystem must permit also IAEA review and inspection, at least of representative facilities, if not of the entire U.S. nuclear industry.

It is reasonable to expect that other nations will be concerned if nuclear material in the U.S. were unaccounted for, and perhaps fell into the hands of an unfriendly neighbor or a dissident national faction. Other nations will want careful control of the enormous special fissionable material stocks in the U.S. nuclear industry. U.S. industry also wishes to have an efficient safeguards system. Rigorous protection of the public from violence or even the threat of physical harm from stolen material seems essential if the nuclear-power industry is to gain general acceptance.

Important parts of an acceptable national safeguards system are clear statements of goals, objectives, and strategies. These must be followed by explicit directives or regulations. Thus far, the national system has lacked such statements. If they have been made by government, they have not been heard by the leaders of the nuclear industry (see Chapter 8 below). The following outlines the objectives which some in industry believe should be set forth by the U.S. government:

The U.S. national safeguards system must prevent misuse, as explosives, of special fissionable material under U.S. control, through

1. Maintenance of a record system that analyzes inventories and transactions.

2. Establishment of inventory control and measurement systems for each

---

[21] Letters of February 28, 1972, sent to Kerr-McGee Corporation and Nuclear Materials and Equipment Corporation from Director of Regulation, U.S. Atomic Energy Commission, *AEC Public Documents* 18 (March 1972):42.

facility that accurately define material quantities, types and kinds of losses under control.

3. Maintenance of an independent audit capability that seeks to test and improve the various systems.

4. Establishment of control and alarm systems that deter and signal theft.

5. Institution of search and recovery procedures for prompt and effective recovery of stolen or diverted materials.

All these procedures must be compatible with (1) those required by the IAEA, and (2) the industrial operations characteristic of the competitive nuclear industry. Each must be performed at an incremental cost that still permits nuclear power to compete economically with other fuels for energy and power.[22]

Any national system must have explicit and rational priorities for nuclear material control levels and control efforts. Criteria for government priorities based on monetary worth (or strategic value) and quantities of material at risk have been proposed.[23] Similar criteria based in part on values of weapons (or effects of misuse of weapons material) could well be used to establish control priorities within industrial organizations.[24] The national records system can provide accurate information on quantity, type, and location of materials. It can also be used to uncover measurement bias between plants. This bias can be accidental, but it could also be deliberately introduced for commercial advantage or to hide diversion. While in principle all the data necessary for comparison to reveal bias have been collected, they are not now used by the AEC for this purpose.

In any national system of controls over nuclear material, the vulnerability of transportation media to direct assault must be recognized. Transportation links must be protected through industry or government action. Nuclear weapons and weapons components are transported under government control. It can be argued that civilian nuclear materials that can readily be transformed into weapons should have similar physical protection. It can be further argued that the security of the nation is especially threatened in the transportation phase of the nuclear fuel cycle, and that ensur-

22 Results of deliberations on May 23, 1972, Subcommittee on Research and Development, Atomic Industrial Forum Committee on Nuclear Materials Safeguards, Stanford Research Institute, Menlo Park, California.

23 E. M. Kinderman and R. R. Tarrice, "Criteria for Special Nuclear Materials Inventory and Control Procedures," *Nuclear Materials Management*, pp. 31-41.

24 Suggested by C. D. W. Thornton in an address to the Atomic Industrial Forum, October 17-21, 1971, reported in *Nuclear Industry* 18 (October-November 1971):38.

ing adequate protection should be a general burden of government, rather than the financial and legal responsibility of the industry.

Finally, it should be recognized that the trustworthy employee is the cornerstone of any material control system. He acts to secure the success of the system and observes others to see that they do likewise. All industrial organizations attempt to find honest persons for positions of trust. The security investigation and clearance procedures of the U.S. government could be used to obtain additional assurance of employee trustworthiness in nuclear industry. The expense of this procedure relating to the national security might well be borne by the government.

In addition to all the factors discussed above, the author believes that industrial management must fully comprehend and strongly support national safeguards for an effective system to be developed. The basic steps in material control take place within the nuclear industry. Management action and attitude determine the priorities, the quality, and the effectiveness of control. Without wholehearted industry support in this difficult and important task, a nation's safeguards system cannot promote the common defense and security, protect health, and minimize danger to life or property.

## CONCLUSION

An effective and credible national safeguards system is needed to protect our own national security and to provide other nations with assurance that nuclear material will not be stolen from the U.S. nuclear industry and used to threaten them. The national safeguards system must protect against diversion and theft of very small quantities of special fissionable material from the enormous amounts contained in the inventories of major U.S. nuclear facilities. Moreover, the system must be organized to maximize the chance of recovery of stolen material. Clear statements of goals and strategies are essential and overdue.

# Part III

# Possibilities for Nuclear Diversion

# CHAPTER 6

# Diversion by National Governments

## VICTOR GILINSKY

### INTRODUCTION

This chapter deals with diversion, at the direction of a national government, of civilian nuclear materials and facilities to uses related to nuclear weapons.[1] The main purpose is to assess the extent to which such an improper use of materials and facilities may be affected by the application of international safeguards, as envisioned under the NPT.

The analysis which follows is restricted to fission weapons. Thermonuclear weapons pose a higher order of technical problems. All the present nuclear-weapon powers first progressed through the stage of fission weapons, and nothing has happened so far to suggest that a future nuclear power could easily bypass that stage. Thus a country constructing thermonuclear weapons would be well past the diversion possibilities of concern here, and would already have a large, visible nuclear weapon effort. Full-scale nuclear testing would probably be essential as part of that effort.

---

[1] I wish to acknowledge work undertaken jointly with William Hoehn of the RAND Corporation related to an unpublished report, "Nonproliferation Treaty Safeguards and the Spread of Nuclear Technology," which I have drawn upon extensively in preparing this paper.

Governmentally authorized diversion to a national nuclear weapon program, discussed here, differs substantially from non-governmental diversion, considered in Chapter 7. Governmental diversion can take place only in a political environment which leads persons in authority to conclude that possession of nuclear weapons will improve their country's strategic or political position. Moreover, such diversion involves governmental decision-making, various technical support activities, and military preparations. On the other hand, diversion by a non-governmental group does not necessarily require an underlying political rationale. There would presumably be a black market for any material with the economic and strategic value weapons-grade uranium or plutonium. Furthermore, non-governmental diversion need not be related directly to activities for the further processing of the diverted material.

This chapter emphasizes *clandestine* diversion, which IAEA/NPT safeguards are intended to deter by the threat of early exposure. However, governmental diversion of civilian nuclear material and facilities to a nuclear weapon program can take many forms. At the outset, the context of the problem is examined in order to place in perspective the possibility of clandestine diversion and the role of international safeguards.

## A SHORT CUT TO NUCLEAR WEAPONS

Diversion from civilian facilities is not the only way to obtain materials for nuclear weapons. They may be produced directly for military purposes independently of any civilian program. This is, in fact, the way in which the United States, the Soviet Union, Britain, and China proceeded. Of the present nuclear powers, only France had a civilian nuclear program before it decided to produce nuclear weapons.[2] However, it seems likely that a future nuclear-weapon power would rely more heavily on fissionable material obtained from a civilian nuclear program, at least at the start, than has been done in the past.

When the nuclear weapon programs of the present five nuclear

[2] Although France started with civilian plutonium production reactors, as Bertrand Goldschmidt comments (*The Atomic Adventure* [New York: Macmillan, 1964], p. 81), the military "aspect of the atomic problem had been much present in the minds of those responsible for the plan."

powers got under way, there were essentially no civilian nuclear programs from which to divert material. For example, in the years immediately after World War II, the U.S. and Soviet civilian nuclear programs were minuscule offshoots of military nuclear programs. Until recently, there have been no significant nuclear programs in non-nuclear-weapon countries. As described in Chapter 3, civilian nuclear programs will soon dwarf, by any reasonable measure, corresponding military nuclear programs. In particular, the civilian nuclear programs under way in many non-nuclear-weapon countries will be substantially larger, in a few years, than any hypothetical military programs which such states could reasonably be expected to develop if they were to decide to produce nuclear weapons. As a result of the reversal of scale, the opportunity will soon exist to take a short cut to nuclear weapons by diversion of a relatively small fraction of a much larger overall civilian nuclear effort.

## DIFFERENCES IN NUCLEAR WEAPON INCENTIVES AND CAPABILITIES

There is a tendency to speak loosely of a country's "going nuclear" as if all nuclear weapons were equivalent. In fact there is a spectrum of possible types of nuclear weapons which may be combined into a broad range of nuclear force programs, varying as to size, level of sophistication, and mode of delivery. The variety of nuclear force postures reflects profound differences among countries in both strategic interests and technical capabilities. For purposes of discussion, it is useful to group possible nuclear programs according to the potential adversaries against whom such forces might be primarily directed. This procedure reveals the requirements a national nuclear weapon program must meet.

### Nuclear Force Directed against a Superpower

The Federal Republic of Germany is probably the only non-nuclear-weapon country in which any nuclear weapon program would clearly threaten a superpower—the Soviet Union. A German nuclear weapon program must therefore be structured to cope with a broad range of threats on the part of the Soviet Union. A Japanese program may or may not fall into the same category. Other states, for example, Sweden or Switzerland, might conclude that possession of a small defense nuclear force would permit them to deter a narrowly limited range of Soviet threats, but nothing more.

The standards of military sophistication and required nuclear force levels are obviously very high for would-be superpower deterrent forces. The Federal Republic of Germany or Japan could not reasonably consider the acquisition of anything less than the nuclear force levels of the United Kingdom or France, and they would probably set their sights considerably higher. This implies, ultimately, the production of low-weight thermonuclear weapons[3] deployed on highly sophisticated strategic delivery vehicles and directed by elaborate command and control systems. Probably submarine-based missiles would be necessary because of the difficulty in deploying survivable land-based missile forces so close to the Soviet Union or China. Therefore, any suggestion that the Germans or the Japanese might base a military strategy on a few "bombs in the basement" borders on the ridiculous, whatever the technical possibilities.

In order to have a relatively short-term option to develop nuclear weapons for deployment against the Soviet Union or the United States, a country must have the facilities to produce large quantities of weapons-grade fissionable material, as well as special laboratories and manufacturing facilities. Such countries cannot take chances with unpredictable or inferior weapons, nor can the number of weapons be small.

A credible nuclear force for the Federal Republic of Germany or Japan would seem to involve a minimum of one hundred warheads. Such a weapons program would probably require at least 1,000 kilograms of plutonium or many thousands of kilograms of highly enriched uranium. Fuel reprocessing facilities or uranium enrichment facilities of sufficient capacity would be

---

3 J. Carson Mark, *Impact of New Technologies on the Arms Race*, ed. B. T. Field et al. (Cambridge, Mass.: MIT Press, 1971), p. 136:

> The main thrust of weapons work in the past 10 or 15 years has been to obtain effective weapon packages at weights suitable for rocket vehicles—as single warheads in the first instance and as units for multiple warheads in more recent instances. Efforts along these lines have been quite successful, to the extent that improvements in yield per pound of something like a factor of 100 over the first fission of bombs have been realized. This brings the yield per pound up to a few times 100,000 larger than a high explosive, which is to say close to within an order of magnitude of the ideal, hundred percent advantage factor of 17 million (for fissile material without any assembly hardware) or 3 or 4 times larger for bare unpackaged thermonuclear fuel.

needed to obtain this material. At the present time, the Federal Republic of Germany has only a small fuel reprocessing facility, with a capacity of about 40 tonnes per year, which yields about 200 kilograms of reactor-grade plutonium per year but a much smaller amount of relatively pure plutonium-239. On commercial grounds, the Federal Republic of Germany has decided not to expand its fuel reprocessing capacity for some years because of the overcapacity which presently exists in other Western countries.[4] Japan is constructing a larger chemical reprocessing plant which will have a capacity of about 250 tonnes when completed in 1974. Even after this plant is operating, Japan will still have to send much of its fuel abroad for reprocessing.

It should be noted that the Federal Republic of Germany is constructing a small gas centrifuge enrichment plant in the Netherlands.[5] Later plants may be located in Germany. Japan has been actively studying enrichment technology and is approaching a decision as to whether to construct an enrichment plant independently or in cooperation with other industrial states. It is possible that both the Federal Republic of Germany and Japan will have independent access to sources of highly enriched uranium in militarily significant amounts in the 1980s,[6] and perhaps earlier.

In any event, capability should not be mistaken for intent. Neither of these countries would lightly make a decision which could jeopardize its civilian nuclear power program. These programs, while very large, are not entirely self-sufficient. Germany and Japan will both continue for some years to depend heavily on the United States, especially for fuel services.

## Nuclear Force Directed against Another Major Nuclear Power

It is difficult to imagine new nuclear forces directed against Britain and France, but nuclear weapon programs in some countries— India is an obvious example—would presumably be directed pri-

[4] For the situation of the nuclear fuel cycle in West Germany see G. Wirth, "Der Stand der Brennstoffkreislaufindustrie in der BRD," *Atomwirtschaft* (August-September 1971), p. 455.

[5] See "German Fuge Plant Underway," *Nuclear Industry* 18 (June 1971):44. The plant's design capacity is about 25 tonnes SWU per year. In principle, this capacity could be used to produce about 100 kilograms of highly enriched uranium per year.

[6] That is, they will have independent access to enrichment capacities of the order of 1,000 tonnes SWU per year. In principle, such a facility could produce about 5,000 kilograms of highly enriched uranium per year.

marily against the People's Republic of China. Japan is a mixed case, for it may, in the event it develops nuclear weapons, decide to choose this modest course, attempting to avoid a posture which might threaten the Soviet Union. Australia and Taiwan, if the latter could manage the effort, are potential candidates for this group.

India presently has independent ready access to weapons-grade nuclear material (plutonium) and thus has the option to develop nuclear weapons. Moreover, India does not intend to adhere to the NPT. The other countries could not acquire special production facilities for special fissionable material, much less nuclear weapons, for at least five years and probably for a good deal longer. As of mid-1972 Australia had not purchased its first nuclear power plant. Furthermore, the acquiescence of one or more of the principal nuclear supplier states would be necessary for Australian development of nuclear weapons; without such acquiescence much more time would be required for Australia to acquire a reasonably self-sufficient nuclear fuel cycle.

### Nuclear Force Directed against Another Incipient Nuclear Power

A local arms race between countries with modest industrial resources might take on nuclear dimensions in the future. In a local arms race even a few nuclear weapons, using "reactor-grade" plutonium, and without any special delivery vehicles, could play an important role. Most countries in this category do not and will not have independent access to special fissionable material, at least for many years. However, if nuclear technology spreads on a national rather than a commercial basis, it is conceivable that even these countries may purchase small fuel reprocessing facilities or perhaps small enrichment plants.

### Nuclear Force Directed against Non-Nuclear Countries

There are a number of relatively advanced states which may at times feel "cornered" politically and militarily and which might, in some circumstances, choose to defend themselves with nuclear weapons against numerically superior forces. Israel is commonly put in this category. The presence of a relatively small number of Israeli nuclear weapons would radically alter the situation in the Middle East. Because a superpower might intervene to balance the side of the conventionally armed adversary, the incentive to keep an Israeli nuclear weapon capability secret even after it were acquired would be especially strong. Since Israel has not signed the NPT thus far and may decline to do so in the future, one of the countries most often suspected of clandestine nuclear activities is probably not going to be subject to international safeguards to the full extent required by the NPT.

## REASONS FOR DIVERSION
## OF CIVILIAN NUCLEAR INDUSTRY

As noted previously, the principal reason for diversion of nuclear material or facilities from civilian to weapons purposes is to reduce the time interval from the governmental decision to produce nuclear weapons to their initial deployment. A secondary incentive is simply to conserve resources by not duplicating facilities. The relative importance of these incentives would obviously depend on the specific context of the diversion. If a fairly large military program were envisioned, it would probably entail the eventual construction of military production facilities, but it seems clear that speed in moving from decision to deployment will be an increasingly important factor in almost every likely future context.

Paradoxically, the need for rapid acquisition of nuclear weapons, once a governmental decision has been reached, would seem to increase in rough proportion to the success of the NPT. While the NPT does not incorporate explicit sanctions for intervention, it nevertheless could provide both a pretext and an improved political climate for action against any new nuclear power, whether or not it is or was a party to the Treaty.

Assuming relatively widespread acceptance and implementation of the NPT, the United States and Soviet Union, either individually or perhaps in some wider context, may be more inclined to take pre-emptive action against incipient members of the nuclear club. The prospects for such action may be further enhanced by agreement between the two nuclear superpowers on strategic arms limitations. As a result of a growing shared interest of the United States and Soviet Union in maintaining the nuclear status quo, countries bent on the acquisition of nuclear armaments may feel they cannot afford the luxury of a visible production program for weapons material, and they would logically place a premium on speed in the deployment of a new nuclear force.

A non-nuclear-weapon country which feared an incipient nuclear force might respond forcefully itself or might succeed in mobilizing a collective international response. Altogether, these possibilities suggest that the period between the first overt manifestation of the intent to develop nuclear weapons and the deployment of a significant nuclear force will be a particularly dangerous interval for a newcomer to the nuclear club. Therefore, a potential nuclear power will try to shorten this interval as much as possible.

Other activities which are associated with the acquisition of nuclear weapons and precede manufacture—initial planning, warhead design, and even non-nuclear testing—are relatively easy to hide compared with the construction of a set of military reactors or special enrichment plants for obtaining highly enriched uranium. If the initial inventory of weapons-grade nuclear material could be obtained from a civilian program it would no longer be necessary to start early on the construction of highly visible facilities. In short, a strong incentive exists for diversion from the civilian sector even if the diversion is not concealed from public view.

It may be argued that in the case of open diversion there would still be an interval during which the program was visible and before weapons were deployed. But it would take time to mobilize any international counteraction. If the interval of maximum vulnerability can be reduced from years to months, the prospects for a new nuclear force coming to maturity unscathed may be significantly enhanced.

The reasons for saving time by diverting material from the civilian nuclear fuel cycle also constitute an argument for keeping diversion secret as long as possible. The main objective of clandestine diversion is to achieve strategic surprise. A country may wish to keep a nuclear weapon capability secret even after it is acquired, intending to reveal its existence only in the event of war. It seems evident, as mentioned earlier, that if Israel were to possess nuclear weapons, it would not hasten to display them. Another reason for proceeding secretly is that a country may merely want to create an option to develop nuclear weapons without incurring obvious political costs. For purposes of weapons research and development, it would need a small amount of weapons-grade nuclear material. The risks of discovery would be slight. The objects of research and development activities are often sufficiently ambiguous, sometimes even to those involved, to be explained away without difficulty.

## THE NPT AND ALTERNATIVE ROUTES
## TO NUCLEAR WEAPONS

The act of adherence to the NPT confirms that the government of a non-nuclear-weapon state has no present intention to acquire nuclear weapons. Thereafter, the NPT is intended to deter a non-nuclear-weapon party from changing its policy of nuclear forbearance. The IAEA safeguards which the NPT requires on civilian nuclear activities serve as an important part of the deterrent against acquisition of nuclear weapons by creating a risk of detection of weapons manufacture using material diverted from civilian nuclear industry. The possibilities for clandestine diversion and the possible role of IAEA safeguards must, therefore, be related to the alternative routes to nuclear weapons open to a party to the NPT. If, then, the government of a non-nuclear-weapon party to the NPT decides to acquire nuclear weapons, how might it proceed?

The simplest course of action would be to withdraw from the Treaty at the time that the decision is made. While this is perhaps the most honorable approach, many countries will regard it as the most foolish. In any event, the decision to acquire nuclear weapons may not be taken at any one time. Rather, it is more likely to take the form of a series of incremental, option-widening steps. Indeed, the faction within a government which favors acquisition of nuclear weapons may be able to use the state's status as a party to the NPT to undercut resistance to such steps, arguing at each step that it does not constitute a change in policy since adherence to the NPT continues. Thus, open withdrawal from the NPT in the early stages of weapons acquisition by a non-nuclear-weapon party is not expected.

A second course of action is to make all the preparations that can be carried out secretly, and then announce withdrawal as late as possible consistent with the NPT. The Treaty prohibits the "manufacture" of nuclear weapons. Thus, a state can come arbitrarily close to manufacture without clearly violating the NPT, and in the process it can lay a substantial foundation for a nuclear weapon program.

A third alternative is to engage in clandestine development, manufacture, and perhaps even deployment of nuclear weapons without withdrawing from the NPT. In most cases, such a course of action would be impossible to complete successfully even without any safeguards being applied. It would be too difficult to mask all intelligence indicators of a nuclear weapon program. But this is not to say it might not be attempted in a situation where the penalty for public acknowledgment of such a program even in the final states of the weapons acquisition process would outweigh the political cost of being branded a violator of the NPT. IAEA safeguards under the NPT apply mainly to the third alternative. The safeguards system is an alarm system to detect and announce the clandestine use of civilian nuclear material for illegal military purposes. Thus, safeguards are focused on a narrow band of the spectrum of proliferation possibilities: clandestine manufacture of nuclear weapons, by a party to the NPT, prior to withdrawal from the Treaty.

## CLANDESTINE DIVERSION ALTERNATIVES

The best places in the nuclear fuel cycle to divert special fissionable material are where they are in fairly pure form and in a condition to be fabricated into nuclear explosives or easily transformed to that condition. These are fuel reprocessing plants where plutonium separation occurs, uranium enrichment plants, fuel fabrication plants, and connecting transportation links. Countries which lack such facilities will lack direct, independent access to special fissionable material. A number of diversion modes must be considered. It should be kept in mind, however, that this analysis is necessarily speculative and hypothetical.

### Clandestine Small-Scale Diversion

The diversion mode most often discussed is the slow diversion of small amounts of weapons-grade nuclear material until some militarily significant amount has been accumulated. The detection of such diversion is often treated as a problem in statistics, and the design of elaborate detection systems has absorbed the efforts of many of the organizations charged with responsibility for safe-guarding nuclear material. The problem is to recognize the difference between normal fluctuations and uncertainties in processing losses, on the one hand, and intentional diversion, on the other.

Statistical detection systems are clearly relevant to the problem of non-governmental diversion. However, they are far less relevant on the international level to detection of diversion pursuant to a governmental decision. There are different reasons for this in countries with large and with small civilian nuclear industries, that is, in large industrially advanced countries and in small, less developed countries. In a country with a large civilian nuclear industry the long-term diversion of small amounts of material would be plausible if that country were faced with a national security threat that could be balanced by a very few nuclear weapons. However, it is difficult to find a country in such circumstances. As the previous analysis indicated, the *strategic* military potential of a few nuclear weapons is likely to be small for industrially advanced countries. Thus, the size of the nuclear weapon program required in a major industrialized country appears to militate strongly against clandestine weapons development, whether or not safeguards are applied to its civilian nuclear industry.

A more plausible possibility would be a small diversion of civilian nuclear material to an option-widening research and development program. Since kilogram amounts may be sufficient for this purpose, there is probably not a great deal that can be done to prevent such hard-to-detect activities. Moreover, it is unclear as to which of these activities are prohibited by the NPT. In certain less developed countries with small civilian nuclear industries, a few primitive nuclear weapons may have strategic importance. In such countries the clandestine diversion of small amounts of material from civilian facilities to a nuclear weapon program might seem plausible. However, the inventory of special fissionable material in the civilian program of a less developed country would normally be much smaller than the inventory in a major industrialized country, and therefore the amount of material that could be diverted beneath the detection threshold would be smaller. Even in the unlikely event that a less developed country had the essential nuclear facilities (enrichment, reprocessing, or fabrication) for the production of special fissionable material, the motivation for these facilities would constantly be suspect since they would be difficult to justify in economic terms. Nuclear weapon development in such a country would take place in an environment with a much lower technological "noise" level. The program would be more conspicuous and, therefore, more easily detected. The slow accumulation of weapons-grade nuclear material diverted from civilian industry does not, therefore, appear to be a very attractive mode of diversion for governments of either advanced or less developed countries.

## Clandestine Large-Scale Diversion

The objective of this mode of diversion is to shorten as much as possible the vulnerable period between disclosure of a nuclear weapon program and deployment of an operational nuclear force. This may be worthwhile even if the entire interval cannot pass by without detection, for even after detection other countries would need time to organize a response. As previously noted, an effective response would be particularly difficult if it depended on collective rather than on unilateral action. A gain of even a few months' lead time may significantly reduce the risk to the incipient nuclear power.

Tactically, a government directing massive diversion would count on the delays inherent in the system of inspection and material control to result in a delay in exposure of the diversion. At any moment in time, the nuclear material inventory disclosed internationally through the IAEA safeguards system will lag behind the real inventory within a country. The IAEA inventory may be only one month or many months out of date, depending on the intensity and efficiency of the safeguards applied. The discrepancy will increase with the size of the inventory, other things being equal. Thus rapid massive diversion might well be a plausible course of action for a country with a large civilian nuclear industry.

## Disclosed Diversion with a Clandestine Purpose

As discussed in Chapter 4, the NPT permits use by a non-nuclear-weapon party of special fissionable material for any military purpose which does not involve the manufacture of explosives.[7]

---

[7] Note that the NPT does not forbid non-nuclear countries to engage in military

At the same time, military facilities are not directly covered by the IAEA/NPT safeguards system. In principle, a country could transfer a large amount of special fissionable material to a military program, ostensibly for the development of submarine power plants, and then use that material for nuclear explosives. The announced transfer of significant amounts of material to a military facility would, however, arouse suspicions. Although IAEA inspectors could not follow the material diverted to a non-explosive military use, the public knowledge of such diversion could substantially help in targeting the efforts of national intelligence networks. If a government feels compelled to choose this path, IAEA/NPT safeguards will at least disclose its intentions, although ambiguously, sooner than would have occurred without the Treaty.

## Clandestine Unreported Facilities

There exists the possibility that a country may secretly construct facilities for the production of weapons-grade nuclear material such as plutonium production reactors or uranium-enrichment facilities, although in general it is fairly difficult to hide facilities of significant size during construction or operation. Operation of clandestine production reactors alone would not provide a country with a secret supply of plutonium for nuclear explosives because fuel fabrication and chemical reprocessing would also be necessary. These activities might conceivably be carried on in clandestine facilities or secretly within facilities which are subject to safeguards. In any event, there is only a small chance that all these clandestine activities would escape detection by an external authority.

The clandestine construction of facilities for uranium enrichment, though technically more demanding, is another possibility. In effect, only one type of facility would be needed, an enrichment plant, assuming the uranium were available in suitable form. As described in Chapter 3, most of the separative work required to produce highly enriched uranium is carried out in the production of reactor-grade uranium fuel. Therefore, slightly enriched uranium might be diverted from the civilian fuel cycle to a small

nuclear activities other than the manufacture of explosive devices. Such activities would not be subject to international inspection. See Mason Willrich, *The Non-Proliferation Treaty: Framework for Nuclear Arms Control* (Charlottesville, Va.: Michie, 1969), p. 93.

clandestine enrichment plant. In typical circumstances the clandestine plant need be only one-fifth the size required if natural uranium were used as feed material in order to produce the same amount of weapons-grade uranium. On the other hand, slightly enriched uranium would be subject to more stringent safeguards than natural uranium, and the risk of detection of its diversion would also be greater than in the case of natural uranium.

With respect to clandestine facilities generally, the primary risk of detection comes not from the international safeguards system, since IAEA/NPT safeguards are not designed to uncover clandestine facilities, but rather from national intelligence services.

## Governmental Diversion from Another Country

For a country with no independent access to special fissionable material but with the determination and technical resources to produce nuclear weapons, the theft of the necessary material from another country (or its purchase on a black market) may be a tempting course of action. This mode of diversion would have especially insidious effects, although very little attention has been given to it thus far. Although admittedly a bizarre and improbable course, diversion from another country's civilian nuclear industry may appear to a government preferable to diversion from its own industry. It would, for one thing, avoid the need for the early involvement of nuclear industry officials and workers who might be unreliable accomplices in an illegal enterprise. The possibility of governmental diversion from another country must be dealt with primarily by national safeguards systems, rather than the IAEA/NPT system. Indeed, this is one important reason why strong national safeguards systems are needed. The problem is discussed further in Chapter 7.

## EFFECTIVENESS OF INTERNATIONAL SAFEGUARDS IN DETERRING CLANDESTINE DIVERSION

In large part, safeguards are useful in proportion to the degree that they introduce added constraints into the decision-making process of the potential diverter. To what extent do IAEA/NPT safeguards increase the risks to the government contemplating clandestine diversion? What features of the safeguards system are particularly effective in this regard? It is sometimes implied that considerations of effectiveness are not very important—that the significance of safeguards is mainly "political" or "symbolic" and that their actual accomplishments are less important than what they appear to accomplish. This may be true to some extent, especially since most countries have no experience with the application of safeguards, and hence no appreciation of the capabilities of such a system. At the least, international safeguards serve as a highly visible reminder of a country's international obligations. However, the operational performance of the IAEA safeguards system under the NPT will be carefully examined by those concerned. The usefulness of safeguards in deterring governmental diversion will depend ultimately on critical assessments of the actual effectiveness of the system in providing reliable early warning of diversion. Thus, in the long run, credibility will rest heavily on the technical effectiveness of the system.

### Importance of a Timely Alarm

In order to have a value beyond the symbolic one mentioned above, the safeguards system must sound a reliable alarm before disclosure of diversion would normally occur by other means. Otherwise, it will not contribute to the risks perceived by a government contemplating diversion. In fact, in order to increase the real risk assumed by a government which diverts, the alarm system must be capable of sounding a warning in time to permit other states to plan, organize, and implement a counteraction before the purpose of the diversion is accomplished.

Until recently, the IAEA reporting system appeared to be six months behind actual events. Efforts are being made to reduce this time lag in the system, but the rapid growth of civilian nuclear power programs, as well as expansion in the IAEA's safeguards responsibilities under the NPT, are compounding the difficulty. Unless this lag is dealt with effectively, in a few years a number of countries may be capable of initial deployment of an operational nuclear force using material diverted from civilian industry before the diversion is even detected by the IAEA/NPT safeguards system.

### False Alarms

A safeguards system is commonly pictured as a careful and continuous watch over all of the activities in nuclear facilities for any signs of diversion. If any such signs are detected at any point, an alarm goes off. The wrongdoer is then promptly summoned for judgment. However, a government engaged in clandestine diversion is not likely to exhibit unambiguous evidence of such activities. Whatever suspicious indicators exist in records may or may not be significant because of the inevitable presence of random measurement errors, incomplete inventories, and normal operating inaccuracies and processing losses, especially when a new facility starts up. Thus it is necessary to establish criteria for activating the alarm system.

It may be asserted that any suspicious signal should sound the alarm. However, an international safeguards system is at best a politically fragile instrument, and the number of false alarms which it can tolerate without a breakdown is probably small.[8] The dilemma is this: to keep the false alarm rate low, the threshold signal strength must be kept high; but a high signal threshold implies low effectiveness for the system.

There are two types of alarm errors that a safeguards system can make: it can sound an alarm when there has been no diversion, or it can fail to sound an alarm when a diversion has taken place. For a given frequency of false alarms one would like to choose a test that minimizes the frequency of alarm failures. But for a given signal sample size (in effect, level of intrusiveness) one cannot reduce the false alarm frequency without incurring, at the same time, increasingly large numbers of alarm failures. In this somewhat abstract discussion all types of input data are lumped together. In practice, there are many, possibly incommensurate, types of signals.

In practice, there will also be times when a safeguards test result has exceeded the alarm threshold but there is no certainty that a diversion has actually occurred. In such cases, given the possibility of error in measurement, an inspector can only state that on the basis of a theoretical model of the nuclear facility in question and with a specified degree of confidence, standard tests suggest a diversion of a given amount of material. Presumably, this information will then be transmitted by international inspectors to higher authorities. If the degree of confidence is, for example, 95

---

[8] This is one reason why the subnational diversion problem is best left to national inspection systems—they can tolerate a much higher false alarm rate.

percent, then 5 percent of the results exceeding the threshold are false alarms. Which 5 percent are the false alarms is, of course, unknown when the statement is made.

What the higher authorities in the IAEA inspectorate do with such an inspection report will depend very much on the circumstances. They can call for an explanation from the government or facility manager concerned or for more thorough on-the-spot investigation. They may meet with cooperation and may clarify the nature of the situation that triggered the alarm, or they may not. It is possible that persons directly involved in the administration of the safeguards system and having a vested interest in its continued existence may be reluctant to deal promptly and resolutely with what may, after all, be a false alarm.

## Operation of Safeguards in a Crisis

It is often said that an international safeguards system provides a country with assurance that other countries, perhaps some of its neighbors, are not developing nuclear weapons. Such an assurance is particularly important during a period of international tension or crisis: it reduces a nation's incentive to "go nuclear" out of fear that it may be left behind. Yet IAEA charges that a nuclear weapon program is under way may aggravate the crisis and possibly trigger other decisions to produce nuclear weapons. The tolerable false alarm rate may well decrease in such circumstances, resulting in paralysis of the inspection system. The difficulty is compounded if the intelligence derived from reports and inspections lags relatively far behind events. Furthermore, as previously noted, the NPT does not prohibit states from taking actions which are very close to the manufacture of nuclear weapons. When a large number of states are thus poised on the threshold of the nuclear club, the NPT safeguards system may fail to provide adequate assurance to keep some of them from crossing the threshold for fear that others may do so. It is clear, therefore, that the safeguards effort would be greatly helped by measures to prevent the accumulation of certain critical materials, facilities, and technology—the preconditions of a weapons program. In fact, the prevention of such accumulations may be a precondition for the long-term effectiveness of safeguards.

# CHAPTER 7

# Diversion by Non-Governmental Organizations

## THEODORE B. TAYLOR

### INTRODUCTION

National governments are not the only organizations that may divert weapons-grade nuclear material from civilian industry. Persons not acting on behalf of any national government may seek to acquire such material by either covert or overt theft. Possible motives for theft of material include its sale to national governments and to extremist or terrorist organizations and the clandestine construction of nuclear explosives, either for coercive use by the organization responsible for the theft or for sale to other organizations. Although the safeguards required by the NPT are intended to deter non-nuclear-weapon parties from diverting nuclear material for use in explosives, the threat of non-governmental diversion should have a direct bearing on the way in which those international safeguards are implemented. The importance of that threat depends on its credibility and on the character of present national efforts to cope with it.[1]

---

[1] These dangers have been recognized for a number of years, particularly since the publication of the findings of the USAEC's Ad Hoc Committee on Nuclear Safeguards in

Present nuclear safeguards are aimed primarily at the detection of material losses after they have occurred, rather than at the prevention of theft through various physical protection measures. As described in Chapters 4 and 5, the IAEA/NPT and the U.S. national safeguards systems are mainly techniques for auditing nuclear material balances in the various facilities which comprise the nuclear fuel cycle in order to determine whether any discrepancies have occurred that cannot be accounted for by normal process losses. If the auditing procedures are sufficiently accurate to detect such losses, they can be used both to deter and to detect diversion by the managers or other employees of a nuclear facility. Thus nuclear safeguards now function in a manner analogous to the use of auditing procedures in a bank to detect embezzlement by its employees. However, banks do not rely on such procedures to inhibit all types of theft. They use vaults, alarms, and often armed guards to detect attempts at theft by outsiders at once and to make a successful theft difficult. The absence of effective physical protection measures to prevent the theft of nuclear material by non-governmental organizations is a major weakness in the entire system of international and national safeguards on which the NPT depends.

In assessing the risk that nuclear material will be stolen, a key question is: how difficult is it to construct nuclear explosives using material taken from nuclear industry? A major part of this chapter is devoted to exploring this question. We find that a small number of individuals with some experience in the fields of nuclear engi-

1967 (*Report of the Ad Hoc Committee on Nuclear Safeguards* [Washington, D.C.: AEC, 1967]). Several rather detailed studies of the problem and of possible corrective actions have been made since that time. See, for example, "Preliminary Survey of Non-National Nuclear Threats," SSC-IN-5205-83, September 17, 1968, prepared for the Army Research Office by Stanford Research Institute (Unclassified); "The Unconventional Nuclear Threat—A Preliminary Survey," SRI-9-429, May 1969, prepared for the Advanced Research Projects Agency by Stanford Research Institute (Secret RD); "A Study of Non-Attributable Nuclear Threats," IRT-70-8, November 1970, prepared for the Advanced Research Projects Agency by International Research and Technology Corporation (Confidential). These studies conclude that present and formally planned national and international nuclear material safeguards measures are not adequate barriers to the theft of fissionable material by determined people with resources similar to those that have been used in the past for major thefts of other valuable materials. They also conclude that the likelihood that such material may be stolen by non-governmental organizations is increasing rapidly with time. Concern has also been registered in a number of recent public statements by U.S. government officials and private individuals (Congressman Craig Hosmer, Keynote Address, *Proceedings of Symposium on Implementing Nuclear Safeguards,* Kansas State University, Manhattan, Kan., October 25-27, 1971 [New York: Praeger, 1972]; Charles Thornton, *ibid.*).

neering and high explosives technology, using information contained in unclassified publications, could secretly design and build easily transportable nuclear explosives with yields in at least the one-kiloton range.

A second question that bears on the likelihood of non-governmental diversion is whether present physical protection measures are generally adequate against determined groups of people with resources comparable to those used in major robberies of other valuables in the past. Despite continued improvements in national safeguards systems, our answer is no.

A third, and much more difficult, question is what types of non-governmental organizations might want to use nuclear explosives and for what purposes? Although this question is explored below, no clear answers emerge. An enormous variety of non-governmental threat scenarios can be written. Which, if any, appear credible is a matter of individual judgment; fortunately, we have no historic examples to draw upon for the answer. Another issue is less speculative: how likely is it that a group of people might steal special fissionable material for clandestine sale to national governments? If a flourishing international black market in this material develops, it is possible, if not probable, that a national government which decides to acquire nuclear weapons would find black market purchases preferable to diversion from its own civilian nuclear program.

Clearly, physical protection measures must form an integral part of an effective system of safeguards applicable to peaceful nuclear activities. The concluding sections of this chapter discuss principles on which those safeguards could be based and various ways of implementing them.

## RESOURCES REQUIRED FOR CRIMINAL PRODUCTION OF NUCLEAR EXPLOSIVES

### Definitions

For purposes of this discussion, a "nuclear explosive" is a device that derives most of its energy from nuclear fission and is capable of the explosive release of at least ten times as much energy as a conventional high explosive of a weight equal to the total weight of the nuclear device. "Explosive" means energy that is released during less time than is required for a sound wave to pass through the device. "Total weight" is the sum only of those parts which, fuse, detonate, or explode the device. This definition excludes nuclear reactors, which could conceivably be used as radiation weapons to deliver lethal doses of gamma rays or neutrons, since the energy is not released explosively. It also excludes explosive devices that derive most of their energy from thermonuclear reactions.

It may be argued that a minimum yield-to-weight ratio of 10 kilograms of high-explosive equivalent per kilogram of the nuclear explosive device is too small to qualify a device as a nuclear explosive. A minimum ten-to-one ratio is, however, appropriate in terms of possible non-governmental uses in attacks on gatherings of people, individual buildings, or large vehicles, such as ships or transport aircraft. Here a fission yield equivalent to as little as 1 tonne of high explosive from a device weighing 200 kilograms could kill hundreds or even thousands of people.

The important point is that this definition includes, but is not limited to, devices that are crude and inefficient, with highly unreliable nuclear yields compared to the types of nuclear weapons that have been developed for national military uses. Such nuclear explosives are nevertheless far more destructive than any weapons which depend on the release of stored chemical energy.

## Special Fissionable Material

A fission explosion is produced by rapidly assembling more than one critical mass of highly enriched uranium, plutonium, or uranium-233. The fissions must be predominantly caused by fast neutrons. If the assembly contains too high a concentration of light elements, the chain reaction is maintained primarily by neutrons slowed by collisions with non-fissionable nuclei. If the "slowing-down time" is large compared to the time required for the device to disassemble, the reaction will not be explosive. The materials used, therefore, must not contain too many moderating atoms per atom of fissionable material. At normal densities, fast breeder reactor fuels, such as uranium or plutonium oxide, as well as metallic forms of special fissionable material, can be used to make nuclear explosives.[2]

[2] David B. Hall, *ibid.*

The spherical critical mass of uranium-235 metal is approximately 50 kilograms without a reflector[3] and about 20 kilograms with a reflector consisting of several centimeters of common metals, such as steel or copper. The corresponding critical masses of plutonium-239 metal are approximately 10 and 5 kilograms, respectively.[4] Critical masses of highly enriched uranium or plutonium oxides are somewhat larger. The amount of any of these materials required for a fission explosive depends on its chemical composition and density, as well as on the type and thickness of the reflector, the required explosion efficiency and yield, and other characteristics of the device.

As noted in Chapter 3, natural uranium must be enriched with respect to the isotope uranium-235 for use in nuclear explosives. The level of enrichment required for its use in fission explosives is not well defined, partly because the fraction of fast neutron fissions varies with the enrichment. In any case, the critical mass of a uranium assembly decreases as the enrichment increases. Published data indicate that the critical mass of an unreflected sphere of metallic uranium decreases from about 150 kilograms at 30 percent enrichment to 100 kilograms at 50 percent and 50 kilograms at 100 percent.[5] In other words, the mass of uranium-235 required for an explosive that uses 30-percent-enriched uranium is about three times the mass required if the enrichment is 100 percent. Below 30 percent enrichment the fast critical mass of uranium increases rapidly until it becomes categorically impossible to make a critical assembly that does not rely primarily on fission by slow neutrons to sustain a chain reaction. This happens at an enrichment substantially above the 4 or 5 percent level that is typical of the fuel used in present light-water-moderated nuclear power reactors. Thus, the term "highly enriched uranium" is generally used to mean uranium enriched above 20 percent.

Fast critical assemblies can be made with a variety of forms of highly enriched uranium diluted by other materials. The allowable amount of dilution depends on the degree of enrichment and on the size of the critical mass that is deemed acceptable. Typical uranium fast breeder reactor fuels include uranium oxide, uranium

[3] H. C. Paxton, *Los Alamos Critical Mass Data*, LAMS-3067 (Los Alamos, Calif.: Los Alamos Scientific Laboratory, 1964).

[4] *Ibid.*

[5] H. C. Paxton et al., *Critical Dimensions of Systems Containing $U^{235}$, $Pu^{239}$, and $U^{233}$*, TID-7028 (Oak Ridge, Tenn.: Oak Ridge National Laboratories, 1964).

carbide, various alloys of uranium and other metals, and uranium metal. As long as sufficient quantities of such materials are used and the uranium enrichment is sufficiently high, some kind of nuclear explosive could be made from any of them.[6] Since the presence of other materials tends to increase the mass of highly enriched uranium required, more efficient nuclear explosives may be produced from diluted uranium if it is converted to metallic form. Detailed descriptions of the chemical and metallurgical processes involved are widely published and well known to technicians who have worked in plants processing fissionable material, as well as to many students of nuclear engineering.[7]

Fast critical assemblies can be made with plutonium having any composition of the various plutonium isotopes now in use or contemplated for use in nuclear reactors. At one time, the belief was widespread that in order to make plutonium usable in any type of nuclear explosive, the concentration of plutonium-240, which undergoes spontaneous fission, releasing neutrons, would have to be kept well below the concentration typical in irradiated power reactor fuels. This was officially refuted by the Atomic Energy Commission in 1952.[8] Therefore, as noted in Chapter 3, so-called reactor-grade plutonium can be used to make crude nuclear explosives.

Plutonium is extremely toxic, especially if taken into the lungs in air containing very small particles of it. However, it is easy to handle safely in solid form or as a liquid in some kind of container. Machining or otherwise processing plutonium in ways that might release small particles is hazardous unless done in protective laboratory hoods, which are readily available.

As with uranium, detailed information concerning the design and operation of facilities for conversion of plutonium compounds to forms suitable for nuclear explosives has been widely published, along with detailed instructions for safe handling of the material in all forms and under all conditions that might be relevant to a clandestine operation.[9]

[6] Ibid.

[7] W. D. Wilkinson, Uranium Metallurgy (New York: Interscience, 1962).

[8] See Hall, in Symposium on Implementing Nuclear Safeguards. The reference is to a 1952 speech by Lewis L. Strauss, AEC Chairman.

[9] A. S. Coffinberry and W. N. Miner, The Metal Plutonium (Chicago: University of Chicago Press, 1961); C. R. Tipton, The Reactor Handbook, vol. 1: Materials, 2d ed. (New York: Interscience, 1960).

## Conversion to Metallic Form

It is difficult to establish a realistic estimate of the minimum resources, time, and skills required for the clandestine conversion of uranium or plutonium oxide, or uranium or plutonium nitrate in solution, to metallic form. However, there is no basis for arguing that it is much higher than what is required in some other clandestine technical operations, such as the conversion of morphine base to heroin, an activity that has flourished for years in southern France. Since heroin production bears on several aspects of the credibility of clandestine nuclear operations of several types, it will be described in some detail.

Converting opium to morphine base is a relatively simple process that can be carried out by workers without special skills using crude equipment. However, the subsequent conversion of morphine to heroin is rather complicated. Moreover, this activity presents severe health hazards because of the high toxicity of heroin and other precursor chemicals suspended in air and the narrow temperature range (15°C) between the operating temperature for morphine base and the temperature at which the mixture explodes violently.[10] Explosions in clandestine heroin laboratories apparently act as a continuing deterrent to criminals who undertake amateur chemistry.[11] Moreover, the toxic and corrosive materials used in the process can leak into the air, requiring forced ventilation and the use of laboratory hoods similar to those often used in industries processing nuclear chemicals.[12]

Illicit heroin production is similar in several other respects to potential clandestine nuclear processing operations. The bulk value of heroin is about $9,000 per kilogram, approximately the same as the U.S. AEC's "buy-back" price for plutonium, in effect until recently. The larger illicit heroin plants produce as much as a metric ton or more of heroin per year. These facilities have an estimated value on the order of $100,000.[13] The specific steps and risks involved in converting uranium or plutonium nitrate to metal are comparable to those taken in the conversion of mor-

[10] Alvin Moscow, *Merchants of Heroin* (New York: Dial, 1968), pp. 61-63.

[11] *Ibid.*

[12] *Ibid.*

[13] U. S., Congress, House of Representatives, Committee on Appropriations, *Hearings, Departments of State, Justice, Commerce, the Judiciary, and Related Agencies, Appropriations for 1970,* 91st Cong., 1st sess., 1969, p. 959.

phine base to heroin. Criminal organizations have a proved ability to recruit the highly skilled manpower required to design and operate heroin plants. These factors suggest strongly that criminal organizations could successfully design and operate clandestine nuclear material processing facilities if they wished to do so.

The above discussion pertains to nuclear materials that are sufficiently free of radioactive fission products for safe handling without gamma ray shielding. Before chemical reprocessing, irradiated power reactor fuels generally contain special fissionable material at concentrations of a few percentage points by weight, along with comparable concentrations of fission products. The fuel is so intensely radioactive that it cannot be safely approached without massive gamma ray shielding. Nuclear materials at this stage of the fuel cycle are therefore self-protected, compared with "clean" fuel materials, and are unattractive targets for theft, which would require handling massive objects weighing many tons. Moreover, the subsequent processing required to convert the stolen material to a form suitable for nuclear explosives would be much more difficult than converting "clean" fuel material: the processes involved are not secret, but they require extensive use of shielding and remote-handling equipment.

### Design and Fabrication of Nuclear Explosives

Assuming nuclear material is available in suitable form, a criminal organization would need the appropriate knowledge, skilled manpower, non-nuclear material and components, and fabrication facilities. Each class of requirements will be discussed separately.

*Knowledge.* The knowledge of nuclear explosives a criminal organization would need does not necessarily include detailed understanding of the major physical phenomena associated with the detonation and explosion of a chain reaction system. Criminals will only need to know how to fabricate and put together components that will detonate to produce a nuclear yield in the approximate range desired for their purposes. This kind of information can be found in published books or periodicals, in unclassified reports that have not had wide distribution, in classified publications, and in classified or unclassified drawings, notes, computer tapes, printouts, punched cards, etc. Such knowledge is also found in people's heads. Important information, such as

identification of useful paths to investigate among several alternatives, can be transferred in a large variety of ways, and determined
efforts to pass information out of a security system without
detection are likely to be successful.

A brief survey of the physical principles involved in the assembly and explosion of a nuclear device will often be much more
useful to a small organization that wants to assemble some crude
nuclear explosives relatively quickly and easily than, for example,
a complete set of sophisticated hydrodynamic and neutron transport computer programs would be. The former type of information is also much more readily available than the latter.[14] The
knowledge of physics required to design fission explosives depends
on the type of explosive and on the other information the persons
involved possess. Very little knowledge of basic physics is needed
if detailed drawings of a device are available, along with instructions on how to proceed. If efficient and light explosives are
required, and drawings or detailed recipes are not available, a great
deal of knowledge is necessary. In either case, all the necessary
basic physics is well known throughout the world.[15]

The theory of chain-reacting systems has been widely described in print; it is intended for use in nuclear-reactor design but
is presented in forms applicable to the design of nuclear explosives.[16] Extensive data on the critical masses of various combinations of fissionable and other material, in many types of reflectors,
and in configurations relying on various neutron energies for
fission, are found in the open literature.[17] These critical mass data
can be used both for relatively "quick and dirty" designs of fission
explosives and for experimental tests of detailed neutron transport
calculations. Explanations of the theory of hydrodynamics, in
forms suitable for making calculations of both the assembly and
disassembly of fission explosives, are also found in the literature.
Some forms of the equations of state of chemical high explosives,
fissionable material, and material that might be used as reflectors

[14] R. Serber and E. U. Condon, *The Los Alamos Primer*, LA-1 (Los Alamos, Calif.:
Los Alamos Scientific Laboratory, 1943); Samuel Glasstone, *Sourcebook on Atomic
Energy*, 2d ed. (Princeton, N.J.: Van Nostrand, 1959); Samuel Glasstone, ed., *The
Effects of Nuclear Weapons* (Washington, D.C.: AEC, 1962), pp. 18, 19.

[15] *Ibid.*

[16] *Ibid.*

[17] Paxton et al., *Critical Dimensions*.

are published.[18] The phases through which a nuclear explosive proceeds during assembly and nuclear disassembly are described at least qualitatively in the open literature, so that a designer can determine what he should think about, and how he should think about it, when he analyzes a given design concept.[19] Simple methods for estimating the efficiencies of fission explosives are also described. The physics and applied mathematics required for detailed calculations can be formulated by any competent group of theoretical physicists and applied mathematicians, using modern computer methods.

Assembly systems for nuclear devices require the use of high explosives or propellants. Since the end of World War II there has been extensive unclassified experimentation with and theoretical study of high explosives for a variety of purposes directly related to their use for fission explosives. Descriptions of techniques for making high-explosive lenses, for accelerating metal plates to the required velocities, and for casting and fabrication of a wide variety of especially energetic high explosives are available in the literature.[20] The information necessary for the design of effective fusing and firing systems for many different types of fission explosives can be obtained from published information directly or can be derived from it by reasonably competent high-explosive and electronics specialists. In summary, the information required for the design and construction of nuclear explosives of various types is there. The performance of the explosives designed by a clandestine group will depend on its access to certain classified information, on its understanding and ingenuity, or both.

*Skilled Manpower.* Three kinds of people would be useful to a criminal organization that wants to construct nuclear explosives:

1. People with direct experience in designing, building, or testing nuclear explosives. There are thousands in this category. Most of them reside in the five nuclear-weapon nations. Perhaps

---

[18] U. H. Tillotson, "Metallic Equations of State for Hypervelocity," Report No. GA-3216 (San Diego, Calif.: General Atomic Division of General Dynamics, 1961).

[19] *Ibid.*

[20] See Robert J. Eichelberger, "Re-examination of the Theories of Jet Formation and Target Penetration by Lined Cavity Charges," Ph.D. diss., Carnegie Institute of Technology, 1954; R. Westwater, "Shaped Charges: What They Are and What They Do," *Colliery Engineering* 24 (1947):5-9; "A Scientific Approach to the Industrial Application of Shaped Charges," *Experimental Engineering* 25 (1947):171-83.

several hundred of these have recently lived, or are now living, for extended periods in other countries.

2. People with developed skills and a basic knowledge of the specific technical fields required. There are at least tens of thousands in this category throughout the world in the industrialized nations, concentrated in those nations which carry on extensive research and development programs in civilian nuclear technology. Especially relevant professional disciplines include theoretical and experimental reactor physics and nuclear engineering, theoretical and experimental plasma physics, chemistry and metallurgy of uranium and transuranium elements, and the applied mathematics of chain-reacting systems.

3. People with basic skills but without specific knowledge or experience in the fields required (e.g., people with training and experience in related engineering fields). There are millions in the last category—scientists, engineers, and skilled technicians with education and experience in the physical sciences and engineering.

At the beginning of 1943, no one had experience in the detailed design or construction of nuclear weapons. Two and one-half years later the first implosion bomb was successfully tested. Most of the work done to make the original atomic bomb explode has been published. It should be expected, therefore, that a small group of professionals and technicians from the third category above would, in the future, be capable of constructing nuclear explosives.

*Non-Nuclear Materials and Components.* In addition to the core materials, what is primarily required for the manufacture of nuclear explosives are high explosives or propellants for achieving rapid assembly of the nuclear core, material for a reflector or "tamper" to reduce the core mass required for criticality and to contain it during the initial stages of the explosion, and material to provide a source of neutrons to initiate the chain reaction. All of these materials can easily be obtained practically anywhere in the world, either purchased from ordinary commercial outlets or stolen. They should be no more difficult to acquire than the components of clandestinely assembled high-explosive bombs that are now used for terrorist or other destructive purposes.

*Construction and Assembly Facilities.* The hand and machine tools found in many home workshops would be adequate to construct the components of relatively heavy, inefficient fission explosives with unpredictable yields. The more sophisticated and predictable the design, the greater the need for precision equipment. In any case, nuclear particle or gamma ray counters, which can be purchased commercially, would be needed to monitor the assembly process in order to identify dangerously high fission levels in the core materials during fabrication of a device.

## RESOURCES REQUIRED FOR THEFT
## OF SPECIAL FISSIONABLE MATERIAL

The national safeguards system in the United States is described and analyzed in Chapter 5. For purposes of discussion here, it is useful to summarize the measures in effect which are intended to ensure physical protection of nuclear material against theft. (Measures designed to account for material inventories may be useful in detecting a theft but do not serve the critical function of preventing it.)

Special fissionable material in transit must be transported under the established procedures of a common or contract carrier which provide a system for the protection of valuable material in transit. Shippers must notify receivers of the time of departure, estimated time of arrival, and the identity of the carrier for each shipment. Licensees must conduct prompt tracking investigations of any overdue shipments and immediately report to the AEC any incident in which an attempt has been made, or is believed to have been made, to commit a theft or unlawful diversion.[21]

Special fissionable material not in transit must be in the continuous personal custody of an authorized individual, but he need not be armed. Quantities of more than 5 kilograms of such material are to be used only in an area encompassed by physical barriers and to which access is controlled by an authorized person. When not in use or transit, fissionable material must be stored in a security container or kept within a locked building constructed of stone, brick, cinderblock, concrete, steel, or comparable materials which are capable of preventing or impeding unauthorized entrance. Buildings or containers must be protected either by an intrusion alarm system that will bring armed guards within fifteen minutes or by an armed guard or unarmed watchman who will

[21] 73 Code of Federal Regulation 73.31.

patrol at intervals of four hours or less.[22] As described in Chapter 4, IAEA safeguards do not contain any provisions for physical protection except what may be implied by the presence of IAEA inspectors at facilities or by material accounting audit techniques.

With these protection provisions in mind, let us examine a few examples of skills and resources that have been used in the past to defeat security measures for the protection of other valuables. These famous thefts will provide points of reference for determining the kind of physical protection that should be provided for special fissionable material, assuming that future attempts to steal such material may well involve resources and planning on a comparable scale.

### The Brinks Robbery, Boston, Massachusetts, January 1950

Eleven men, picked for their various skills by an experienced thief with a reputation for detailed planning, took part in this theft of about $2.8 million. Planning and training for the operation went on for two years. The gang surreptitiously entered the Brinks premises thirty to forty times at night while the vaults were closed in order to conduct rehearsals for the robbery. Keys were made for all the interior and exterior doors; three motor vehicles were stolen for the operation, as were large sums of money to support the gang members and to purchase other equipment during the preparation period. The actual operation took approximately twenty minutes; the locked building was entered with a key, other keys were used to open intervening interior doors, the group of Brinks employees was surprised while they were placing the day's proceeds in the vault, they were bound, and the sacks of money and checks were dragged to a waiting truck. Police unwittingly interrogated all of the members of the group responsible for the robbery during the exhaustive manhunt that followed. Seven years later, several members of the group defrauded one of their number of his share of the proceeds, with the result that he turned state's evidence.[23] Otherwise, all would probably have escaped criminal penalty.

---

22 *Ibid.*, p. 32.

23 Joseph J. O'Keefe, *The Men Who Robbed Brinks* (New York: Random House, 1961).

## The Brockville Trust and Savings Co. Robbery, Brockville, Ontario, May 1958

Five men carried out this robbery, which took no more than a month to plan. The thieves several times entered the building in which the bank vault was located, both before and after working hours, found that the vault had no alarm system, and determined the thickness of its walls. They cut their way through the ceiling of the bank office and through a wall four bricks thick, then cut an entry through the steel plate three-eighths of an inch thick that formed the inner wall of the vault. Once inside, they cut holes in the faces of three safes, withdrew the locking bolts, and obtained access to the contents. The equipment used in the robbery had been stolen previously and included acetylene tanks and torches, sledgehammers, chisels, metal working tools, and respirators to permit work when flames from the cutting torch generated smoke and fumes. Only one of the burglars was ever caught; he was identified only because his bank passbook dropped from his pocket during the robbery and was found later by police. Negotiable bearer bonds in the amount of $1,750,000 were never recovered and are believed to have been disposed of successfully.[24]

## The Mail Train Robbery, England, August 1963

On August 8, 1963, the Glasgow-London mail train was robbed of the equivalent of $7 million. Planning was extensive and evidently included making a movie of the area through which the train would pass, to be used during training. Mail trains traveled nightly from Glasgow to London with no fixed schedule. The robbers apparently had no difficulty in identifying the train to rob. They set up false railroad beacon signals to slow the train and then bring it to a stop. The regular beacons were masked, notwithstanding the presence of an alarm system that was supposed to be set off when they were tampered with. When the train halted, the engineer and firemen were overpowered. Although the robbers were successful in compelling the engineer to follow their directions, they had included an experienced engineer in their group to drive the engine in case the train's engineer refused to cooperate. Without attracting the attention of anyone on board, the thieves

[24] Private communication, Brockville Police Department, December 1969.

operated the manual and mechanical brakes and uncoupled the engine and first two cars from the remainder of the train. The engineer was then compelled to drive the train a mile further and to stop at an intersection with a country road. The participants in the robbery then formed a line, and, in bucket-brigade fashion, moved 120 sacks of money from the train into waiting trucks, in which they departed. Railroad employees, discovering that the engine and forward cars were missing, attempted to use emergency telephones located along the track. Despite alarms designed to prevent tampering, the telephones were made inoperable.[25] British authorities have succeeded in imprisoning several persons for complicity in the robbery, but no one has confessed to it.

### Other Major Thefts

In the last fifteen years more than two dozen major thefts from modern alarmed vaults wired directly to a protective agency have been reported. Alarm systems connected only to the door of the secured place have been circumvented, and comprehensive alarm systems have been successfully disconnected. Burglars have used diamond-tipped steel drills, acetylene torches, twenty-millimeter antitank guns, thermic lances, explosives, and other highly specialized equipment to penetrate cement-filled doors, steel-reinforced concrete vault walls, steel vaults, and steel vault doors as much as two feet thick.

A majority of thefts of armored cars have occurred during the transfer of the valuables at pickup or delivery points. Several robberies have taken place en route, with the thieves often using prefabricated vehicle keys to enable them to drive the armored car away from a stop en route. Train robberies require more detailed planning and are more difficult to accomplish than truck robberies. There have been a number of incidents in which valuables being transported by air have unaccountably disappeared, but armed robberies at airport freight terminals, which are often under light or no guard, are more frequent and successful. Thieves have successfully stolen large weights of valuables—$500,000 in dimes, several tons of gold, and up to 28 tons of non-precious metal. One theft involved containers weighing 700 pounds each.[26]

---

25 *Boston Herald Traveller*, August 9, 1963, p. 1; *New York Times*, August 9, 19, 1963, p. 1.

26Theodore B. Taylor et al., *A Study of Non-Attributable Nuclear Threats*, First

In most parts of the U.S. civilian nuclear fuel cycle, plutonium and highly enriched uranium are less effectively protected by physical barriers, intrusion alarm systems, and armed guards than are large quantities of money stored in banks or shipped by armored cars, both of which, as noted above, continue to be successfully robbed. Therefore, present security precautions for deterring theft of special fissionable material from parts of civilian nuclear fuel cycles would be ineffectual against operations involving the kinds of skills and resources used for large-scale thefts of other valuables in the recent past. It is reasonable to conclude that thefts of quantities of fissionable material sufficient to make at least one nuclear explosive can now be carried out in any country having physical protection safeguards comparable to those now in force in the United States.

## RATIONALE FOR DIVERSION BY NON-GOVERNMENTAL ORGANIZATIONS

There are two main reasons why a group not acting directly on behalf of a national government might covertly or openly steal special fissionable material: for sale to other organizations and for construction of one or more nuclear explosives to serve its own purposes. In addition, stolen special fissionable material might be used in other insidious ways: less than a kilogram could be used in a critical assembly as a crude radiation weapon; a few grams of plutonium powder placed in the air-conditioning system of a large modern skyscraper could render the building useless permanently. However, arson, scattering of chemical or biological poisons, or chemical explosives could produce equal or more destructive effects, in many cases, with less effort. Such non-explosive uses of very small amounts of fissionable material will not be discussed further.

### Theft for Profit

In analyzing the profit motive for theft of weapons-grade nuclear material, several possibilities should be considered. Stolen material might be sold to non-governmental organizations that plan to use it to make one or more nuclear explosives. It might be sold to

Quarterly Report, IRT-R-17 (Washington, D.C.: International Research and Technology Corporation, January 30, 1970), pp. 2.1-2.24.

national governments contacted and offered the material after the theft. A national government might "commission" thefts in order to avoid diversion of material from its own nuclear facilities (which might be subject to international safeguards) or to avoid undertaking the large-scale effort required to obtain its own enriched uranium or plutonium. Such a purchase would presumably be for the purpose of acquiring a nuclear weapon capability. Finally, sales of stolen nuclear material might be made to middlemen in a black market who would resell it to national governments or non-governmental organizations. Whether a non-governmental organization would prefer to acquire nuclear material by engaging in theft itself or by purchase in an illegal market would depend on its character and its assessment of the risks associated with a theft and with dealing with the members of the organization supplying the material.

The profits from such sales could be extraordinarily high. The current market price of plutonium is over $9,000 per kilogram in the United States.[27] It seems reasonable that groups wanting plutonium or highly enriched uranium for use in nuclear explosives would consider paying considerably higher prices than those prevailing on the legal market.

### Theft for Explosive Uses

It is difficult to draw firm conclusions concerning the likelihood that non-governmental organizations might want to use nuclear explosives to threaten or attack society or various social groups and institutions. Their concern with "overkill" is evidenced by the warnings that, often, but not always, are given prior to terrorist bombings with conventional high explosives. In all previously recorded cases of terrorist bombings, however, the number of people killed was much smaller than the number that would be killed by a nuclear explosive with a yield as low as a few tens of tons of conventional high explosives detonated in a densely populated area. A nuclear explosive with a yield of one kiloton, detonated in the center of the New York City financial district during a working day, for example, would kill more than 100,000

27 *Ibid.*, p. 32.

people. Would any extremist political or terrorist organization be willing to carry out such mass destruction? Would responsible government officials or the public in the target area take such threat seriously? There are no firm answers to these questions.

Our previous analysis showed that a sufficiently motivated non-governmental organization could acquire a few low-yield nuclear explosives that could be carried by a few people on a small vehicle. Based on this assumption, we can make several points relevant to the credibility of nuclear acts of violence by non-governmental organizations.

The threat of nuclear retaliation, which many consider to be the primary deterrent against nuclear attacks by national nuclear forces, would generally not exist against a terrorist organization. The threatening organization need not identify itself to achieve large-scale disorder or to force compliance with its demands. Furthermore, the organization's members are likely to be unknown or at least dispersed throughout population. The qualitatively greater destructive power of nuclear explosives than of conventional arms or explosives and the widespread public fear of the effects of nuclear radiation offer opportunities for revolution or coercion which are at present, so far as we know, beyond the reach of any but a large national military organization. For example, a terrorist organization might distribute small nuclear explosives in a densely populated or otherwise important target area, then issue a public threat to detonate the explosives one by one until certain demands were met, and then conduct a demonstration explosion in some remote, unpopulated area. Thus, nuclear explosives might give an alienated group an extremely powerful lever to use against society, if it were willing to go to such extremes.

History is punctuated by terrorist activities, including explosions which kill or maim hundreds of innocent bystanders and cause widespread damage to property, and the headlines of daily newspapers around the world prove that terrorism is not going out of style—in fact, all the evidence is to the contrary. On the basis of history and all that is known about human nature, it would be foolish indeed to conclude that the threat or use of nuclear violence by one group against another in society, or against society itself, is incredible.

## WAYS TO INCREASE THE PHYSICAL PROTECTION
## OF SPECIAL FISSIONABLE MATERIAL

A complete systems approach is needed in the design, assessment, and implementation of integrated physical protection systems for all special fissionable material used, produced, and processed for civilian purposes throughout the world. Nothing less will provide the necessary level of security and, at the same time, allow nuclear industry to expand rapidly to meet increasing demands for energy. Patchwork "fixes" are likely to be less effective and more costly.

In order to assure adequate levels of physical protection some steps in the fuel cycle will have to be more extensively modified than others. Certain stages in the transport of fission-product-free plutonium, for example, are now especially vulnerable to overt theft. Improvements such as continuous communications between transport vehicles and monitoring stations, extremely heavy fuel shipping containers, and armed couriers are likely to increase transportation costs considerably. However, the resulting increase in overall fuel cycle costs is not likely to be unacceptable. Methods should be developed, therefore, for fairly allocating the added costs of effective physical protection measures among the various segments of the nuclear industry.

There are likely to be many opportunities for modifying nuclear fuel cycle components and operations in ways that not only increase the effectiveness of safeguards but also benefit the industry as a whole economically. The co-location of fuel reprocessing and fuel fabrication plants, for example, would remove a troublesome transportation link. Perhaps co-location could also decrease overall fuel cycle costs by allowing detailed optimization of both types of processes for maximum throughput of fuel at lowest cost. As another example, massive shipping containers, as well as specially designed transport vehicles, might be used both for safe shipment of irradiated fuel assemblies to reprocessing plants and for secure shipment of new fuel assemblies from fuel fabrication plants to reactors.

There are two guiding principles that would help considerably in designing and implementing systems of physical safeguards for fissionable material. The first is the principle of containment, which may be stated as follows: restriction of the flow and storage of all fissionable material within physically identified, authorized channels. Present national and IAEA safeguards procedures are primarily designed to detect diversion or theft after it has happened. Application of the principle of containment strongly implies prevention of unauthorized removal of fissionable material from authorized places. On this principle, physical barriers and other methods, including armed guards if necessary, would be used to prevent the flow of materials through unauthorized channels. In other words, the idea is to concentrate attention on the presence and flows of special fissionable material at any point where it is not supposed to be.

This does not imply that the present material balance approach should be discarded, but only that it should not be the principal basis for safeguarding nuclear material. It is difficult, if not impossible, to achieve material balances in large fuel reprocessing or fabrication facilities accurate enough to detect losses of tens of kilograms per year. It is quite possible, however, to achieve extremely high sensitivities for detecting small quantities, grams or less, of special fissionable material flowing through channels in which no such material whatever is authorized.

The containment principle might be applied to a plant that fabricates fuel containing plutonium in the following way. Imagine that all the plant operations involving plutonium are enclosed in a big box. The openings in the box for authorized input of plutonium (from, for example, a fuel reprocessing plant) and output of fuel elements are monitored. In addition, sides, top, and bottom of the box are visually or instrumentally monitored to detect any movement of small quantities of plutonium through the barrier. All openings in the box which are not used for the flow of plutonium—employee entrances and exits, channels for input and output of water, air, chemicals, equipment, etc.—are also continuously monitored. In addition, heavy storage containers, metal walls, and obstructing fences are used inside the plant to impede the transport of material from authorized to unauthorized channels. Automatic alarm systems to detect attempts to penetrate the barriers are used as signals for rapid deployment of armed guards. Finally, a secondary containment system of peripheral fences and movable barriers that can be placed along vehicle routes surrounds the entire complex.

The second principle of physical protection, which is the principle of security in depth, has a double purpose: impeding thefts in progress and at the same time facilitating the deployment of reserve forces to the scene of the theft as such reinforcements become necessary. Security in depth requires not only a number of physical impediments to theft but also a system of alarms, communications, and transport methods that will allow reinforcements to be brought to the scene before fissionable material can be removed from places under surveillance and control. The strength of the protection forces is determined by the capability of the criminal force for which the system is designed. Such a system should be able to deal with a criminal force somewhat greater than that previously used in any non-military theft. It should be capable of coping with several dozen heavily armed individuals using several different types of vehicles for forced entry and getaway, as well as hundreds of pounds of high explosives.

## IMPLEMENTATION OF PHYSICAL PROTECTION MEASURES

There has been considerable discussion within and outside the IAEA concerning the Agency's responsibilities under the NPT for providing assurance that special fissionable material is physically protected against theft.[28] The consensus both inside and outside the Agency appears to be that national governments should have the responsibility for physical protection safeguards. It is clear, nevertheless, that the threat of clandestine diversion or overt theft of nuclear material by unauthorized individuals or groups is an international problem. Weapons-grade material sold through an international illegal market could be used in nuclear explosives that either become part of a national military stockpile or are used by non-governmental organizations for the purposes discussed above. Thus, measures to prevent diversion or theft of material by non-governmental organizations appear to be a necessary part of an international safeguards system, even if the exclusive purpose of such a system is to strongly inhibit further national proliferation of nuclear weapons.

If sole responsibility for physical protection measures continues to reside in national governments, there are no guarantees

---

28 In March 1972 the Agency convened a panel of experts which produced a report containing recommendations to states for physical protection of nuclear material; see *Recommendations for the Physical Protection of Nuclear Material* (Vienna: IAEA, 1972).

that national safeguards systems will be effective in preventing non-governmental diversion. A nation may be seriously threatened by nuclear explosives made from material stolen from some other nation with an ineffectual national safeguards system. As a further assurance that special fissionable material subject to IAEA safeguards is protected from theft, the IAEA could establish international physical protection standards to guide development of national safeguards systems. Once such standards were established, several possibilities would follow.

1. The Agency could widely publish its physical protection standards and leave to governments the decision whether or not to develop and implement a national safeguards system in conformity with them. National governments would also determine for themselves whether other governments had adopted physical protection measures which met those standards. This procedure would be analogous to present methods for attempting to assure that radioactive materials are safely handled and shipped throughout the world: although the Agency has established and published standards for safe handling, it has limited powers to require member states to adhere to them.

2. Having established physical protection standards, the Agency could determine whether nations subject to its safeguards system were abiding by them and could report any deficiencies to the IAEA Board of Governors. This procedure would not necessarily ensure adherence to the IAEA standards. However, it would provide for international scrutiny of serious deficiencies in national systems.

3. Interpreting its somewhat ambiguous responsibilities under the IAEA Statute and Article III of the Non-Proliferation Treaty, the Agency could require effective physical protection measures to be incorporated into all its safeguards agreements. The Agency could rely on individual nations to implement appropriate measures but retain the right to verify that the measures were adopted. This would represent a major increase in the responsibility of the IAEA, as compared with the previous alternative in which the Agency would be responsible only for reporting observed inadequacies in national physical protection safeguards.

4. A remote possibility would be for the IAEA to assume direct responsibility for providing effective physical protection measures for all special fissionable material subject to its safeguards. It is difficult to imagine that such a strong role for the

Agency would be acceptable, since it would seem tantamount to the establishment of an international police force that would infringe heavily upon the sovereign rights of nations.

The first two alternatives would require the consent and cooperation of a majority of the IAEA members, or at least a strong consensus of the Board of Governors. Neither the third nor the fourth alternatives could be adopted without the consent of each state to which they would be applied. The second and third alternatives appear worthy of further study. The first essentially ignores the international aspects of the physical protection problem. The fourth is probably impractical outside the framework of some kind of world government which, desirable or not, appears to be a long way off.

# Part IV

# Implications of
# Nuclear Safeguards

# CHAPTER 8

# Industrial Implications of Safeguards

## EDWIN M. KINDERMAN

### INTRODUCTION

It is impossible to describe accurately the impact of international and national safeguards, whose relationships are just now being defined, on an industry which is rapidly growing and in which various components are in different stages of development. In this chapter, therefore, the author has been forced to mix his knowledge of the history of nuclear safeguards with projections of a future industrial activity which will be substantially influenced by political considerations. The objective is to estimate the likely effect of safeguards on industrial operations, primarily operations in the United States.

The role of material control in industry and the requirements of nuclear material control from the industrial viewpoint will be briefly described, the application of safeguards to the principal industrial operations will be discussed, the impact of safeguards on nuclear industry will be predicted, and ways to accommodate the diverse interests of industry and government in a nuclear safeguards program will be suggested below.

## ROLE OF MATERIAL CONTROL IN INDUSTRY

The control of material inventories is an essential activity in all businesses. To be successful, a small restaurant must have an adequate supply of foods, but it must avoid surplus of perishable items in a rapidly changing inventory. An electric utility which produces power from coal must balance the costs of storage space and large inventories against the unfavorable consequences of a power outage caused by interruption in coal supply. Thus the balancing of adequate stocks to carry on business against the costs of maintaining those stocks is one important facet of the material control problem. Another, and perhaps more difficult, aspect of material control is the prevention of loss. Loss can occur through uncontrolled waste or theft, and, in either case, the result will be financial penalty. The prudent man in every business introduces procedures to minimize such losses. In general, he will try to achieve a balance between the savings achieved by control methods and their costs.

In special cases, material control is more stringent than ordinary business practice would justify. Such measures are usually imposed on businesses by governmental authorities to achieve special purposes. The controls on alcohol manufacturing and warehousing facilities imposed by the Alcohol and Tobacco Division of the U.S. Internal Revenue Service provide one example. The alcohol is cheap, and stringent controls are required by the government in order to protect its interest in tax revenue. The businessman may either comply with such governmental controls, imposed equally on all legitimate business operations in a particular field, or invest his money and talent in a different enterprise.

The nuclear industry must deal with inventory problems whether or not the NPT or IAEA safeguards are applicable. In most nuclear operations the investment in fuel inventories is extremely large and the unit values of most materials are extremely high, compared to other industrial operations. Moreover, the potential use of special fissionable material in the manufacture of weapons justifies stringent controls.

It has been estimated that in 1985 the U.S. nuclear industry will process about 60,000 tonnes of uranium concentrate having a total value of $700 million. This material will be converted to fuel assemblies containing about 10,000 tonnes of low enriched uranium having a value at this stage of about $2 billion. Perhaps as much as 15 tonnes of plutonium with a value ranging from $4,000 to $5,000 per kilogram for recycle in light water reactors to $10,000 to $15,000 per kilogram in breeder reactors will be recovered from fuel irradiated in power reactors operated by electric utilities.[1] These enormous quantities of nuclear material, also suitable for military and criminal uses, will be distributed throughout fuel reprocessing, fuel fabrication, and storage facilities.

## SAFEGUARDS TECHNIQUES FROM THE INDUSTRIAL VIEWPOINT

The techniques used to safeguard nuclear material are those generally used to control valuable material in other operations. Quantities of material are measured upon receipt and shipment; transformations from raw materials to finished products are noted and measured; losses in processing are measured or estimated; and inventories on hand are verified by volume, weight, piece counts, and assay measurements.

However, nuclear materials have several unique characteristics which must be taken into account in making determinations for control purposes. First, they are radioactive and thus have distinctive emanations which are sometimes usable. Second, some of the materials have other distinctive nuclear properties which can be utilized—neutron absorption, for example. Third, since the value of a particular kind of nuclear material is closely related to its isotopic composition, methods to determine isotopic as well as chemical composition are needed. Finally, measurements and analyses are sometimes hampered by the radioactive and otherwise toxic nature of nuclear material and its environment.

### Measurement

Measurements of weight and volume in nuclear fuel cycle operations generally use common techniques such as scales, balances, and volumetrically calibrated tankage or flow measuring devices. The special methods used in quantitative determination of uranium and plutonium and their isotopes have been developed over

[1] These estimates are based upon data of "Forecast of Growth of Nuclear Power," Division of Operations Analysis and Forecasting, USAEC, January 1971, and miscellaneous sources.

the past thirty years, and the techniques are well advanced. The sampling of containers follows common principles with two exceptions; namely, fabricated fuel elements and fuel discharged from a reactor.

The high value of fabricated fuel elements demands that nondestructive testing be used to determine the content of special fissionable material. In other industries, occasional destructive measurements are used as a check on routine non-destructive measurements. This is not practical, however, with respect to nuclear fuel elements. The highly radioactive nature of fuel discharged from a reactor makes it extremely difficult to sample the primary solutions in which the fuel is dissolved prior to reprocessing for residual fuel values. The tanks containing the solutions are large (a capacity of 1,000 liters or more), but the radiation hazards limit the primary sample to about one milliliter. Therefore, obtaining a representative sample requires special care.

The measurement of finished fuel elements and of the products of spent fuel occur consecutively in the nuclear fuel cycle. However, they are made several years apart and are separated by an exposure in a reactor, which changes the composition and material ratios of the fuel. The fuel reprocessing plant measurement is particularly crucial in safeguarding nuclear material since plutonium, which will permeate the fuel cycle, is first identified and measured at this point.

The difficulties of sampling and measurement, the impossibility of exact confirmatory measurements by the reactor operator, and the transformations inherent in fuel irradiation all tend to limit the information that is useful to auditors and safeguards inspectors. On the other hand, if the quantity or quality of fuel charged to a power reactor is significantly different from that specified, the discrepancy is revealed in the performance of the reactor, and if accurate records of the quantities of uranium charged to the reactor are available from the fuel fabricator, the fuel reprocessor can measure the ratio of plutonium to uranium and thus obviate some sampling difficulties.

### Records

A nuclear facility keeps records of all transactions in nuclear materials. The inventories predicted by the records are compared to those established by actual measurements by means of a material balance. The usual balance contains the terms—beginning inventory, ending inventory, receipts, shipments, normal operating loss, and material unaccounted for. Ideally, inventories, receipts, and shipments are determined from direct and independent measurements at a nuclear facility. Each term can be expressed as a sum of individual quantitative measurements. Normal operating loss (NOL) includes anticipated losses not accounted for through measurements, such as material vented to stacks (which might be trapped in filters and later recovered) or trapped in pipe joints and corrosion layers. Operating experience will eventually produce engineering data from which estimates of these losses can be made for the individual facility concerned. Operators of new plants must use experience gained in similar operations until data for the new plant are accumulated.

Material unaccounted for (MUF) is the quantity used as a primary measure of the effectiveness of inventory control. It can be either a positive or negative quantity. No material balance based on physical measurements, with their inherent uncertainties, should come to a zero balance, or zero MUF. However, the MUF should lie in a range determined by the uncertainties of all measurements involved.

## Audits

Audits (i.e., independent examination of records and techniques for measurement, inventory, and estimating) are important ways of verifying that procedures used by plant operators and managers produce accurate information about the valuable materials held and processed in a nuclear plant. Audit and inspection are used to evaluate the completeness, accuracy, and general quality of record-keeping and the adequacy of individual measurements, taking into account the overall precision and accuracy of the methods used. The adequacy of the measurement system as a whole is revealed through estimates of uncertainty of the MUF, called limit of error of MUF or LEMUF. A large LEMUF implies that the nuclear material safeguards system is poorly designed and vulnerable to diversion efforts. Either a large LEMUF or an actual MUF that exceeds the projected LEMUF requires special consideration and suggests a potential diversion.

Large corporations commonly use their own auditors to establish the validity of inventories. This internal review is almost always confirmed by an independent certified public accountant specializing in business audits. For a company engaged in activities that involve nuclear materials, these internal and independent audits are supplemented by further governmental review and audit.

Whether internal, independent, or governmental, auditors are generally authorized to observe operations; to make independent measurements; to take samples for impartial analysis; and to take whatever steps are necessary to assure that the measurements taken are properly recorded and that the recorded data are transferred to accurately maintained central records. In addition to examinations of the in-plant measurements, auditors can analyze shipper-receiver data. Shipper-receiver differences can reveal otherwise undetected losses. While the general techniques for audit are the same in all industries, the nature of nuclear material and its processing requires special technical competence.

A number of industries, such as alcohol and drug manufacturing, are subject to governmental inspection and audit on a regular basis. Nuclear industry is, however, the only commercial activity which may presently be subject to an international inspectorate with full audit authority. International nuclear safeguards establish a precedent that is unique in this respect. In the early phases of the development of the U.S. nuclear industry, plant managers and owners tended to rely on the governmental audit system rather than on internal or independent audits. This tendency was natural since the industry drew heavily upon the personnel and practices of government-owned, industrially operated plants where the nuclear material audit function was in fact a government responsibility. As the quantities and value of nuclear material grow, increased attention is being given to internal company audits and audits by independent certified public accountants.

## Physical Protection

Physical protection measures, such as barriers, alarm systems, and guards, are used in most industrial security and material control programs. The radioactive nature of nuclear materials can be used to augment these common techniques through use of corridor or gate detection systems. Such systems are not always feasible, however, and in all probability they could be defeated by intelligent and determined efforts. Plant design and layout can be used to enhance both physical protection and records and inventory procedures.[2] This aspect of nuclear material control has generally been neglected thus far, with operational convenience and production efficiency the major focus of the plant designer's attention.

## Graded Safeguards

In usual inventory control situation, the businessman makes a judgment about the degree of control to be exercised. Theoretically, he will be willing to expend, directly or indirectly, an amount of money less than or equal to the cost that he might incur through misuse of inventory. He can measure costs of inventory losses and also most costs of inventory control, but he must judge the likelihood of loss. The manager of a nuclear enterprise makes the same calculations and judgments. He is guided, however, by national regulation or by IAEA safeguards agreements and subsidiary arrangements under the Non-Proliferation Treaty.

The IAEA, just like the businessman, is expected to use judgment in determining the degree of control required in implementating safeguards under the NPT. The impact of safeguards on industry will be expressed in requirements for (1) accuracy and precision of measurement and sampling; (2) quality control standards and practices; (3) frequency of inventory-taking, reports, and audits by the plant management; and (4) frequency of inspections by national and/or IAEA inspectors. IAEA judgments concerning specific requirements are expected to vary depending on the quantity of material subject to safeguards, its form, and its suitability for nuclear explosives. Such a "graded safeguards" approach by the Agency is merely an extension of that followed by the prudent businessman, although the Agency cannot rely on monetary worth to measure the value of prevention of loss (diversion).[3]

---

[2] See, for example, the paper by F. Brown et al., "Criteria for the Design of Nuclear Installations To Facilitate the Application of Safeguards," *Safeguards Techniques, Proceedings of a Symposium, Karlsruhe, 6-10 July 1970* (Vienna: IAEA, 1970), 1:389-94.

[3] The principle has been espoused by the U.S. nuclear industry in several recent public statements (remarks of A. Eugene Schubert, Chairman, Committee on Nuclear Materials Safeguards, Atomic Industrial Forum, at the Forum's annual conference, October 17-21, 1971, reported in *Nuclear Industry* 18 [October-November 1971]: 36-37, and elsewhere). The U.S. Atomic Energy Commission has used a graded assignment of audit and control effort for many years (E. M. Kinderman and R. R. Tarrice, "Review of AEC Nuclear Materials Management Systems" [u], SRIA-76, August 1962,

## APPLICATION OF SAFEGUARDS TO PRINCIPAL
## INDUSTRIAL OPERATIONS

### Enrichment

In principle, safeguards systems are concerned with enrichment activities. However, at the present time no enrichment operation is subject to IAEA safeguards, and specific safeguards procedures for enrichment plants have not yet been developed by the Agency. Furthermore, enrichment plants are (or can be) used to make, simultaneously, high- and low-enrichment fuel for civilian power reactors, fuel for naval propulsion reactors, and material for nuclear weapons. The latter two uses of the plants for military purposes would place them beyond IAEA/NPT safeguards. Enrichment plants in the United States are presently government-owned. If in the future these or additional plants are transferred to or constructed under private ownership, presumably they would come within the terms of the U.S. offer to permit the application of IAEA safeguards.

The character of the enrichment process makes accurate inventory-taking difficult. The process equipment used in gaseous diffusion has large surface areas exposed to corrosive gases. Pumps and other rotating machinery are used to maintain gas pressure and flow and to provide the gravitational force necessary for separation in the centrifuge process. The uranium hexafluoride can react with the metallic surfaces to produce uranium-rich solid corrosion products. Leakage through seals can release gas, which is quickly hydrolyzed inside the pump. In this manner large amounts of uranium can be lost from the measurable inventory. It is recoverable, to some undetermined amount, only after the process component, or stage, is removed from service for cleaning or replacement. The quantities involved can only be estimated for purposes of routine material balances. The engineering data necessary for accurate estimation will not become available in new plants until equipment replacement has begun and the old equipment is cleaned.

The plant inventory is contained in many operating units. As a practical matter the plant operation cannot be stopped and the

Secret), although some doubt exists as to whether the approach will continue to be followed in the future. Moreover, a graded safeguards system has been in practical use by the IAEA in its selection of frequencies and durations of inspection of facilities.

plant "flushed out" for inventory. The temperature, pressure, gas composition (generally assumed to be pure uranium hexafluoride), and isotopic composition must be determined simultaneously at all parts of the operating system before a meaningful inventory can be taken. Each sampling point must represent the conditions of the cell or section sampled. Intimate knowledge of plant design and operating characteristics are thus necessary before the operator, auditor, or inspector can design or take a plant inventory.

The inventory quantities and plant throughput times are substantial. For example, a plant with a capacity of 10,000 tonnes of separative work units (SWU) per year will produce approximately 3,000 tonnes of low-enrichment uranium from 20,000 tonnes of natural uranium annually. The inventory in such a plant will be worth more than $100 million, assuming a plant residence time of two months. Moreover, a new plant can require many months to reach an equilibrium condition. These factors contribute to the difficulties of efficient plant management, inventory control, and audit.

At present, national security restrictions make the information necessary for a proper external audit difficult to obtain, whether by a professional auditor, a government auditor, or the IAEA staff. It is likely that full access to information on plant design and operations, bolstered by some form of resident inspection, will be necessary for credible control over this portion of the nuclear fuel cycle. The degree of control required is related to the nature of plant operations and products. If the plant is designed and operated to produce slightly enriched uranium only, and it is clear that such is the case, there is less reason for concern over inventory discrepancies.

## Fuel Fabrication

At present, the nuclear materials in fuel fabrication plants are mainly natural and low-enriched uranium. Relatively small quantities of highly enriched uranium and plutonium are processed. However, this situation will change in the near future. Plutonium-bearing fuels will be recycled in light water reactors which presently use slightly enriched uranium fuel, and substantial quantities of highly enriched uranium are required for high-temperature gas-cooled reactors. Moreover, large quantities of plutonium will also be required for breeder reactors. For example, a fuel charge of

2.5 tonnes or more of plutonium will be required for a 1,000-megawatt commercial breeder reactor.

All safeguards systems include fuel fabrication facilities in their area of concern. At this stage the nuclear material is clean, containing no radioactivity other than its own, is usually in solid form, and is readily transportable. This is the only point in the nuclear fuel cycle at which these conditions exist, and thus the fuel fabrication plant presents perhaps the most tempting target for diversion. The fuel fabricator receives uranium as either a fluoride, a metal, or an oxide. Preparation of metal creates refractory slags of uncertain composition, while conversion of fluorides to oxide creates dilute liquid waste streams and powdered residues. All of these are difficult to measure accurately or precisely.

Effective material control systems require estimates, on the basis of engineering experience, of the special fissionable material content of these waste products. However, engineering-based estimates are generally not adequate for control if highly enriched uranium is involved. Further measurements are required, preferably after the materials are chemically treated and converted from heterogeneous scrap to solutions that can be sampled and measured.[4]

The principal activity of the fuels processor is the fabrication of oxide fuels. Powder must be compacted into briquettes, and they must be fired and sized by grinding. The briquettes are then loaded into fuel rods and assemblies. The high quality standards required for reactor operation result in substantial reject material and scrap. Processing results in dust, which is "tracked out" or trapped in air ducts and filters. Scrap recycle and losses to the ventilating system complicate efforts to achieve accurate inventory accounting.

The modern power reactor uses several uranium enrichments at one time, even in one fuel rod. The fuel fabrication plant operator has difficulty in segregating the wastes properly to maintain isotopic balances. Careful control of operations is also required to assure that the proper material is in place in the rod or assembly. The matter is complicated by the apparent sameness of

---

[4] Much effort is now being exerted to develop methods suitable for measuring the fissile material content of heterogeneous scrap directly. See, for example, papers by G. R. Keepin et al., F. Brown et al., T. Gozani et al., K. Baumung et al., in *Safeguards Techniques* 2:79-191.

materials of different isotopic composition. Careful record-keeping must be combined with good material segregation and non-destructive testing for effective production control, as well as for safeguards.

The finished product is encased in expensive fuel rods and assemblies. As previously noted, destructive testing of fabricated fuel is not a feasible method of quality control or safeguards. Non-destructive methods based on the gamma-ray emission of uranium-235, neutron transmission, or neutron capture, which have been used to measure fissionable content, all have technical limitations. As they are improved, non-destructive techniques are gaining acceptance for rod measurements but are generally not acceptable as a method of measuring the fissionable material content of entire assemblies.

The measurement and control problems associated with fuel fabrication are intensified if plutonium is substituted for some of the low-enrichment uranium in fuel elements. Plutonium-bearing fuel fabrication is conducted by remote control in enclosed hoods or shielded boxes. Both these techniques confine the material but also make inventory control more difficult. Clean-up of the boxes or hoods is difficult, and material can be misplaced. Detection and measurement of plutonium is aided by neutron emission, but accurate knowledge of the isotopic composition of the material and the chemical content of the mixture being analyzed is still required. Studies are under way to determine the contribution that plant design can make to effective inventory management and control. The fuel fabrication operation is also seriously considered in connection with the strategic points concept, discussed more fully below.

### Reactor Use

At the reactor, control over nuclear material is simplest. The valuable material is encased in containers that can be labeled and counted as units. The continuous charge-discharge (CANDU, AGR) reactors have many more units to account for, and piece-by-piece control at these installations is more tedious than at the batch charge-discharge light water reactors.

Material as a unit can be well controlled, but the exact content of the units at the end of reactor exposure is not known. The nuclear transformations which are at the heart of the process are well understood theoretically. However, practical calculations of the quantities and isotopic nature of the plutonium produced and the depletion of uranium-235 and uranium-238 are still under review and development. These require a detailed knowledge of the heat balances in the reactor and heat transfer sections of the nuclear plant. Estimates are also required of the average temperature and effective behavior of the neutrons in all segments of the reactor at all times. Since only part of a reactor core is discharged at one time, the heat balances and detailed calculations are less certain than would be possible if the full core were discharged. In any event, the operator, auditor, and inspector must have detailed knowledge of plant design and operating data as a proper basis for their estimates.

### Reprocessing

The accounting link between reactor operator and fuel reprocessor has already been discussed from the viewpoint of the operator. The reprocessor receives spent fuel elements which he cannot assay. He must perform physical and chemical operations on the assemblies until he has reduced the fissionable material to a homogeneous solution. This is a somewhat difficult task. The oxide fuel is refractory, and residues are difficult to dissolve. Samples of the solutions taken for assay are a small part of the total volume—one part in a million or less. Mixing and sampling are important operations that can easily be slighted if control over the operations is not vigilant. The processing produces dilute waste streams whose fissionable material content cannot be easily measured with precision or accuracy. The equipment is remotely operated: cleaning out for inventory is time-consuming, and it is difficult to be sure that it is complete. The products, uranium and plutonium, are in the form of pure compounds in solution or solid oxides. These materials can be sampled and assayed with precision and accuracy if proper care is taken.

Material control inventories must be taken at the end of processing campaigns. It is expensive and time-consuming to close out a process run. Material losses increase during starting up and closing down. The uncertainty of individual input measurements ranges from 1 to 5 percent depending on plant design and the analytical methods used. Product measurements can be made with high accuracy and precision of 1 to 2 percent. The uncertainty of waste stream measurements is perhaps 50 percent. Because of these quantitative uncertainties and the possibility of material being held up in the equipment, the material balance taken in a reprocessing plant can be significantly biased without detection. For this reason resident inspection or operation in bond has been suggested.

## Transportation

The usual methods of measurement, inventory, and audit do not apply to the principal activities involved in the transportation of nuclear materials. The transport agency accepts a unit, or units, of packaged material at one location. It transfers the material to another location to complete its assignment. The transfer may use several types of vehicle and require warehousing, but the essential activities are simple and do not involve chemical or physical transformations. Diversion of material, if it occurs, will most likely be achieved through theft of the entire shipment.

## IMPACT OF SAFEGUARDS ON U.S. INDUSTRIAL POLICY AND OPERATIONS

The U.S. nuclear industry is ambivalent about the imposition of national and international safeguards. On the one hand, industry spokesmen have repeatedly stated their willingness to cooperate with the U.S. government in the advancement of the objectives of the NPT.[5] On the other, they have expressed concern about the effect of safeguards on their particular competitive positions in relation to each other and to their international competitors; they are also concerned about the competitive position of nuclear industry generally in relation to other fuel sources.[6] Unwitting transmission of trade secrets or special manufacturing procedures to competitors could destroy a technical or operational advantage established through expensive and imaginative effort. Strict insis-

[5] A. Eugene Schubert, reported in *Nuclear Industry* 18 (October-November 1971): 37.

[6] For example, see the comments of Ralph J. Jones, Atomic Industrial Forum annual conference, reported in *ibid.,* p. 41: "We have also seen in recent months the imposition of requirements and license conditions on some licensees that are different and more strict than those imposed on other licensees. We have seen, in fact, license conditions on one part of a process that were different from those already in effect on another part of the same process."

tence on complete inventories on dates not compatible with normal plant production schedules and operating procedures could
increase nuclear costs relative to other fuels. Discriminatory application of international safeguards, or unequal stringency of national safeguards, could give a competitive advantage to other nations
or enterprises within those nations. In most instances, proper or
prudent commercial inventory control practices will provide the
information necessary for application of national or IAEA safeguards. However, the cost of any extra effort required solely for
achievement of the national objectives of the U.S. government
remains unsettled and is a major concern to nuclear industry.

## Industrial Secrets

Commercial and industrial secrets exist in every industry, and they
are especially important in those industries whose technological
base is rapidly changing. Much of the nuclear refining, conversion,
and reprocessing technology in the United States was developed
under government sponsorship and was freely published in furtherance of the Atoms for Peace program, especially in the period
1957-1964. Other reprocessing technology has been developed
under industrial sponsorship. This technology is protected by
patents, but detailed information on design and operations is also
guarded by the company. Such information would be valuable
to both competitors and buyers of a company's nuclear products
or services.

For example, in the field of oxide fuel fabrication for light
water reactors, many of the details of the production technology
required to produce fuel to meet stringent quality standards have
been developed by the individual fuel fabrication organizations.
The basic technology is well understood, but the specific techniques necessary for efficient, low-cost production have been
developed at a high cost. Industry will question, therefore, the
necessity of permitting inspectors to observe, in the course of
inquiries essential to safeguards, such details of process design and
procedures.

U.S. government employees are subject to severe penalties if
they knowingly reveal to other industrial organizations information acquired in the course of their inspection activities. The
operation of this law is well understood by the U.S. nuclear

industry, and, as a result, AEC inspectors are tolerated. As discussed in Chapter 4, the IAEA is required to take "every precaution" to protect commercial and industrial secrets in the course of implementing NPT safeguards. Nuclear industry remains suspicious of the Agency's ability to adhere strictly to this injunction, however.

## Interference with Operations

Potential interference with plant operations by safeguard inspectors, with a resultant increase in production costs, is of substantial concern to industrial organizations. Such interference can occur in many ways. A member of an inspection team inevitably requires attention from middle management and technical staff. An inspector who requests separate samples from the dissolver or head-end tanks of a fuel reprocessing plant can delay closely integrated operations throughout the plant and perhaps cause additional radiation exposure to workers. A separate sampling, for inventory purposes, of an entire enrichment cascade would be an expensive operation, requiring the services of a large number of the plant's operating staff. If an inspector does not accommodate his inspection schedule to the plant's, employees can be made idle and penalties for late delivery and interest on fuel costs can be incurred; electric utility may be forced to purchase other power at higher cost or disrupt service during the inspection period.

IAEA safeguards require its inspectors to "avoid hampering or delaying the construction, commissioning or operation of facilities, or affecting their safety." However, U.S. industry has no experience with an international inspectorate, with the exception of IAEA test inspections of one fully operational commercial reactor (Yankee Atomic), one reprocessing plant (Nuclear Fuel Services), and one fuel fabrication facility. All inspections have been viewed as experimental. In the case of the Nuclear Fuel Services inspection, several research projects were conducted to assess the effectiveness and intrusiveness of inspection, and the company was reimbursed, at least in part, for the extra work involved. The industry fears that IAEA inspections, whether concurrent with or separate from U.S. AEC inspections, will add extra costs and create management problems. Indeed, there is concern about the costs of U.S. inspections alone. The IAEA inspection of the fuel fabrication facility was reported to be "less than burdensome."[7] However, only experience will dispel or reinforce nuclear industry's present doubts about the burden of U.S. national and IAEA safeguards on daily operations.

## Competitive Position

The U.S. industrialist views himself as an individual competing with others. He pits his skills in technology, management, and the use of capital against those of other entrepreneurs at home and abroad. He jealously guards his advantages and resents or envies the advantages of others. In the nuclear field much of his basic technology has come from government-sponsored research and development, but even so, the industry questions the impact of government policy on its competitive position, especially in relation to firms in other countries. His foreign competitors could enjoy an advantage in the nuclear fuel cycle through two levels of discrimination in the implementation of safeguards: first, requirements specified in the NPT Safeguards Agreements or in the Subsidiary Arrangements between the Agency and individual might be unequal; second, and the more likely form of discrimination in the case of U.S. industry, the operations of the various *national* systems might work to the disadvantage of the U.S. businessman.

Those who are suspicious see the Atomic Energy Commission acting as a potential adversary of U.S. industry. The Commission is cast in the role of imposer of a tough national safeguards system on U.S. industry and of supporter of extensive IAEA inspection and audit procedures. At the same time, the suspicion exists that authorities in other countries will adopt relaxed national safeguards systems and will defend their industrial enterprises against interference by or annoyance from Agency inspection. These beliefs are derived primarily from the greater government-industry cooperation existing in other countries. For example, in the Federal Republic of Germany the only reprocessing plant presently operating is an experimental facility that is owned by the Federal Republic and the state of Baden-Wurttemburg, although it is operated by a company that is jointly owned by private interests. In

---

[7] Remarks of David J. Haymon at the Symposium on Implementing Nuclear Safeguards, Kansas State University, Manhattan, Kansas, October 25-27, 1971, reported in *ibid.*, p. 18.

the U.K., industrial fuel cycle activities are conducted by British Nuclear Fuels, Ltd., a company with a large government participation in ownership. Somewhat similar arrangements exist in France and Italy.

Despite these fears of a potential adverse impact of safeguards on the competitive position of U.S. industry, IAEA/NPT safeguards may, in fact, give that industry advantages over certain foreign competitors. First, IAEA safeguards will probably not be widely applied to nuclear facilities in the U.S., although the U.S. offer to submit voluntarily to IAEA inspection is about as broad as the NPT requirement. The IAEA is not likely to implement safeguards on more than a few selected nuclear facilities in the United States because of its limited resources. Second, the actual number, intensity, and duration of IAEA inspections must be determined by the Agency on the basis of various criteria, including "the extent to which the operators of facilities are functionally independent of the State's accounting and control system." This implies that if the relationship between industry and government in the United States is truly an adversary one, the industry should be subject to less intense IAEA inspection than a foreign plant whose operations are owned or otherwise controlled, even indirectly, by the government.

## Resident Inspection—A Special Problem

The requirements for an effective international control and inspection system related to civilian nuclear industry have been estimated and debated for many years. A recurring argument is the form of and need for resident inspection. An extreme form, not contemplated either by IAEA/NPT or by non-NPT safeguards, calls for external guards as well as inspectors.[8] Most of the work force, under this proposal, would guard the perimeters of all nuclear installations and accompany all shipments. This has the appearance of a supranational, paramilitary operation and would require a staff numbered in the thousands. It has also been proposed that smaller teams of technically trained persons be stationed inside the monitored area. They would observe and possibly perform in duplicate some or all of the technical opera-

---

[8] "The Technical Possibility of Internal Control of Fissile Material Production," ENDC/60, August 31, 1962 (quoted in Sir Michael Wright, *Disarm and Verify* [New York: Praeger, 1964], pp. 234ff.).

tions of safeguards—measurements, records, material balances, etc. However, complete duplication of plant operations and services related to safeguards seems clearly unfeasible.

The IAEA/NPT safeguards specify a maximum total effort for routine inspections which precludes large resident inspection staffs for any nuclear facility. No single reactor can have an inspector in continuous residence. However, facilities processing plutonium and/or enriched uranium could have small staffs in residence according to the formulas adopted in the IAEA/NPT system. A small processing facility having a throughput or inventory of 100 kilograms of plutonium would require the minimum inspection effort of 1.5 man years and thus qualify for one resident inspector, if that were desirable. A larger facility having a 1,000-kilogram throughput or inventory could have 2.5 man years of routine inspection effort and thus use resident inspectors. Some investigators have concluded that "resident (or nearly continuous) inspection is currently a necessary and effective means of providing independent control over a continuous operation. . . . Resident inspection is also a valuable means of monitoring plant safeguards practices to assure that such practices meet national safeguards requirements."[9] Others have stated that "surveillance is certainly more timely and effective if it is continuous."[10]

Nevertheless, the resident inspector faces many problems in performing his duties effectively. Perhaps the most severe is that caused by the fact that he is simultaneously an international inspector and a resident at the facility. He must maintain his role as adversary and his independence as an inspector, at the same time, he must establish relationships of confidence and trust with industry officials which will permit him the necessary free access to their activities. Rotation of assignment, job security, inculcation of pride in the organization, adequate local staff, appropriate salary scales, prestige, and positive supervision will be necessary to keep the inspector's morale high and maintain his effectiveness. The presence of large groups of resident inspectors would undoubtedly be resisted by the nuclear industry. One or a very few

[9] R. A. Schneider et al., "Evaluation of the U.S. Resident Inspection Experiment," BNWL-SA-2671, November 1, 1969.

[10] H. J. C. Kouts et al., paper prepared for presentation at the Fourth International Conference on the Peaceful Uses of Atomic Energy, September 6-16, 1971, Geneva, Switzerland.

can undoubtedly be accommodated without major disruption of plant organization and activities, but the smaller the group, the more susceptible it might be to coercion or to less than vigorous performance of its inspection duties.

### Strategic Points Concept—A Novel Solution

The strategic points concept has been advanced by several groups, most notably the one at Karlsruhe, Federal Republic of Germany.[11] The concept is attractive, especially to nuclear industry, because it apparently excludes the inspector from process operations, and thus affords greater protection to industrial secrets than other safeguards approaches.

Strategic points are viewed as control stations which connect separate contained systems or activities. Entrances and exits to nuclear facilities are important strategic points, but not the only ones. Others are located between important operations conducted within the facilities. Measurements must be made of all special fissionable material which passes these points. Substantial use of seals is also envisioned. Process inventory is to be estimated by calculating the difference between quantity in and quantity out of a subsystem or unit. Inventory is brought out for measurement at selected or specified times. It then becomes a measured flow.

The accuracy and precision of receipt and shipment measurements required in this system are usually much higher than those required for inventory-taking. It can be argued that an inventory deduced from the receipt-shipment difference is more accurate than an inventory directly measured for a substantial period of time after plant startup.[12] A complete plant cleanout at intervals would permit application of the strategic points method indefinitely. On the other hand, the effectiveness of the strategic points concept depends primarily on whether the strategic points are located in such a way that all input and output flows are covered. The inspector must be able to confirm that the plant operator has indeed covered all flows. To do this he must have access to

[11] See, for example, W. Haefele et al., "Safeguards System Studies and Fuel Cycle Analysis," *Proceedings of the International Conference on the Constructive Uses of Atomic Energy, Nov. 10-15, 1968,* ed. Ruth Farmakes (Washington, D.C.: American Nuclear Society, 1969), pp. 161-79.

[12] F. W. Dresh et al., "Statistical and Inventory Procedures Applied to Nuclear Materials Management," SRIA-115P49-1, April, 1966; W. L. Coggshall, Jr., "Optimal Control Schemes for Strategic Materials," Ph.D. diss., Stanford University, 1969.

detailed plant designs and, on occasion, to the plant itself. Thus the plant operator will forfeit some of the privacy that the strategic points concept is supposed to ensure.

## ACCOMMODATION OF INTERESTS

### Development of Techniques

The proceedings of two IAEA-sponsored symposia on safeguards show that substantial progress in measurement methods has been achieved in the five years from 1965[13] to 1970.[14] Particular attention has been given to non-destructive measurements of fuel elements and heterogeneous scrap. Several of the more promising methods are being tested in plant operations.[15] One concern of industry is the capital and operating cost of some of the more elaborate techniques.[16] Further developments are expected which will increase the precision and accuracy of these important measurements. They will improve safeguards by improving the accuracy of receipt, shipment, and inventory measurements. However, it is noteworthy that safeguards experts expect continued reliance to be placed on conventional analytical methods.

Research has also been directed to the development of reliable seals or secondary labels that will define or preserve the identity of units. Inventory-taking can be simplified and measurement variables eliminated to the extent that sealed containers need not be remeasured. Seals can also be applied to completed fuel assemblies, transport containers, and other units containing nuclear materials.

The IAEA is hampered in its own research and development activities by a very small budget. However, it encourages other agencies to undertake particular research tasks of special value to safeguards. It regularly reviews progress through sponsorship of small, relatively informal meetings and large symposia of the type cited in this chapter. Major research efforts are sponsored by the

[13] *Proceedings of the Symposium on Nuclear Materials Management, Vienna, August 30-September 3, 1965* (Vienna: IAEA, 1963).

[14] *Safeguards Techniques*, vols. 1 and 2.

[15] D. L. Crowson, "Progress and Prospects for Nuclear Materials Safeguards," *Safeguards Techniques* 1:23-34.

[16] J. E. Lovett, remarks during panel discussion, "Views on Progress in Safeguards Techniques and Future Activities," *Safeguards Techniques* 2:471.

U.S. AEC; lesser contributions directly related to safeguards are made by industrial organizations. All of these efforts must be increased if safeguards techniques are to keep pace with the growth of nuclear industry.

## Improvement of Systems

Safeguards control systems are of two types. The first is designed for use in a single nuclear facility. It utilizes all techniques common to control of other valuable material—input and output measurements, inventory measures, record-keeping, material balances for the entire facility and for physically separable subdivisions, and surveillance and other physical protection measures. The development of this type of control system has been vigorously pursued for several years, and much effort has been expended in this regard by the United States, the United Kingdom, the Federal Republic of Germany, and the IAEA staff. This effort builds upon traditional material balance area concepts.

The second type of control is concerned with a larger system, such as a national nuclear industry. It depends upon the actions and measurements of the first system, it relies upon the adversary actions of multiple shippers and receivers to reveal potential measurement bias which could be used to conceal diversion of material. This type has not been investigated thoroughly.[17] It is my opinion that it should be developed through national and Agency-sponsored research, for it is particularly applicable to assessment of material flows and discrepancies in the larger systems.

Systems of any kind must take into account the limited resources available for safeguards,[18] the adversary who wishes to overcome them, and the time interval before detection. The proper consideration of these topics, and of the needs of national or IAEA safeguards, will lead to formulation of specific goals and

[17] The second type was suggested by research of F. W. Dresh, "Statistical and Inventory Procedures," and W. L. Coggshall, Jr., "Optimal Control Schemes."

[18] E. M. Kinderman and R. R. Tarrice, "Criteria for Special Nuclear Materials Inventory and Control Procedures," *Symposium on Nuclear Materials Management*, pp. 31-41. See also R. Avenhaus and D. Gupta, "Effective Application of Safeguards Manpower and Other Techniques in Nuclear Fuel Cycles," *Safeguards Techniques* 1:345; C. A. Bennett, "Progress in Systems Analysis," *ibid.*, 2:247; F. Morgan, "The Usefulness of Systems Analysis," *ibid.*, p. 265; Kinderman and Tarrice, "Review of AEC Nuclear Materials Management Systems."

objectives. In the near future increased attention to safeguards goals and objectives is essential if improved safeguards systems are to keep pace with the rapid increase in special fissionable material used for peaceful purposes.

## The Roles of the IAEA, the U.S. Government, and Industry

The concern of the nuclear industry over the effects of safeguards, mentioned above, must be balanced against the interest of government and the general public, including business executives and workers in nuclear industry, in the prevention of acts of nuclear violence. The balance between these interests ultimately determines the extent of the nuclear safeguards effort. That balance has not yet been struck.

The U.S. nuclear businessman will ask why he must adhere to rules that are meant to prevent nations from acquiring nuclear weapons when our nation already has these weapons in abundance. He will declare his willingness to submit his industrial activities to IAEA safeguards as part of a major effort towards world peace, but he will object when that action may be costly. He is apparently not yet entirely convinced that diversion of special fissionable material from stocks in the United States, which amount to nearly one-half of the world total, could contribute to the proliferation of nuclear weapons in other countries or to mass destruction here at home by an extremist revolutionary group. He wants to exert whatever degree of inventory control will minimize his financial loss, and that calculation or judgment he derives from the market value of special fissionable material as fuel for the power industry and the probability that this material may be stolen. He acknowledges there may be other, higher values for special fissionable material based on potential military use, but he does not believe that the criminal can exploit these higher values. Neither the national government nor the IAEA has yet defined these values for the businessman in workable terms. The wholehearted acceptance of external controls by the industry, therefore, depends on the ability of the government and the IAEA to explain and define safeguards in language intelligible to the businessman, as well as to make clear the reasonableness of demands made in their name.[19]

[19] This has been said in another way by J. O. Tattersall of the South African Atomic Energy Board, who stated:

The U.S. government may have been impeded in its attempts to communicate effectively with the industry both because of traditional government-industry attitudes and "arms-length" relationships where regulatory matters are at issue and because of its insistence on a high degree of secrecy in all matters pertaining to the manufacture of nuclear weapons. The IAEA has no direct lines of communication with U.S. industry since diplomatic protocol limits it to dealing with the U.S. government. Whatever the cause, public position statements have been made by both industry and government and private meetings have been held, but no better understanding or acceptance of divergent opinions on either side has resulted.[20] Obviously, much remains to be done.

---

As a comparative newcomer to the safeguards field, I have listened with great interest to the proceedings of this Symposium. However, I am left with the feeling that while a substantial amount of elegant work has been and is being done in developing safeguards measurements and inspection techniques, in evaluating their quantitative capabilities and in studying their theoretical and practical application in safeguards systems, the primary objective of all this work is still only vaguely defined. In general terms, of course, the motive is clear, but it seems to me that development of the techniques has progressed to the point where a proper judgment of how adequate they are, cr are likely to be, and of how future efforts should be steered can be reached only if the target is defined in much more precise and quantitative terms. The definition of a logical and practical target may well be difficult, but I think it is important at this stage and worthy of a concerted effort by leading safeguards experts from several countries, perhaps coordinated by the Agency. Clearly, account must be taken of many things, including the limited acceptability of safeguards systems and possible extensions in the future.

"Views on Progress in Safeguards Techniques and Future Activities (Session IX)," *Safeguards Techniques* 2:473.

[20] See, for example, the reports in *Nuclear Industry* 18 (October-November 1971) of the annual meeting of the Forum, 1971, and of the Symposium on Implementing Nuclear Safeguards at Kansas State University.

# CHAPTER 9

# Political Implications
# of Safeguards

## LAWRENCE SCHEINMAN

### INTRODUCTION

The Non-Proliferation Treaty (NPT) is a significant step in the evolution of international arms control arrangements. It is evidence of the capacity of the United States and the Soviet Union, the two principal protagonists in the current international system, to act in concert in matters they consider vital to world order. The Treaty also codifies a presumption, now widely shared, that further proliferation of nuclear weapons is not legitimate, and thus it represents for the major powers generally an indispensable step along the long road of arms control.

A controversial aspect of the NPT is the provision for the application of international safeguards to the nuclear industry of non-nuclear-weapon states party to the Treaty. As pointed out in Chapter 2, NPT safeguards on peaceful nuclear activities are considerably less comprehensive than the system proposed in the Baruch Plan of 1946, yet in the context of the evolution of post-World War II arms control and disarmament negotiations, the NPT safeguards system constitutes an important landmark. Prior to the NPT, bilateral and international safeguards (aside from

Euratom) usually provided either exporting states or international agencies with a right of access within the territory of the recipient state in order to determine that nuclear material supplied by or through them was not being diverted from peaceful to military uses. NPT safeguards go much further. They apply to *all* peaceful nuclear activities in a non-nuclear-weapon state which is a party to the NPT, regardless of whether the nuclear material involved is imported or indigenously produced.

The bilateral safeguards and inspection arrangements concluded prior to the NPT could be rationalized as commercial conditions applied to international transactions. However, the NPT represents an unprecedented voluntary derogation of the principle of national sovereignty. On the one hand, the non-nuclear-weapon parties agree "not to manufacture or otherwise acquire nuclear weapons or other nuclear explosive devices."[1] Thus they accept a constraint on the dimensions of their national nuclear development and on the orientation of their peaceful nuclear technology. On the other hand, non-nuclear-weapon parties agree to accept in principle the presence of international inspectors on their national territories for the purpose of verifying fulfillment of their respective international treaty obligations. Acceptance of this derogation by a large plurality of states is significant, even apart from the question of the effectiveness of NPT safeguards, for it indicates a reconsideration by nation-states of the scope and limitations of sovereignty.

The political value of an international safeguards system depends primarily on the extent to which the system satisfies two criteria: acceptability and credibility. Many observers support the proposition that the more credible the safeguards system, the more intrusive it must be on national sovereignty; and the more intrusive the system, the less likely it is to be accepted by the largest possible number of states. Those who hold this opinion argue that, since there is a close relationship between the level of nuclear development and the probable intensity of safeguards inspection required, those countries most likely to resist implementation of a credible safeguards system are precisely those which are industrially and technologically most able to convert their peaceful nuclear programs to military ends. This school of

[1] Treaty on the Non-Proliferation of Nuclear Weapons, Article II.

thought concludes that any safeguards system that is acceptable to all or nearly all non-nuclear-weapon states has doubtful credibility.

Against this analysis, others assert that even a relatively modest safeguards system is adequate to detect a nuclear diversion in a state which is technologically and industrially advanced. Their argument rests on the assumption that such an advanced state could profit only from possession of a rather large nuclear force and that a large-scale (hence, detectable) diversion would be necessary to provide a basis for such a force. Nuclear diversion in a smaller, less developed state with a smaller force requirement would be readily detectable with a relatively unobtrusive system.[2]

These divergent views arise out of a difference in what constitutes credibility or, more precisely, what degree of security one seeks from international safeguards. Without choosing between these positions, this chapter offers a political evaluation of the existing IAEA/NPT safeguards system. In approaching this task, we assume that safeguards are neither irrelevant to, nor panaceas for, the problems inherent in arms control; but that they should be regarded as reinforcing mechanisms for certain of the obligations undertaken by parties to the NPT.

First, we consider IAEA/NPT safeguards in relation to the principal incentives for the acquisition of nuclear weapons—security and prestige. Next, we examine the functions and limitations of safeguards from the perspective of national decision-making. We go on to analyze the political aspects of the main operational problems associated with the IAEA/NPT safeguards system. Finally, we explore the limitations and opportunities of that system over and above the immediate question of its operational effectiveness.

## NUCLEAR SAFEGUARDS AND NATIONAL SECURITY

The underlying objective of the NPT is to reduce the risk of nuclear war by restricting access to nuclear weapons and inhibiting the acquisition of such weapons by non-nuclear-weapon states. This objective must be realized in an international system composed of nation-states interacting in an atmosphere of mutual mistrust. Indeed, mistrust and resultant fear are substantial causes of arms races. To the extent that this is true, each member of the

[2] See, for example, Myron Kratzer, "A New Era for International Safeguards," *Nuclear News* (February 1971), pp. 40-43.

international system can reduce suspicion and build confidence by convincing every other member that it is fulfilling the obligations it has undertaken.

Safeguards are prescribed as the vehicle for each party to communicate to the international community the fact that it is fulfilling its obligations under the NPT. Safeguards are not intended to prevent the diversion of nuclear material from peaceful to weapon purposes, but rather to provide "timely detection of diversion of significant quantities of nuclear material from peaceful nuclear activities to the manufacture of nuclear weapons or of other nuclear explosive devices for purposes unknown, and deterrence of such diversion by the risk of early detection."[3]

Of course, the emphasis on detection and deterrence and the absence of prevention and positive control constitute a weakness of the IAEA/NPT safeguards system. In short, NPT safeguards deal with symptoms, not causes. What extent, then, can IAEA/NPT safeguards contribute to a state's national security? Can safeguards be regarded as credible for purposes of national defense? In other words, will they provide adequate security? Answers to these questions depend on an evaluation of the effectiveness of the safeguards system.

It is difficult to generalize about the relationship between safeguards and security. A general improvement in the global security climate does not necessarily increase the security of each member state of the international system. By reducing the risk of nuclear war, the inhibition of nuclear-weapon proliferation may enhance the overall stability of the current international system. However, non-proliferation may do relatively little to increase the security of a country in such special circumstances as, for example, those of Israel. Furthermore, in evaluating the relationship of nuclear safeguards to national security, some decision-makers may be impressed by the strategic argument, voiced a decade ago by the French general Pierre Gallois, that "thermonuclear weapons neutralize the armed masses, equalize the factors of demography, contract distance, level the heights, (and) limit the advantages which until yesterday the Big Powers derived from the sheer dimensions of their territory"[4]—in short, that nuclear weapons

---

[3] IAEA, INFCIRC/153, par. 27, "The Structure and Content of Agreements between the Agency and States Required in Connection with the Treaty on the Non-Proliferation of Nuclear Weapons."

[4] Quoted in Raymond Aron, *The Great Debate*, trans. Ernst Powell (New York: Doubleday, 1965), p. 102.

not only are great levelers of nations, but an added increment to security as well.

The value of non-proliferation and the potential role of nuclear armament as an equalizer or leveler will thus depend on particular national circumstances, and the impact of nuclear safeguards on security must be judged in particular contexts. For example, the situation of the Federal Republic of Germany must be distinguished from that of Japan, and India from that of Israel. The principal threat to the security of the Federal Republic is from the Soviet Union, while Japan may perceive a threat from China as well as the Soviet Union. Both the Federal Republic of Germany and Japan are allied to a nuclear superpower, the United States. Neither can expect to deter independently the potential nuclear threats of their adversaries with anything less than a full-scale nuclear force. For these two countries, therefore, the acquisition of nuclear weapons for security purposes appears to make little sense as long as the international system remains what it is today.

Of course, changes in the international system may lead to national re-evaluations of current non-nuclear policies. It is important to remember that adherence to the NPT does not foreclose this possibility. Indeed, the treaty explicitly provides that each party has a right to withdraw "if it decides that extraordinary events, related to the subject matter of this Treaty, have jeopardized the supreme interests of its country."[5] The disintegration of NATO, or the withdrawal of American troops from Europe, or substantial evidence that the United States would not respond to a Soviet nuclear attack on Europe might well cause the Federal Republic of Germany to devalue its commitment to non-proliferation. The articulation of the Nixon doctrine and the incipient evolution of Sino-American relations may lead eventually to substantial modifications in the pattern of international relations in Asia, affecting Japan especially. It is not yet clear whether the Nixon doctrine means selective involvement or generalized withdrawal of the United States from the Asian theater, nor whether its greater emphasis upon self-reliance of Asian states entails increased reliance by the United States on nuclear weapons in honoring its Asian commitments. It is clear, however, that a perceptible altera-

[5] Treaty on the Non-Proliferation of Nuclear Weapons, Article X.1.

tion of American commitments under the Japanese-United States Security Treaty could cause Japan to reconsider its three non-nuclear principles: not to manufacture, to possess, or to allow nuclear weapons on Japanese territory. Even a U.S. promise of "no first use of nuclear weapons" could be interpreted as voiding the security treaty of its substance, leaving Japan vulnerable to conventional attack by a nuclear-weapon state. Government spokesmen have emphasized that nuclear armament for so-called defensive purposes would not violate the Japanese constitution, and political observers have noted the erosion of the "nuclear allergy" that characterized the generation of Hiroshima.[6]

India and Israel, both of whom face regional security threats, have thus far rejected the NPT. India claims to be non-aligned, although its recent treaty with the Soviet Union casts doubt on this position, and India perceives its security to be threatened by a non-nuclear Pakistan, on the one hand, and a nuclear China, on the other. Israel's security is not guaranteed by any formal treaty commitment, and that country faces a multiplicity of threats from the surrounding Arab states underwritten largely by the Soviet Union. The ambiguity of its nuclear intentions and the absence of international safeguards inspectors from its territory may serve Israeli security interests.[7] For both India and Israel, the credibility of possible nuclear guarantees is a more important factor than the effectiveness of safeguards against nuclear diversion in their respective decisions regarding nuclear weapons. Israel could take no comfort from an assurance that Arab arsenals were devoid of nuclear weapons if its forces were being driven into the sea by overwhelming conventional forces. Similarly, India could not tolerate defeat with conventional armaments by a nuclear-armed China.[8]

In summary, nuclear safeguards do not appear to increase substantially the national security of those countries which seem to face particularly acute national security dilemmas. Nevertheless, acceptance by those countries of IAEA/NPT safeguards on their

[6] See George Quester, "Japan and the Nuclear Non-Proliferation Treaty," *Asian Studies* 10 (September 1970):765-78.

[7] See George Quester, "Israel and the Nuclear Non-Proliferation Treaty," *Bulletin of the Atomic Scientists* 25 (June 1969):7-9, 44-45.

[8] For an analysis of the Indian situation see Shelton L. Williams, *The United States, India and the Bomb* (Baltimore: Johns Hopkins Press, 1969); Krish Nanda, "Will India Go Nuclear?" *Bulletin of the Atomic Scientists* 27 (December 1971):39-41.

nuclear programs might well be perceived as increasing the security of countries which are threatened by them; for example, the countries of Eastern Europe in the case of the Federal Republic of Germany and Pakistan in the case of India. Moreover, given two hostile non-nuclear-weapon states which are both subject to IAEA/NPT safeguards, it is plausible to hypothesize that a safeguards system with proven credibility may serve to deter one from exercising its nuclear weapon option because it is confident that diversion in the other will be detected in good time. If both perceive safeguards in this way, the system may be credited with deterring proliferation and helping to confine hostilities to the conventional level.

## NUCLEAR WEAPON PROLIFERATION AND PRESTIGE

The functional limits of non-proliferation safeguards become apparent when prestige factors are analyzed. The benefits which safeguards may offer a state are essentially unrelated to the political and psychological elements of national prestige. Considerations of prestige have motivated, in some measure, the nuclear weapon programs of all five of the states which presently possess nuclear forces. Prestige may appear to weigh more heavily in national decisions in the middle powers than in the superpowers. For example, the acquisition and maintenance of status as a nuclear-weapon power appeared to be a logical step for Great Britain and France as former major world powers, vested with the trappings of great-power status (as permanent members of the United Nations Security Council and occupying powers of a defeated Germany) in the postwar international system.

We have previously noted the argument that advanced industrial states, such as the Federal Republic of Germany or Japan, would require very large nuclear weapon programs and, therefore, that a moderately comprehensive safeguards system would detect the kind of large-scale diversion from nuclear industry which would contribute significantly to such a program. The argument would hold if a nuclear weapon capability were primarily intended to deter one of the superpowers, but not if such a capability were intended largely for such symbolic purposes as prestige or global or regional status.

For example, in undertaking a military nuclear program, the Fourth Republic of France started out to demonstrate something of a symbolic-political nature and to acquire a political advantage within the North Atlantic Alliance. Its objective was not an eventual *force de dissuasion,* but recognition of equality with Great Britain. It was some years later that, under General De Gaulle, the French nuclear program was transformed into an instrument for supporting a revisionist policy with global, as distinct from intra-alliance, objectives and for giving increased credibility to an independent foreign policy. The point is that, in its initial phases, the French nuclear weapon program was related to prestige and international standing, rather than to specific national defense requirements. In the future other states, such as India or Brazil, which have major-power ambitions, in regional contexts at least, and which thus far have refused to adhere to the NPT, may follow a similar course of action.

This could create a perverse situation. A state in a given region might decide for prestige reasons not to become party to the NPT, despite the adherence of its neighbors. While remaining free of the Treaty itself, such a state would nevertheless benefit from the collective good (increased security) derived from the adherence of others. A state might thus satisfy its own security concerns with regard to its neighbors while avoiding the costs associated with the acceptance of international safeguards and other constraints imposed by the NPT. Thereafter, the non-party state might attempt to use its nuclear weapon option to bargain for political objectives unrelated to nuclear affairs. To the extent that a non-party state is successful in carrying out such a policy, it profits from ambivalence on proliferation and the NPT suffers.

There emerges from these considerations an evident need for policies ancillary to safeguards, particularly policies designed to discourage proliferation for prestige (or, for that matter, for security) reasons. Other nations which observed the evolution of the Anglo-American "special relationship" in nuclear matters in the 1950s may have felt that similar benefits would flow to them if they acquired nuclear weapons. However, it may be argued that France was never rewarded in NATO for attaining nuclear weapon status and that this may have dampened the expectations of other potential nuclear-weapon powers. The United States thus reinforced the concept of non-proliferation to the extent that it did not respond to French possession of nuclear weapons with rewards.

The problem for the proponents of non-proliferation is how to prevent the advantages of a comprehensive non-proliferation system paid for by others from accruing fully to the recalcitrant state. The solution must be found either in the framework of the NPT system itself or in other, perhaps unrelated, areas. In the implementation of Article IV of the NPT, regarding peaceful nuclear development, or Article V, concerned with sharing the benefits of possible uses of nuclear explosions for peaceful purposes, preferential treatment might be offered by the major nuclear powers to NPT parties. Outside the immediate NPT framework, the major powers could reverse the game being played by a state seeking benefits without obligations. They might refuse to give or renew security guarantees to non-party states or refuse to sell such states conventional armaments, or they might apply economic or diplomatic pressure to bring around the recalcitrant state. Collective action of a similar nature could be exercised by regional or global organizations. The success of such sanctions would depend on the development of a strong consensus among the major powers, and on the absence of alternative sources of supply or support. It may be doubted whether these conditions are likely to exist in any given situation because not all of the nuclear-weapon states, nor all the states which supply nuclear material, are parties to the NPT.

## SAFEGUARDS AND NATIONAL DECISION-MAKING

Our discussion up to this point has been predicated on a state-centered model of the international system. In such a model the nation-state is the only relevant actor, and it appears to act as a monolithic unit with set purposes and a singular "national interest." We have thus spoken of Indian or Japanese security, French or British prestige, as though all of the relevant elites in those political systems shared the same views of their nation's security problems or of its international image. Analysis confined to this classic model of international politics is deficient in a number of respects, not the least of which is the fact that it tends to oversimplify the political process at both the national and international levels. It is not necessary to discard the state-centered model completely in order to examine the competition among governmental, sub-governmental, and non-governmental units for a dominant role in defining national interests and in shaping supportive policies, but it is necessary to recognize the fact that states consist of competitive groups, organizations, and bureaucracies and that particular national interests are defined at particular points in time by the outcome of struggles among these groups.

In the setting of this disaggregated international political system some of the more salient effects of IAEA/NPT safeguards come to light, and Victor Gilinsky's assertion in Chapter 6 that "safeguards are useful in proportion to the degree that they introduce added constraints into the decision-making process of the potential diverter" is important. The present nuclear-weapon states attained their status when there was no widely shared assumption that such a step was illegitimate. Public opinion recoiled at the thought of nuclear war, and nuclear weapons were developed to contain, deter, or prevent such a war. There was, however, no community-wide consensus against proliferation, and such consensus as did exist was not formalized and codified.

As a consequence of the NPT, a national decision to acquire nuclear weapons must now be reached in the face of a well-articulated agreement that non-proliferation is desirable. Non-parties to the NPT may avoid legal barriers to proliferation, though not the political handicaps that such a decision might entail. Parties to the Treaty which may consider acquiring the material for nuclear weapons through diversion from nuclear industry will face not only legal and political barriers but also the additional risks and costs of detection as a result of international safeguards.

The initial French "decision" to acquire nuclear weapons was the product of a series of incremental decisions made by a small group of persons (administrative, executive, military, and legislative, in roughly that order of importance) operating through informal channels of communication outside the mainstream of political activity. In a very real sense the final decision to exercise the nuclear option was imposed on the responsible political authorities almost as a *fait accompli*. Internally, public debate was non-existent; externally, the only constraints were American disapproval and a policy of controlled nuclear assistance which precluded the use of imported nuclear material for military purposes. The European Atomic Energy Community, which established the first international safeguards system, left each member state free to develop nuclear weapons if it chose to do so.[9]

Since IAEA/NPT safeguards are based on a national system of accounting and control applicable to all nuclear material in peaceful nuclear activities, decision-making patterns similar to those which obtained in the Fourth Republic would quickly surface in the future. The probability of benign neglect of the implications of incremental nuclear decisions would be sharply reduced. IAEA/NPT safeguards, while not preventing a decision to divert or to acquire nuclear weapons, place those decisions in a radically different context than that which previously existed. Three points deserve particular emphasis in this respect.

First, the existence of a safeguards system forces politically responsible authorities to make hard decisions. Only a conscious and considered decision by these authorities could start a program of governmental diversion. A properly functioning national safeguards system subject to international verification minimizes the risk of diversion by default. Moreover, most states will wish to keep international inspection and verification to a minimum. Thus, they will have a stake in maintaining a sophisticated and efficient national safeguards system which will, in turn, produce a thorough and effective information flow to responsible political leadership. A safeguards system publicizes national developments and conditions to a broad audience (national and international), which increases the probability that dubious or suspect patterns will be spotted and brought into the open for discussion, clarification, and debate.

Second, safeguards systems may strengthen the hand of those within a particular country who support adherence to a nonproliferation policy. National elites opposed to deceptive nuclear practices or to the acquisition of nuclear weapons by their country will be able to support their positions by pointing out not only the obligations undertaken in the NPT but also the risk of detection and sanction associated with the Treaty's safeguards. Thus safeguards play a double role in national decision-making: they serve

[9] French policy and Euratom are both analyzed in Lawrence Scheinman, *Atomic Energy Policy in France under the Fourth Republic* (Princeton: Princeton University Press, 1965).

to alert national elites to incipient nuclear weapons policies, and they provide an argument against further implementation of those policies.

Third, and perhaps most important, the internal debate suggested above would be likely to be noticed outside the state in which it was occurring. This would give other countries (e.g., the superpowers or other states whose actions were perceived as threatening) an opportunity to take appropriate action. If security concerns were the source of the state's anxiety, these might be met with an appropriate guarantee or other assurance; if prestige were the stimulant, substitutes might be offered. Finally, if the circumstances warranted drastic action and there were a major-power consensus, sanctions or the threat of sanctions might be considered, although their application prior to actual diversion or the acquisition of nuclear weapons by other means seems unlikely. In any event, publicity before consummation of the act is what is important. If IAEA/NPT safeguards can create such publicity, they will have served a valuable, though limited, purpose.

## THE OPERATION OF INTERNATIONAL SAFEGUARDS

The extent to which IAEA/NPT safeguards work positively in the manner described above depends on whether their operation is perceived favorably by the relevant national elites. The economic and technocratic elites of a given state may assign a low priority to the achievement of nuclear weapon status or they may doubt the claims made on behalf of the utility of nuclear weapons to the national defense. It does not follow, however, that these groups are indifferent to the country's status, security, or international standing. Rather, the indicators of national influence and power are different for them than for their pro-weapon counterparts. Their assessment of and support for NPT safeguards will be grounded not on the moral goodness of safeguards, but on cost-benefit analysis, with economic, commercial, and technological variables substituting for strategic or symbolic factors. This introduces the problem of the implementation and operation of the IAEA/NPT safeguards system.

Once the principle of international safeguards is accepted, the key operational concepts that must be dealt with are *equity* and *credibility*. These concepts will be analyzed in turn.

## Equity

Equitable treatment has been a recurrent theme throughout the negotiation both of the NPT and of the IAEA safeguards system it generated. Two sets of concerns are evident: parity of treatment for peaceful nuclear activities in nuclear-weapon and non-nuclear-weapon states and parity of treatment among non-nuclear-weapon parties to the NPT. Concern has been expressed about the imbalance of obligations in the NPT between nuclear-weapon and non-nuclear-weapon states; the risk of industrial espionage resulting from the access of international inspectors to industrial information and facilities; the risk of commercial disadvantage resulting from the imposition of extra burdens on industry in non-nuclear-weapon states, including added cost factors and interference with plant operations; and a vague fear that implementation of IAEA/NPT safeguards would be tantamount to the extension of the nuclear imperialism of the weapon states into the peaceful nuclear sector.

The economic arguments against safeguards were rapidly assimilated and forcefully espoused by political opponents of the NPT, who were themselves unwilling or unable to address the issue in stark political terms. This tended to raise doubts about the legitimacy of those claims among the advocates of IAEA/NPT safeguards. It is, however, important to understand that collectively those claims represent a complex blend of economic, political, and psychological reactions to the *explicit* acceptance of the principle of intrusion on national sovereignty which the NPT requires. Earlier bilateral safeguards agreements could be rationalized as cost factors built into commercial transactions, and Euratom safeguards could be viewed as a price to be paid for the pursuit of integration. IAEA safeguards, however, are an essential element in a discriminatory treaty that sanctifies the division of the world into two classes of states—those with nuclear weapons and the rest.

Countries like the Federal Republic of Germany and Japan, which have substituted economic and technological leadership for earlier traditions of military prominence, are likely to object strongly to any form of discrimination between themselves and the nuclear-weapon states below the level of the acquisition of nuclear weapons or other "explosive devices." Indeed, both explicitly regard scientific research and development and technological excellence as the way to enhance national prestige and international standing. German and Japanese officials have taken the position that in the last analysis the IAEA/NPT safeguards system can actually increase their country's sovereignty if applied in a non-discriminatory fashion. They assert that once subject to safeguards, a nuclear facility can be placed anywhere (by this they mean that uranium enrichment or plutonium separation facilities may be constructed on the territory of non-nuclear-weapon states) and that there is no basis upon which to deny any nuclear research and development activities in non-nuclear-weapon states aside from those directly prohibited by the NPT. In sum, by accepting a diminution of legal sovereignty, the Federal Republic of Germany and Japan (and non-nuclear-weapon states generally) may enlarge their empirical sovereignty. One of the conditions *sine qua non* for Japanese and German submission to IAEA/NPT safeguards is implementation of the U.S. offer to place all its nuclear facilities except those with "direct national security" significance under the same safeguards applicable to industry in the non-nuclear-weapon states. There are still many points at issue concerning this offer, including the role of private industry in selecting facilities to be subject to IAEA/NPT safeguards and in determining the conditions of inspection.

A number of advanced industrial states have insisted that the safeguards applied to any nuclear industry be no more intrusive or onerous than those applied to American facilities. Countries such as Sweden and Canada are less concerned with this issue, for they regard IAEA inspection of U.S. facilities as a high-cost-low-payoff procedure in relation to the objective of non-proliferation. However, they see some value in taking up the U.S. offer because its implementation would keep the United States aware of problems associated with international safeguard procedures and would help develop a common point of view in the worldwide nuclear industry. The symbolic value of inspection of nuclear industry in nuclear-weapon states is that it helps minimize perceptions of discrimination by placing all industries under the same psychological burdens and subject to the same risks to their competitive positions.

A second concern, mentioned previously, relates to parity of treatment among non-nuclear-weapon states, specifically the role of national safeguards systems and the frequency and intensity of international inspections. Without the participation of Euratom member states and Japan, an IAEA/NPT safeguards system would lose its *raison d'être*. A major Japanese objective throughout the negotiation of IAEA/NPT safeguards has been to obtain equality of treatment among non-nuclear-weapon states. Euratom has been the particular target of Japanese allegations that safeguards could create discriminatory treatment among the non-nuclear-weapon states. On their side, the non-nuclear-weapon Euratom states have been intent on protecting their regional system and avoiding any duplication of safeguards.

The IAEA/NPT system recognizes national safeguards systems as integral parts of the overall international system and contains the possibility for equal or near-equal roles for national and regional safeguards systems. This should go far, in principle, toward meeting Japanese concerns, while still being satisfactory to the Euratom countries. As pointed out in Chapter 2, it really could not have been otherwise, for the IAEA would probably never have developed the capability to perform its safeguards duties in all non-nuclear-weapon parties to the NPT without the aid of national or regional systems.

However, formal recognition of equality of status of national and regional safeguards systems does not *a priori* eliminate the problem of discrimination. Specific control measures will be spelled out in subsidiary arrangements negotiated between each state or regional grouping and the IAEA. It thus remains possible that the discrimination alleviated by the national control concept will be reintroduced through the subsidiary arrangement process. As these arrangements are private, not public, agreements, differences perceived by states between the verification procedures applied to them and to other states might be interpreted as discrimination, once more raising the problem of equity.

Negotiations between Euratom and the IAEA were concluded in July 1972. Euratom appears satisfied that it has secured its goal of a minimum verification arrangement consistent with the basic obligations of the NPT. IAEA appears equally satisfied that it has retained the integrity of the universal safeguards system. Whether this mutual satisfaction will facilitate Agency negotiations with Japan remains to be seen. Even if agreement is facilitated, the possibility should not be ruled out that problems may recur in the implementation of those agreements as one or the other perceives discriminatory treatment by the Agency.

The frequency and intensity of IAEA inspections raise additional operational problems in relation to equal treatment of all non-nuclear-weapon parties to the NPT. The actual number of inspections and their intensity, duration, timing, and mode depend, among other things, on the type of material in question and the effectiveness of the national safeguards system. These questions will be resolved in the subsidiary arrangements between the IAEA and the state concerned. Already some difficulty has arisen: Sweden, one of the first states to negotiate a safeguards agreement following ratification of the NPT and one of the more ardent advocates of the Treaty, objected to the frequency and intensity of inspection of Swedish facilities suggested by the IAEA on the grounds that they would place undue burdens on the facility operators and create a risk of revealing industrial secrets.

In many of the non-nuclear-weapon states, especially those with major civilian nuclear industries, nuclear development is largely in the hands of private industry. The reluctance of Japanese private industry to submit to anything more than modest inspection, for example, has been widely publicized. Any agreement between the IAEA and Japan will have to take the relationship of industry to government in that country into account. Japanese sensitivity to international inspection is based not only on the traditional catalogue of fears discussed earlier but on experience as well. In October 1970 the IAEA carried out a series of inspections at the Tsurugu Power Plant under a trilateral US-Japan-IAEA safeguards agreement. The inspections were so extensive (every part of the plant was subject to surveillance) and so frequent (they were carried out four times a day over a period of days and took place at midnight as well as during the day) that Japanese industry spokesmen and government representatives went to the IAEA ad hoc Safeguards Committee meetings in 1971 determined to secure assurance that the system would henceforth operate with maximum simplification and minimum intrusiveness.[10] Where government exerts a dominant influence over nuclear industry and is committed firmly to the principle of interna-

[10] For a report on this sequence of events, see "Too Strict International Inspection; Industry Circles Make Representation of Protest," *Daily Summary of the Japanese Press,* November 5, 1970, pp. 39-40; "Establishment of Nuclear Fuel Inspection Techniques Demanded," *Daily Summary of the Japanese Press,* November 6, 1970, p. 9.

tional inspection, problems of this nature may be easier to resolve, but no government is likely to accept voluntarily more onerous burdens than those accepted by others.

The issues of the relation between international and national safeguards and of the frequency and intensity of inspection present potential operational problems for the IAEA, as well as for the states concerned. Evaluations of the quality of national safeguards systems may differ because the states in question have different combinations of facilities and technological expertise. While a more frequent or intense IAEA presence might simply imply the relative weakness of a national control system, another implication might be that the state in question is, for some reason, more suspect or less trustworthy than other states. Can the IAEA deal differently with equal states without making implicit political judgments concerning reliability? And would any discrimination by the IAEA compromise the Agency's position as an objective participant in the safeguards system? These questions suggest that the interposition of national safeguards systems between the IAEA and national nuclear industries complicates, as well as facilitates, the task of implementating IAEA/NPT safeguards.

### Credibility

Our discussion of the problem of equity has emphasized concessions to expressed national concerns. The purpose of those concessions is to make the IAEA/NPT safeguards system broadly acceptable. It is frequently asked whether a system that is acceptable to a large number of states can be regarded as credible in view of the fact that it probably represents a consensus based on the lowest common denominator. Credibility, however, is a relative, not an absolute, concept, and one must ask "credibility for what?" We concluded previously that in the near future states are not likely to view safeguards as credible assurances of national security or as adequate substitutes for other national security measures. We also concluded, however, that states are likely to regard safeguards as a credible means for the detection of significant diversions of nuclear material. Thus, measured against the expectations and understandings of the main participants, there is no *a priori* reason to discount the credibility of the IAEA/NPT safeguards system.

Nevertheless, there are limitations in the present system, some of which have been considered earlier. Several others will be discussed here. The operational scope of the IAEA/NPT system is based upon a declaration of its nuclear facilities by a state negotiating a safeguards agreement with the IAEA. The IAEA cannot undertake intelligence operations to verify the accuracy of that declaration, although inputs from national intelligence networks may offset this deficiency to a degree, nor does the system cope with the problem of possible clandestine facilities built subsequent to its declaration, although the IAEA could inquire into allegations that such facilities were being built. Nor does the IAEA/NPT system cover nuclear material withdrawn from the fuel cycle for a military use, such as a nuclear submarine program, that is not prohibited by the NPT. Thus, the IAEA cannot necessarily verify that withdrawn material is in fact used for the declared purpose.

Yet in any of these circumstances the suspect state may invite international inspection of its facilities in order to reassure others that it is fulfilling its Treaty obligations. Successful verification by invitation may not only reduce tension derived from a suspected violation but also demonstrate the effectiveness of earlier inspections of the suspect state. Finally, if material is withdrawn from safeguards under the NPT system, the act of withdrawal becomes a matter of public knowledge and alerts the international community to developments in the state in question. The publicity alone means that, in such circumstances, safeguards can fulfill their expected function.[11]

On balance, a strong case can be made that the short-term objective in implementing the IAEA/NPT safeguards system should be to achieve the widest possible coverage of nuclear industries and facilities in the shortest possible time because nuclear industry and stocks of special fissionable material are growing rapidly. In order to exert any international control, some access must first be gained. Since a maximum-security system appears

[11] It might be pointed out that under an international as distinguished from a bilateral safeguards system, major nuclear powers who supply political allies with nuclear assistance are relieved of the tensions that could arise from their having to investigate third-party claims of diversion in the recipient state. The United States has enjoyed this relief through the intercession of Euratom between the United States and the Euratom member states. IAEA/NPT safeguards would extend this relief to other countries and would also provide the Soviet Union with a means to exercise surveillance over East European states without creating or raising unnecessary bilateral tensions.

unattainable at this time, efforts should not be made to assault the sovereignty of the nation-state frontally but rather to modify that sovereignty by intruding upon it to the extent that is presently feasible. In this way, safeguards may become increasingly global-ized, institutionalized, and effective.

A useful analogy can be drawn between the process by which international safeguards can be developed and the process by which the West European states attained their current level of integration. The first postwar efforts to unite Europe were aimed at the creation of supranational institutions to which national governments would transfer substantial political authority. This proved to be too radical a step for even the relatively homogene-ous states of Western Europe. Instead, a gradual, incremental, and functional approach to integration was adopted by those states most committed to restructuring the nation-state system in that region. Europe is still not united in any formal political sense, but multiple interdependencies have been created over the past two decades, so that each participating state now finds the values of interdependence and integration greater than those of complete national autonomy. The promise for the future of safeguards would seem to lie in a similar gradualist approach, rather than in an effort to go beyond what sovereign states are willing to toler-ate. Of course, safeguards may not evolve into an irreversible set of interdependencies, but an incremental approach is more likely to lead to globalized and institutionalized verification of arms control measures than any sweeping and compulsory requirement. The argument here assumes that there is a basic consensus favoring international safeguards and that the starting point on the path of incremental growth will not be so low that the system lacks all credibility. Once the political principle is clearly established and fully accepted, then what constitutes minimal frequencies or in-tensities of inspection becomes a technical issue.

## EXTERNAL POLITICAL FACTORS

The political implications of safeguards cannot be evaluated only in terms of the system's operation. Whether IAEA/NPT safeguards will have significant arms control value depends in good measure on the international political environment in which they function. A hospitable environment will not only facilitate operation of the system but could also lead to the extension of safeguards principles to other arms control and disarmament measures. A hostile or adverse environment could make even the most unobtrusive safeguards system ineffective.

## Participation in the NPT

If the principal states which have the ability to acquire nuclear weapons fail to ratify the NPT eventually, the Treaty will turn out to be merely a gesture toward the idea of community control over national destiny. The fact would nevertheless remain that a large number of states seriously considered voluntarily surrendering part of their sovereignty by accepting the principle of international inspection of important national activities. The effect of the failure of only certain states to adhere to the NPT is problematical. It would, for example, be plausible to consider the NPT a success even without the participation of India and/or Israel. Both are regarded by many other members of the international community as having special problems for which the NPT may not offer adequate solutions. If India or Israel were to acquire nuclear weapons, the attitudes of other states would change, although in the case of India such an overt move might have no serious global effects and only marginal regional ones. In other words, the acquisition of nuclear weapons by India may be regarded by many states as less serious than the acquisition of such weapons by Israel, Japan, or the Federal Republic of Germany.

The refusal to join the NPT of two nuclear-weapon powers, China and France, does not necessarily render it ineffectual. Since its adoption neither country has in word or in action indicated any intention to contribute to the process of proliferation. Indeed, France has explicitly stated its intention to abide by the principles of the NPT. French (and Soviet) refusal to accept international safeguards on their territory has complicated matters to an extent, but not so seriously as to threaten broad acceptance of the IAEA/NPT safeguards system.

## Conduct of the Nuclear-Weapon States

Our starting premise was that the NPT is one of a series of steps toward international control of nuclear development. Numerous countries argue forcefully that proliferation has a vertical as well as a horizontal dimension and that an effective non-proliferation scheme must fortify the NPT provisions with agreements on the limitation and reduction of strategic nuclear armaments, a cutoff in the production of fissionable material for use in weapons, and a comprehensive ban on nuclear weapons tests.[12]

Article VI of the NPT reflects a consensus that the Treaty is not an end in itself, but rather a step toward further arms control measures. It commits all parties "to pursue negotiations in good faith on effective measures relating to cessation of the nuclear arms race at an early date and to nuclear disarmament." This provision does not offset the fact that the NPT bears unequally on the nuclear-weapon and non-nuclear-weapon states. The non-nuclear-weapon parties accept immediate responsibilities and obligations, while the nuclear-weapon parties agree only to seek further arms control measures. But as the SALT talks have made clear, the United States and the Soviet Union are taking seriously their obligations to bring the nuclear arms race under control. The conclusion to which we are inevitably drawn is that the political implications of IAEA/NPT safeguards depend as much on the acceptance by the major nuclear-weapon powers of mutual limitation and self-restraint as they do on the acceptance by non-nuclear-weapon states of an efficient, effective, and equitable safeguards system.

[12] The position of the non-nuclear-weapon states on these and other problems related to the context of the NPT are discussed in Lawrence Scheinman, "Nuclear Safeguards, the Peaceful Atom, and the IAEA," *International Conciliation* (March 1969), p. 572.

# Part V
## Conclusion

# CHAPTER 10

# International Safeguards and Nuclear Industry

## MASON WILLRICH

The preceding chapters were written by individual members of the safeguards working group of the Panel on Nuclear Energy and World Order sponsored by The American Society of International Law. These chapters reflect the views of the individual authors, tempered by the criticism of other members of the working group and the panel as a whole. We did not attempt to reach agreement as a group on matters of detail and emphasis: an effort to do so would probably have failed and, even if successful, would have led to an undesirable softening of the analysis. What follows is an attempt to outline the basic themes which I believe have emerged from our study.

An inevitable consequence of the widespread use of nuclear fuel to generate electric power will be the production, processing, and use of very large amounts of special fissionable material in nuclear facilities dispersed in many nations throughout the world. A very small amount of such material—for example, a few kilograms of plutonium—is enough to make a nuclear explosive capable of mass destruction, and the manufacture of such an explosive is within the capability of many groups. The exploitation of nuclear energy for peaceful purposes thus involves substantial risks

247

to the security of nations and to the social order within them. The character and magnitude of these risks is without precedent in the history of civilian industry.

The need for international safeguards to ensure that nuclear material intended for power production or other peaceful uses is not diverted to the manufacture of nuclear explosives was largely foreseen when the nuclear era dawned at the end of World War II. It took twenty-five years, however, for the community of nations to establish the framework for a system of safeguards. Fortunately, it took almost as long to develop the technology required to produce nuclear power economically. For the foreseeable future, nuclear fuel will be used to meet an increasing share of the growing demand for electric power in many nations and every region of the world. This trend appears irreversible if

1. power reactors and other facilities in the nuclear fuel cycle are safely operated without major accidents resulting in widespread radiation damage to public health or the natural environment;

2. major nuclear war is avoided (of course, both arms control and nuclear deterrence are intended to contribute to the achievement of this goal);

3. there are no major diversions of material from the nuclear power industry which lead to the use of nuclear explosives for illicit purposes; IAEA/NPT system of safeguards, in conjunction with national safeguards systems, is intended to assure that no such diversion occurs.

It is important to emphasize that the substantial benefits of peaceful applications of nuclear energy are likely to be fully developed and widely shared only if the inherent security risks from diversion are effectively controlled. If for any reason the risks from nuclear diversion become a reality in the future, the governments of nations might well be compelled to take drastic, repressive action, surely against nuclear industry and possibly against other groups, in order to preserve national security and to prevent chaos within their respective societies.

The IAEA/NPT safeguards system provides by far the most feasible basis on which to develop the global control system required to provide the world community with reasonable assurance that nuclear material is not diverted from civilian industry for use in explosives. Despite certain limitations and weaknesses, it does not seem practicable to scrap the present system and attempt to develop a new and more effective one. Rather the IAEA/NPT system must first gain wide acceptance and then be gradually strengthened. In any event, it must be complemented by strong national safeguards systems.

The various chemical compounds and isotopic compositions of nuclear material flowing through the fuel cycle present a wide range of control opportunities and problems. The different types of reactors and associated nuclear facilities and their deployment and internal arrangement create tradeoffs from a safeguards point of view. Safeguards opportunities, problems, and tradeoffs should be carefully analyzed as a part of every major decision at the industrial, national, and international levels concerning the development and use of nuclear energy.

The development of safeguards technology—hardware, processes, and organization—has been neglected up to now in comparison with, for example, the development of technology for power reactor safety. It should now be given a high priority, and research and development programs in this field ought to receive ample financial support in every nation with a major nuclear power program. Appropriate cooperative arrangements should be made between government and industry within various nations to share the development effort and costs; such arrangements could also be worked out internationally between the governments concerned in order to avoid unnecessary duplication and to share results. The IAEA should serve as a coordinating mechanism but not be the primary vehicle for safeguards technology development. In short, the priority assigned to the development of safeguards technology should be raised substantially, but existing organizational frameworks could be used for the expanded effort.

Success in implementing the IAEA/NPT system of safeguards depends now and in the future on many political uncertainties. The viability of non-proliferation as a policy, and of international safeguards as a major element of that policy, is closely related to continued progress on other nuclear arms control measures. The initial agreements concluded in Moscow in May 1972 between the United States and the Soviet Union on limitations on strategic armaments appear to signify that the two superpowers are mindful of their obligations concerning nuclear disarmament under the NPT and, indeed, that they are determined to create conditions where proliferation of nuclear weapons is less likely, but it remains unclear where these initial agreements will lead. Similarly, the successful implementation of IAEA/NPT safeguards depends largely on the overall political environment in Europe, in Asia, and elsewhere, but it is impossible to predict how political attitudes towards non-proliferation will evolve.

Apart from these uncertainties, the IAEA/NPT system of safeguards will not be effective unless governments and nuclear industries throughout the world become firmly committed to making it work. Such a commitment appears lacking at present in most nations that have already established major nuclear power programs. There are many understandable reasons for this—resentment of the discrimination inherent in any division of the world into nuclear-weapon and non-nuclear-weapon states, unwillingness to permit international inspectors to intrude on national territory, the wish to protect the competitive position of nuclear industries at home, and fear that the complex operations of costly nuclear facilities will be disrupted. All this, however, must not be permitted to obscure the essential function of international and national safeguards nor to delay their timely and effective implementation: for nuclear industry to develop and prosper, not only must nuclear accidents and nuclear war be avoided, but nuclear explosions for any purpose with diverted material must be prevented.

Thus far, the development of safeguards to deal with the international and domestic security problems which underlie nuclear industry has been the work of a small group of experts. Government officials at the highest levels participated briefly in the discussions surrounding presentation of the Baruch Plan in 1946 and the Atoms for Peace proposals in 1953 and in the final stages of negotiation of the NPT in the late 1960s, but they have devoted insufficient attention to the complex security issues raised by nuclear industry. Moreover, top officials in the industry have resisted safeguards in principle and have treated their application to industry operations either as a bureaucratic intrusion to be firmly resisted or as a technical problem to be minimized by their experts.

At this writing—and for at least several years to come—any evaluation of the IAEA/NPT safeguards system must be somewhat tentative. The system is new, and operational experience is limited. Experiments under controlled and generally favorable conditions offer the only basis for prediction. The legal instruments already agreed upon lay the foundations for an effective and credible safeguards system that should be acceptable to the governments of all nations willing to support a policy of non-proliferation of nuclear weapons. Moreover, the IAEA/NPT system can be expected to operate at a cost which is reasonable in view of the essential function it must perform. It is time for political and industrial leaders to perceive more clearly that an effective system of international and national safeguards is essential to their own interest and to the security of future generations. If such an attitude becomes widely shared, the IAEA/NPT safeguards system will make a major contribution to world peace.

# APPENDIXES

# Treaty on the Non-Proliferation of Nuclear Weapons

*The States concluding this Treaty,* hereinafter referred to as the "Parties to the Treaty,"

*Considering* the devastation that would be visited upon all mankind by a nuclear war and the consequent need to make every effort to avert the danger of such a war and to take measures to safeguard the security of peoples,

*Believing* that the proliferation of nuclear weapons would seriously enhance the danger of nuclear war,

*In conformity with* resolutions of the United Nations General Assembly calling for the conclusion of an agreement on the prevention of wider dissemination of nuclear weapons,

*Undertaking* to co-operate in facilitating the application of International Atomic Energy Agency safeguards on peaceful nuclear activities,

*Expressing* their support for research, development and other efforts to further the application, within the framework of the International Atomic Energy Agency safeguards system, of the principle of safeguarding effectively the flow of source and special fissionable materials by use of instruments and other techniques at certain strategic points,

*Affirming* the principle that the benefits of peaceful applications of nuclear technology, including any technological by-products which may be derived by nuclear-weapon States from the development of nuclear explosive devices, should be available for peaceful purposes to all Parties to the Treaty, whether nuclear-weapon or non-nuclear-weapon States,

*Convinced* that, in furtherance of this principle, all Parties to the Treaty are entitled to participate in the fullest possible exchange of scientific information for, and to contribute alone or in co-operation with other States to, the further development of the applications of atomic energy for peaceful purposes,

*Declaring* their intention to achieve at the earliest possible date the cessation of the nuclear arms race and to undertake effective measures in the direction of nuclear disarmament,

*Urging* the co-operation of all States in the attainment of this objective,

*Recalling* the determination expressed by the Parties to the 1963 Treaty banning nuclear weapon tests in the atmosphere, in outer space and under water in its preamble to seek to achieve the discontinuance of all test explosions of nuclear weapons for all time and to continue negotiations to this end,

*Desiring* to further the easing of international tension and the strengthening of trust between States in order to facilitate the cessation of the manufacture of nuclear weapons, the liquidation of all their existing stockpiles, and the elimination from national arsenals of nuclear weapons and the means of their delivery pursuant to a Treaty on general and complete disarmament under strict and effective international control,

*Recalling* that, in accordance with the Charter of the United Nations, States must refrain in their international relations from the threat or use of force against the territorial integrity or political independence of any State, or in any other manner inconsistent with the Purposes of the United Nations, and that the establishment and maintenance of international peace and security are to be promoted with the least diversion for armaments of the world's human and economic resources,

*Have agreed* as follows:

### Article I

Each nuclear-weapon State Party to the Treaty undertakes not to transfer to any recipient whatsoever nuclear weapons or other nuclear explosive devices or control over such weapons or explosive devices directly, or indirectly; and not in any way to assist, encourage, or induce any non-nuclear-weapon State to manufacture or otherwise acquire nuclear weapons or other nuclear explosive devices, or control over such weapons or explosive devices.

### Article II

Each non-nuclear-weapon State Party to the Treaty undertakes not to receive the transfer from any transferor whatsoever of nuclear weapons or other nuclear explosive devices or of control over such weapons or explosive devices directly, or indirectly; not to manufacture or otherwise acquire nuclear weapons or other nuclear explosive devices; and not to seek or receive any assistance in the manufacture of nuclear weapons or other nuclear explosive devices.

### Article III

1. Each non-nuclear-weapon State Party to the Treaty undertakes to accept safeguards, as set forth in an agreement to be negotiated and concluded with the International Atomic Energy Agency in accordance with the Statute of the International Atomic Energy Agency and the Agency's safeguards system, for the exclusive purpose of verification of the fulfilment of its obligations assumed under this Treaty with a view to preventing diversion of nuclear energy from peaceful uses to nuclear weapons or other nuclear explosive devices. Procedures for the safeguards required by this article shall be followed with respect to source or special fissionable material whether it is being produced, processed or used in any principal nuclear facility or is outside any such facility. The safeguards required by this article shall be applied on all source or special fissionable material in all peaceful nuclear activities within the territory of such State, under its jurisdiction, or carried out under its control anywhere.

2. Each State Party to the Treaty undertakes not to provide: (a) source or special fissionable material, or (b) equipment or material especially designed or prepared for the processing, use or production of special fissionable material, to any non-nuclear-weapon State for peaceful purposes, unless the source or special fissionable material shall be subject to the safeguards required by this article.

3. The safeguards required by this article shall be implemented in a manner designed to comply with article IV of this Treaty, and to avoid hampering the economic or technological development of the parties or international co-operation in the field of peaceful nuclear activities, including the international exchange of nuclear material and equipment for the processing, use or production of nuclear material for peaceful purposes in accordance with the provisions of this article and the principle of safeguarding set forth in the preamble.

4. Non-nuclear-weapon States Party to the Treaty shall conclude agreements with the International Atomic Energy Agency to meet the requirements of this article either individually or together with other States in accordance with the Statute of the International Atomic Energy Agency. Negotiation of such agreements shall commence within 180 days from the original entry into force of this Treaty. For States depositing their instruments of ratification or accession after the 180-day period, negotiation of such agreements shall commence not later than the date of such deposit. Such agreements shall enter into force not later than eighteen months after the date of initiation of negotiations.

## Article IV

1. Nothing in this Treaty shall be interpreted as affecting the inalienable right of all the Parties to the Treaty to develop research, production and use of nuclear energy for peaceful purposes without discrimination and in conformity with articles I and II of this Treaty.

2. All the Parties to the Treaty undertake to facilitate, and have the right to participate in, the fullest possible exchange of equipment, materials and scientific and technological information for the peaceful uses of nuclear energy. Parties to the Treaty in a position to do so shall also co-operate in contributing alone or together with other States or international organizations to the further development of the applications of nuclear energy for peaceful purposes, especially in the territories of non-nuclear-weapon States Party to the Treaty, with due consideration for the needs of the developing areas of the world.

## Article V

Each Party to the Treaty undertakes to take appropriate measures to ensure that, in accordance with this Treaty, under appropriate international observation and through appropriate international procedures, potential benefits from any peaceful applications of nuclear explosions will be made available to non-nuclear-weapon States Party to the Treaty on a non-discriminatory basis and that the charge to such Parties for the explosive devices used will be as low as possible and exclude any charge for research and development. Non-nuclear-weapon States Party to the Treaty shall be able to obtain such benefits, pursuant to a special international agreement or agreements, through an appropriate international body with adequate representation of non-nuclear-weapon States. Negotiations on this subject shall commence as soon as possible after the Treaty enters into force. Non-nuclear-weapon States Party to the Treaty so desiring may also obtain such benefits pursuant to bilateral agreements.

## Article VI

Each of the Parties to the Treaty undertakes to pursue negotiations in good faith on effective measures relating to cessation of the nuclear arms race at an early date and to nuclear disarmament, and on a Treaty on general and complete disarmament under strict and effective international control.

## Article VII

Nothing in this Treaty affects the right of any group of States to conclude regional treaties in order to assure the total absence of nuclear weapons in their respective territories.

## Article VIII

1. Any Party to the Treaty may propose amendments to this Treaty. The text of any proposed amendment shall be submitted to the Depositary

Governments which shall circulate it to all Parties to the Treaty. Thereupon, if requested to do so by one third or more of the Parties to the Treaty, the Depositary Governments shall convene a conference, to which they shall invite all the Parties to the Treaty, to consider such an amendment.

2. Any amendment to this Treaty must be approved by a majority of the votes of all the Parties to the Treaty, including the votes of all nuclear-weapon States Party to the Treaty and all other Parties which, on the date the amendment is circulated, are members of the Board of Governors of the International Atomic Energy Agency. The amendment shall enter into force for each Party that deposits its instrument of ratification of the amendment upon the deposit of such instruments of ratification by a majority of all the Parties, including the instruments of ratification of all nuclear-weapon States Party to the Treaty and all other Parties which, on the date the amendment is circulated, are members of the Board of Governors of the International Atomic Energy Agency. Thereafter, it shall enter into force for any other Party upon the deposit of its instrument of ratification of the amendment.

3. Five years after the entry into force of this Treaty, a conference of Parties to the Treaty shall be held in Geneva, Switzerland, in order to review the operation of this Treaty with a view to assuring that the purposes of the Preamble and the provisions of the Treaty are being realized. At intervals of five years thereafter, a majority of the Parties to the Treaty may obtain, by submitting a proposal to this effect to the Depositary Governments, the convening of further conferences with the same objective of reviewing the operation of the Treaty.

### Article IX

1. This Treaty shall be open to all States for signature. Any State which does not sign the Treaty before its entry into force in accordance with paragraph 3 of this article may accede to it at any time.

2. This Treaty shall be subject to ratification by signatory States. Instruments of ratification and instruments of accession shall be deposited with the Governments of the Union of Soviet Socialist Republics, the United Kingdom of Great Britain and Northern Ireland and the United States of America, which are hereby the Depositary Governments.

3. This Treaty shall enter into force after its ratification by the States, the Governments of which are designated Depositaries of the Treaty, and forty other States signatory to this Treaty and the deposit of their instruments of ratification. For the purpose of this Treaty, a nuclear-weapon State is one which has manufactured and exploded a nuclear weapon or other nuclear explosive device prior to 1 January 1967.

4. For States whose instruments of ratification or accession are deposited subsequent to the entry into force of this Treaty, it shall enter into force on the date of the deposit of their instruments of ratification or accession.

5. The Depositary Governments shall promptly inform all signatory and acceding States of the date of each signature, the date of deposit of each instrument of ratification or of accession, the date of the entry into force of this Treaty, and the date of receipt of any requests for convening a conference or other notices.

6. This Treaty shall be registered by the Depositary Governments pursuant to Article 102 of the Charter of the United Nations.

## Article X

1. Each Party shall in exercising its national sovereignty have the right to withdraw from the Treaty if it decides that extraordinary events, related to the subject matter of this Treaty, have jeopardized the supreme interests of its country. It shall give notice of such withdrawal to all other Parties to the Treaty and to the United Nations Security Council three months in advance. Such notice shall include a statement of the extraordinary events it regards as having jeopardized its supreme interests.

2. Twenty-five years after the entry into force of the Treaty, a Conference shall be convened to decide whether the Treaty shall continue in force indefinitely, or shall be extended for an additional fixed period or periods. This decision shall be taken by a majority of the Parties to the Treaty.

## Article XI

This Treaty, the English, Russian, French, Spanish and Chinese texts of which are equally authentic, shall be deposited in the archives of the Depositary Governments. Duly certified copies of this Treaty shall be transmitted by the Depositary Governments to the Governments of the signatory and acceding States.

# International Atomic Energy Agency, The Structure and Content of Agreements between the Agency and States Required in Connection with the Treaty on the Non-Proliferation of Nuclear Weapons

## Part I

### BASIC UNDERTAKING

1.   The Agreement should contain, in accordance with Article III.1 of the Treaty on the Non-Proliferation of Nuclear Weapons,[1] an undertaking by the State to accept safeguards, in accordance with the terms of the Agreement, on all source or special fissionable material in all peaceful nuclear activities within its territory, under its jurisdiction or carried out under its control anywhere, for the exclusive purpose of verifying that such material is not diverted to nuclear weapons or other nuclear explosive devices.

### APPLICATION OF SAFEGUARDS

2.   The Agreement should provide for the Agency's right and obligation to ensure that safeguards will be applied, in accordance with the terms of the Agreement, on all source or special fissionable material in all peaceful nuclear activities within the territory of the State, under its jurisdiction or carried out

---

[1] Reproduced in document INFCIRC/140.

under its control anywhere, for the exclusive purpose of verifying that such material is not diverted to nuclear weapons or other nuclear explosive devices.

## CO-OPERATION BETWEEN THE AGENCY AND THE STATE

3.   The Agreement should provide that the Agency and the State shall co-operate to facilitate the implementation of the safeguards provided for therein.

## IMPLEMENTATION OF SAFEGUARDS

4.   The Agreement should provide that safeguards shall be implemented in a manner designed:

(a)  To avoid hampering the economic and technological development of the State or international co-operation in the field of peaceful nuclear activities, including international exchange of *nuclear material;*[2]

(b)  To avoid undue interference in the State's peaceful nuclear activities, and in particular in the operation of *facilities*; and

(c)  To be consistent with prudent management practices required for the economic and safe conduct of nuclear activities.

5.   The Agreement should provide that the Agency shall take every precaution to protect commercial and industrial secrets and other confidential information coming to its knowledge in the implementation of the Agreement. The Agency shall not publish or communicate to any State, organization or person any information obtained by it in connection with the implementation of the Agreement, except that specific information relating to such implementation in the State may be given to the Board of Governors and to such Agency staff members as require such knowledge by reason of their official duties in connection with safeguards, but only to the extent necessary for the Agency to fulfil its responsibilities in implementing the Agreement. Summarized information on *nuclear material* being safeguarded by the Agency under the Agreement may be published upon decision of the Board if the States directly concerned agree.

6.   The Agreement should provide that in implementing safeguards pursuant thereto the Agency shall take full account of technological developments in the field of safeguards, and shall make every effort to ensure optimum cost-effectiveness and the application of the principle of safeguarding effectively the flow of *nuclear material* subject to safeguards under the Agreement by use of instruments and other techniques at certain *strategic points* to the extent that present or future technology permits. In order to ensure optimum cost-effectiveness, use should be made, for example, of such means as:

(a)  Containment as a means of defining *material balance areas* for accounting purposes;

(b)  Statistical techniques and random sampling in evaluating the flow of *nuclear material*; and

---

[2] Terms in italics have a specialized meaning, which is defined in paragraphs 98-116 below.

(c) Concentration of verification procedures on those stages in the nuclear fuel cycle involving the production, processing, use or storage of *nuclear material* from which nuclear weapons or other nuclear explosive devices could readily be made, and minimization of verification procedures in respect of other *nuclear material*, on condition that this does not hamper the Agency in applying safeguards under the Agreement.

## NATIONAL SYSTEM OF ACCOUNTING FOR AND CONTROL OF NUCLEAR MATERIAL

7. The Agreement should provide that the State shall establish and maintain a system of accounting for and control of all *nuclear material* subject to safeguards under the Agreement, and that such safeguards shall be applied in such a manner as to enable the Agency to verify, in ascertaining that there has been no diversion of *nuclear material* from peaceful uses to nuclear weapons or other nuclear explosive devices, findings of the State's system. The Agency's verification shall include, inter alia, independent measurements and observations conducted by the Agency in accordance with the procedures specified in Part II below. The Agency, in its verification, shall take due account of the technical effectiveness of the State's system.

## PROVISION OF INFORMATION TO THE AGENCY

8. The Agreement should provide that to ensure the effective implementation of safeguards thereunder the Agency shall be provided, in accordance with the provisions set out in Part II below, with information concerning *nuclear material* subject to safeguards under the Agreement and the features of *facilities* relevant to safeguarding such material. The Agency shall require only the minimum amount of information and data consistent with carrying out its responsibilities under the Agreement. Information pertaining to *facilities* shall be the minimum necessary for safeguarding *nuclear material* subject to safeguards under the Agreement. In examining design information, the Agency shall, at the request of the State, be prepared to examine on premises of the State design information which the State regards as being of particular sensitivity. Such information would not have to be physically transmitted to the Agency provided that it remained available for ready further examination by the Agency on premises of the State.

## AGENCY INSPECTORS

9. The Agreement should provide that the State shall take the necessary steps to ensure that Agency inspectors can effectively discharge their functions under the Agreement. The Agency shall secure the consent of the State to the designation of Agency inspectors to that State. If the State, either upon proposal of a designation or at any other time after a designation has been made, objects to the designation, the Agency shall propose to the State an alternative designation or designations. The repeated refusal of a State to accept the designation of Agency inspectors which would impede the inspec-

tions conducted under the Agreement would be considered by the Board upon referral by the Director General with a view to appropriate action. The visits and activities of Agency inspectors shall be so arranged as to reduce to a minimum the possible inconvenience and disturbance to the State and to the peaceful nuclear activities inspected, as well as to ensure protection of industrial secrets or any other confidential information coming to the inspectors' knowledge.

## PRIVILEGES AND IMMUNITIES

10. The Agreement should specify the privileges and immunities which shall be granted to the Agency and its staff in respect of their functions under the Agreement. In the case of a State party to the Agreement on the Privileges and Immunities of the Agency,[3] the provisions thereof, as in force for such State, shall apply. In the case of other States, the privileges and immunities granted should be such as to ensure that:

(a) The Agency and its staff will be in a position to discharge their functions under the Agreement effectively; and

(b) No such State will be placed thereby in a more favourable position than States party to the Agreement on the Privileges and Immunities of the Agency.

## TERMINATION OF SAFEGUARDS

### Consumption or dilution of nuclear material

11. The Agreement should provide that safeguards shall terminate on *nuclear material* subject to safeguards thereunder upon determination by the Agency that it has been consumed, or has been diluted in such a way that it is no longer usable for any nuclear activity relevant from the point of view of safeguards, or has become practicably irrecoverable.

### Transfer of nuclear material out of the State

12. The Agreement should provide, with respect to *nuclear material* subject to safeguards thereunder, for notification of transfers of such material out of the State, in accordance with the provisions set out in paragraphs 92-94 below. The Agency shall terminate safeguards under the Agreement on *nuclear material* when the recipient State has assumed responsibility therefor, as provided for in paragraph 91. The Agency shall maintain records indicating each transfer and, where applicable, the re-application of safeguards to the transferred *nuclear material*.

### Provisions relating to nuclear material to be used in non-nuclear activities

13. The Agreement should provide that if the State wishes to use *nuclear material* subject to safeguards thereunder in non-nuclear activities, such as the

---

[3] Reproduced in document INFCIRC/9/Rev.2.

production of alloys or ceramics, it shall agree with the Agency on the circumstances under which the safeguards on such *nuclear material* may be terminated.

## NON-APPLICATION OF SAFEGUARDS TO NUCLEAR MATERIAL TO BE USED IN NON-PEACEFUL ACTIVITIES

14. The Agreement should provide that if the State intends to exercise its discretion to use *nuclear material* which is required to be safeguarded thereunder in a nuclear activity which does not require the application of safeguards under the Agreement, the following procedures will apply:

(a) The State shall inform the Agency of the activity, making it clear:

(i) That the use of the *nuclear material* in a non-proscribed military activity will not be in conflict with an undertaking the State may have given and in respect of which Agency safeguards apply, that the *nuclear material* will be used only in a peaceful nuclear activity; and

(ii) That during the period of non-application of safeguards the *nuclear material* will not be used for the production of nuclear weapons or other nuclear explosive devices;

(b) The State and the Agency shall make an arrangement so that, only while the *nuclear material* is in such an activity, the safeguards provided for in the Agreement will not be applied. The arrangement shall identify, to the extent possible, the period or circumstances during which safeguards will not be applied. In any event, the safeguards provided for in the Agreement shall again apply as soon as the *nuclear material* is reintroduced into a peaceful nuclear activity. The Agency shall be kept informed of the total quantity and composition of such unsafeguarded *nuclear material* in the State and of any exports of such material; and

(c) Each arrangement shall be made in agreement with the Agency. The Agency's agreement shall be given as promptly as possible; it shall only relate to the temporal and procedural provisions, reporting arrangements, etc., but shall not involve any approval or classified knowledge of the military activity or relate to the use of the *nuclear material* therein.

## FINANCE

15. The Agreement should contain one of the following sets of provisions:

(a) An agreement with a Member of the Agency should provide that each party thereto shall bear the expenses it incurs in implementing its responsibilities thereunder. However, if the State or persons under its jurisdiction incur extraordinary expenses as a result of a specific request by the Agency, the Agency shall reimburse such expenses provided that it has agreed in advance to do so. In any case the Agency shall bear the cost of any additional measuring or sampling which inspectors may request; or

(b) An agreement with a party not a Member of the Agency should, in application of the provisions of Article XIV.C of the Statute, provide that the party shall reimburse fully to the Agency the safeguards expenses the Agency incurs thereunder. However, if the party or persons under its jurisdiction incur extraordinary expenses as a result of a specific request by the Agency, the Agency shall reimburse such expenses provided that it has agreed in advance to do so.

## THIRD PARTY LIABILITY FOR NUCLEAR DAMAGE

16. The Agreement should provide that the State shall ensure that any protection against third party liability in respect of nuclear damage, including any insurance or other financial security, which may be available under its laws or regulations shall apply to the Agency and its officials for the purpose of the implementation of the Agreement, in the same way as that protection applies to nationals of the State.

## INTERNATIONAL RESPONSIBILITY

17. The Agreement should provide that any claim by one party thereto against the other in respect of any damage, other than damage arising out of a nuclear incident, resulting from the implementation of safeguards under the Agreement, shall be settled in accordance with international law.

## MEASURES IN RELATION TO VERIFICATION OF NON-DIVERSION

18. The Agreement should provide that if the Board, upon report of the Director General, decides that an action by the State is essential and urgent in order to ensure verification that *nuclear material* subject to safeguards under the Agreement is not diverted to nuclear weapons or other nuclear explosive devices the Board shall be able to call upon the State to take the required action without delay, irrespective of whether procedures for the settlement of a dispute have been invoked.

19. The Agreement should provide that if the Board upon examination of relevant information reported to it by the Director General finds that the Agency is not able to verify that there has been no diversion of *nuclear material* required to be safeguarded under the Agreement to nuclear weapons or other nuclear explosive devices, it may make the reports provided for in paragraph C of Article XII of the Statute and may also take, where applicable, the other measures provided for in that paragraph. In taking such action the Board shall take account of the degree of assurance provided by the safeguards measures that have been applied and shall afford the State every reasonable opportunity to furnish the Board with any necessary reassurance.

## INTERPRETATION AND APPLICATION OF THE AGREEMENT AND SETTLEMENT OF DISPUTES

20. The Agreement should provide that the parties thereto shall, at the

request of either, consult about any question arising out of the interpretation or application thereof.

21. The Agreement should provide that the State shall have the right to request that any question arising out of the interpretation or application thereof be considered by the Board; and that the State shall be invited by the Board to participate in the discussion of any such question by the Board.

22. The Agreement should provide that any dispute arising out of the interpretation or application thereof except a dispute with regard to a finding by the Board under paragraph 19 above or an action taken by the Board pursuant to such a finding which is not settled by negotiation or another procedure agreed to by the parties should, on the request of either party, be submitted to an arbitral tribunal composed as follows: each party would designate one arbitrator, and the two arbitrators so designated would elect a third, who would be the Chairman. If, within 30 days of the request for arbitration, either party has not designated an arbitrator, either party to the dispute may request the President of the International Court of Justice to appoint an arbitrator. The same procedure would apply if, within 30 days of the designation or appointment of the second arbitrator, the third arbitrator had not been elected. A majority of the members of the arbitral tribunal would constitute a quorum, and all decisions would require the concurrence of two arbitrators. The arbitral procedure would be fixed by the tribunal. The decisions of the tribunal would be binding on both parties.

## FINAL CLAUSES

### Amendment of the Agreement

23. The Agreement should provide that the parties thereto shall, at the request of either of them, consult each other on amendment of the Agreement. All amendments shall require the agreement of both parties. It might additionally be provided, if convenient to the State, that the agreement of the parties on amendments to Part II of the Agreement could be achieved by recourse to a simplified procedure. The Director General shall promptly inform all Member States of any amendment to the Agreement.

### Suspension of application of Agency safeguards under other agreements

24. Where applicable and where the State desires such a provision to appear, the Agreement should provide that the application of Agency safeguards in the State under other safeguards agreements with the Agency shall be suspended while the Agreement is in force. If the State has received assistance from the Agency for a project, the State's undertaking in the Project Agreement not to use items subject thereto in such a way as to further any military purpose shall continue to apply.

### Entry into force and duration

25. The Agreement should provide that it shall enter into force on the date

on which the Agency receives from the State written notification that the statutory and constitutional requirements for entry into force have been met. The Director General shall promptly inform all Member States of the entry into force.

26. The Agreement should provide for it to remain in force as long as the State is party to the Treaty on the Non-Proliferation of Nuclear Weapons.[4]

## Part II

### INTRODUCTION

27. The Agreement should provide that the purpose of Part II thereof is to specify the procedures to be applied for the implementation of the safeguards provisions of Part I.

### OBJECTIVE OF SAFEGUARDS

28. The Agreement should provide that the objective of safeguards is the timely detection of diversion of significant quantities of *nuclear material* from peaceful nuclear activities to the manufacture of nuclear weapons or of other nuclear explosive devices or for purposes unknown, and deterrence of such diversion by the risk of early detection.

29. To this end the Agreement should provide for the use of material accountancy as a safeguards measure of fundamental importance, with containment and surveillance as important complementary measures.

30. The Agreement should provide that the technical conclusion of the Agency's verification activities shall be a statement, in respect of each *material balance area*, of the amount of *material unaccounted for* over a specific period, giving the limits of accuracy of the amounts stated.

### NATIONAL SYSTEM OF ACCOUNTING FOR AND CONTROL OF NUCLEAR MATERIAL

31. The Agreement should provide that pursuant to paragraph 7 above the Agency, in carrying out its verification activities, shall make full use of the State's system of accounting for and control of all *nuclear material* subject to safeguards under the Agreement, and shall avoid unnecessary duplication of the State's accounting and control activities.

32. The Agreement should provide that the State's system of accounting for and control of all *nuclear material* subject to safeguards under the Agreement shall be based on a structure of material balance areas, and shall make

---

[4] See note 1.

provision as appropriate and specified in the Subsidiary Arrangements for the establishment of such measures as:

(a) A measurement system for the determination of the quantities of *nuclear material* received, produced, shipped, lost or otherwise removed from inventory, and the quantities on inventory;

(b) The evaluation of precision and accuracy of measurements and the estimation of measurement uncertainty;

(c) Procedures for identifying, reviewing and evaluating differences in shipper/receiver measurements;

(d) Procedures for taking a *physical inventory*;

(e) Procedures for the evaluation of accumulations of unmeasured inventory and unmeasured losses;

(f) A system of records and reports showing, for each *material balance area*, the inventory of *nuclear material* and the changes in that inventory including receipts into and transfers out of the *material balance area*;

(g) Provisions to ensure that the accounting procedures and arrangements are being operated correctly; and

(h) Procedures for the submission of reports to the Agency in accordance with paragraphs 59-69 below.

## STARTING POINT OF SAFEGUARDS

33. The Agreement should provide that safeguards shall not apply thereunder to material in mining or ore processing activities.

34. The Agreement should provide that:

(a) When any material containing uranium or thorium which has not reached the stage of the nuclear fuel cycle described in sub-paragraph (c) below is directly or indirectly exported to a non-nuclear-weapon State, the State shall inform the Agency of its quantity, composition and destination, unless the material is exported for specifically non-nuclear purposes;

(b) When any material containing uranium or thorium which has not reached the stage of the nuclear fuel cycle described in sub-paragraph (c) below is imported, the State shall inform the Agency of its quantity and composition, unless the material is imported for specifically non-nuclear purposes; and

(c) When any *nuclear material* of a composition and purity suitable for fuel fabrication or for being isotopically enriched leaves the plant or the process stage in which it has been produced, or when such *nuclear material*, or any other *nuclear material* produced at a later stage in the nuclear fuel cycle, is imported into the State, the *nuclear material* shall become subject to the other safeguards procedures specified in the Agreement.

## TERMINATION OF SAFEGUARDS

35. The Agreement should provide that safeguards shall terminate on *nuclear*

*material* subject to safeguards thereunder under the conditions set forth in paragraph 11 above. Where the conditions of that paragraph are not met, but the State considers that the recovery of safeguarded *nuclear material* from residues is not for the time being practicable or desirable, the Agency and the State shall consult on the appropriate safeguards measures to be applied. It should further be provided that safeguards shall terminate on *nuclear material* subject to safeguards under the Agreement under the conditions set forth in paragraph 13 above, provided that the State and the Agency agree that such *nuclear material* is practicably irrecoverable.

## EXEMPTIONS FROM SAFEGUARDS

36. The Agreement should provide that the Agency shall, at the request of the State, exempt *nuclear material* from safeguards, as follows:

    (a) Special fissionable material, when it is used in gram quantities or less as a sensing component in instruments;

    (b) *Nuclear material*, when it is used in non-nuclear activities in accordance with paragraph 13 above, if such *nuclear material* is recoverable; and

    (c) Plutonium with an isotopic concentration of plutonium-238 exceeding 80%.

37. The Agreement should provide that *nuclear material* that would otherwise be subject to safeguards shall be exempted from safeguards at the request of the State, provided that *nuclear material* so exempted in the State may not at any time exceed:

    (a) One kilogram in total of special fissionable material, which may consist of one of more of the following:

        (i) Plutonium;

        (ii) Uranium with an *enrichment* of 0.2 (20%) and above, taken account of by multiplying its weight by its *enrichment*; and

        (iii) Uranium with an *enrichment* below 0.2 (20%) and above that of natural uranium, taken account of by multiplying its weight by five times the square of its *enrichment*;

    (b) Ten metric tons in total of natural uranium and depleted uranium with an *enrichment* above 0.005 (0.5%);

    (c) Twenty metric tons of depleted uranium with an *enrichment* of 0.005 (0.5%) or below; and

    (d) Twenty metric tons of thorium;

or such greater amounts as may be specified by the Board of Governors for uniform application.

38. The Agreement should provide that if exempted *nuclear material* is to be processed or stored together with safeguarded *nuclear material*, provision should be made for the re-application of safeguards thereto.

## SUBSIDIARY ARRANGEMENTS

39. The Agreement should provide that the Agency and the State shall make Subsidiary Arrangements which shall specify in detail, to the extent necessary to permit the Agency to fulfil its responsibilities under the Agreement in an

effective and efficient manner, how the procedures laid down in the Agreement are to be applied. Provision should be made for the possibility of an extension or change of the Subsidiary Arrangements by agreement between the Agency and the State without amendment of the Agreement.

40. It should be provided that the Subsidiary Arrangements shall enter into force at the same time as, or as soon as possible after, the entry into force of the Agreement. The State and the Agency shall make every effort to achieve their entry into force within 90 days of the entry into force of the Agreement, a later date being acceptable only with the agreement of both parties. The State shall provide the Agency promptly with the information required for completing the Subsidiary Arrangements. The Agreement should also provide that, upon its entry into force, the Agency shall be entitled to apply the procedures laid down therein in respect of the *nuclear material* listed in the inventory provided for in paragraph 41 below.

## INVENTORY

41. The Agreement should provide that, on the basis of the initial report referred to in paragraph 62 below, the Agency shall establish a unified inventory of all *nuclear material* in the State subject to safeguards under the Agreement, irrespective of its origin, and maintain this inventory on the basis of subsequent reports and of the results of its verification activities. Copies of the inventory shall be made available to the State at agreed intervals.

## DESIGN INFORMATION

### General

42. Pursuant to paragraph 8 above, the Agreement should stipulate that design information in respect of existing *facilities* shall be provided to the Agency during the discussion of the Subsidiary Arrangements, and that the time limits for the provision of such information in respect of new *facilities* shall be specified in the Subsidiary Arrangements. It should further be stipulated that such information shall be provided as early as possible before *nuclear material* is introduced into a new *facility*.

43. The Agreement should specify that the design information in respect of each *facility* to be made available to the Agency shall include, when applicable:

(a) Identification of the *facility*, stating its general character, purpose, nominal capacity and geographic location, and the name and address to be used for routine business purposes;

(b) Description of the general arrangement of the *facility* with reference, to the extent feasible, to the form, location and flow of *nuclear material* and to the general layout of important items of equipment which use, produce or process *nuclear material*;

(c) Description of features of the *facility* relating to material accountancy, containment and surveillance; and

(d) Description of the existing and proposed procedures at the *facility* for *nuclear material* accountancy and control, with special reference to *material balance areas* established by the operator, measurements of flow and procedures for *physical inventory* taking.

44. The Agreement should further provide that other information relevant to the application of safeguards shall be made available to the Agency in respect of each *facility,* in particular on organizational responsibility for material accountancy and control. It should also be provided that the State shall make available to the Agency supplementary information on the health and safety procedures which the Agency shall observe and with which the inspectors shall comply at the *facility.*

45. The Agreement should stipulate that design information in respect of a modification relevant for safeguards purposes shall be provided for examination sufficiently in advance for the safeguards procedures to be adjusted when necessary.

### Purposes of examination of design information

46. The Agreement should provide that the design information made available to the Agency shall be used for the following purposes:

(a) To identify the features of *facilities* and *nuclear material* relevant to the application of safeguards to *nuclear material* in sufficient detail to facilitate verification;

(b) To determine *material balance areas* to be used for Agency accounting purposes and to select those *strategic points* which are *key measurement points* and which will be used to determine the *nuclear material* flows and inventories; in determining such *material balance areas* the Agency shall, inter alia, use the following criteria:

(i) The size of the *material balance area* should be related to the accuracy with which the material balance can be established;

(ii) In determining the *material balance area* advantage should be taken of any opportunity to use containment and surveillance to help ensure the completeness of flow measurements and thereby simplify the application of safeguards and concentrate measurement efforts at *key measurement points*;

(iii) A number of *material balance areas* in use at a *facility* or at distinct sites may be combined in one *material balance area* to be used for Agency accounting purposes when the Agency determines that this is consistent with its verification requirements; and

(iv) If the State so requests, a special *material balance area* around a process step involving commercially sensitive information may be established;

(c) To establish the nominal timing and procedures for taking of *physical inventory* for Agency accounting purposes;

(d) To establish the records and reports requirements and records evaluation procedures;

(e) To establish requirements and procedures for verification of the quantity and location of *nuclear material*; and

(f)  To select appropriate combinations of containment and surveillance methods and techniques and the *strategic points* at which they are to be applied.

It should further be provided that the results of the examination of the design information shall be included in the Subsidiary Arrangements.

## Re-examination of design information

47. The Agreement should provide that design information shall be re-examined in the light of changes in operating conditions, of developments in safeguards technology or of experience in the application of verification procedures, with a view of modifying the action the Agency has taken pursuant to paragraph 46 above.

## Verification of design information

48. The Agreement should provide that the Agency, in co-operation with the State, may send inspectors to *facilities* to verify the design information provided to the Agency pursuant to paragraphs 42-45 above for the purposes stated in paragraph 46.

## INFORMATION IN RESPECT OF NUCLEAR MATERIAL OUTSIDE FACILITIES

49. The Agreement should provide that the following information concerning *nuclear material* customarily used outside *facilities* shall be provided as applicable to the Agency:

(a)  General description of the use of the *nuclear material*, its geographic location, and the user's name and address for routine business purposes; and

(b)  General description of the existing and proposed procedures for *nuclear material* accountancy and control, including organizational responsibility for material accountancy and control.

The Agreement should further provide that the Agency shall be informed on a timely basis of any change in the information provided to it under this paragraph.

50. The Agreement should provide that the information made available to the Agency in respect of *nuclear material* customarily used outside *facilities* may be used, to the extent relevant, for the purposes set out in sub-paragraphs 46(b)-(f) above.

## RECORDS SYSTEM

### General

51. The Agreement should provide that in establishing a national system of accounting for and control of *nuclear material* as referred to in paragraph 7

above, the State shall arrange that records are kept in respect of each *material balance area*. Provision should also be made that the Subsidiary Arrangements shall describe the records to be kept in respect of each *material balance area*.

52. The Agreement should provide that the State shall make arrangements to facilitate the examination of records by inspectors, particularly if the records are not kept in English, French, Russian or Spanish.

53. The Agreement should provide that the records shall be retained for at least five years.

54. The Agreement should provide that the records shall consist, as appropriate, of:

(a) Accounting records of all *nuclear material* subject to safeguards under the Agreement; and

(b) Operating records for *facilities* containing such *nuclear material*.

55. The Agreement should provide that the system of measurements on which the records used for the preparation of reports are based shall either conform to the latest international standards or be equivalent in quality to such standards.

### Accounting records

56. The Agreement should provide that the accounting records shall set forth the following in respect of each *material balance area*:

(a) All *inventory changes*, so as to permit a determination of the *book inventory* at any time;

(b) All measurement results that are used for determination of the *physical inventory*; and

(c) All *adjustments* and *corrections* that have been made in respect of *inventory changes*, *book inventories* and *physical inventories*.

57. The Agreement should provide that for all *inventory changes* and *physical inventories* the records shall show, in respect of each *batch* of *nuclear material*: material identification, *batch data* and *source data*. Provision should further be included that records shall account for uranium, thorium and plutonium separately in each *batch* of *nuclear material*. Furthermore, the date of the *inventory change* and, when appropriate, the originating *material balance area* and the receiving *material balance area*, or the recipient, shall be indicated for each *inventory change*.

### Operating records

58. The Agreement should provide that the operating records shall set forth as appropriate in respect of each *material balance area*:

(a) Those operating data which are used to establish changes in the quantities and composition of *nuclear material*;

(b) The data obtained from the calibration of tanks and instruments and from sampling and analyses, the procedures to control the quality of measurements and the derived estimates of random and systematic error;

(c) The description of the sequence of the actions taken in preparing for, and in taking, a *physical inventory*, in order to ensure that it is correct and complete; and

(d) The description of the actions taken in order to ascertain the cause and magnitude of any accidental or unmeasured loss that might occur.

## REPORTS SYSTEM

### General

59. The Agreement should specify that the State shall provide the Agency with reports as detailed in paragraphs 60-69 below in respect of *nuclear material* subject to safeguards thereunder.

60. The Agreement should provide that reports shall be made in English, French, Russian or Spanish, except as otherwise specified in the Subsidiary Arrangements.

61. The Agreement should provide that reports shall be based on the records kept in accordance with paragraphs 51-58 above and shall consist, as appropriate, of accounting reports and special reports.

### Accounting reports

62. The Agreement should stipulate that the Agency shall be provided with an initial report on all *nuclear material* which is to be subject to safeguards thereunder. It should also be provided that the initial report shall be dispatched by the State to the Agency within 30 days of the last day of the calendar month in which the Agreement enters into force, and shall reflect the situation as of the last day of that month.

63. The Agreement should stipulate that for each *material balance area* the State shall provide the Agency with the following accounting reports:

(a) *Inventory change* reports showing changes in the inventory of *nuclear material*. The reports shall be dispatched as soon as possible and in any event within 30 days after the end of the month in which the *inventory changes* occurred or were established; and

(b) Material balance reports showing the material balance based on a *physical inventory* of *nuclear material* actually present in the *material balance area*. The reports shall be dispatched as soon as possible and in any event within 30 days after the *physical inventory* has been taken.

The reports shall be based on data available as of the date of reporting and may be corrected at a later date as required.

64. The Agreement should provide that *inventory change* reports shall specify identification and *batch data* for each *batch of nuclear material*, the date of the *inventory change* and, as appropriate, the originating *material balance area* and the receiving *material balance area* or the recipient. These reports shall be accompanied by concise notes:

(a) Explaining the *inventory changes*, on the basis of the operating data contained in the operating records provided for under sub-paragraph 58(a) above; and

(b) Describing, as specified in the Subsidiary Arrangements, the anticipated operational programme, particularly the taking of a *physical inventory*.

65. The Agreement should provide that the State shall report each *inventory
change, adjustment* and *correction* either periodically in a consolidated list or
individually. The *inventory changes* shall be reported in terms of *batches*;
small amounts, such as analytical samples, as specified in the Subsidiary
Arrangements, may be combined and reported as one *inventory change*.

66. The Agreement should stipulate that the Agency shall provide the State
with semi-annual statements of *book inventory* of *nuclear material* subject to
safeguards, for each *material balance area*, as based on the *inventory change*
reports for the period covered by each such statement.

67. The Agreement should specify that the material balance reports shall
include the following entries, unless otherwise agreed by the Agency and the
State:

  (a)  Beginning *physical inventory*;
  (b)  *Inventory changes* (first increases, then decreases);
  (c)  Ending *book inventory*;
  (d)  *Shipper/receiver differences*;
  (e)  Adjusted ending *book inventory*;
  (f)  Ending *physical inventory*; and
  (g)  *Material unaccounted for*.

A statement of the *physical inventory*, listing all *batches* separately and
specifying material identification and *batch data* for each *batch*, shall be
attached to each material balance report.

### Special reports

68. The Agreement should provide that the State shall make special reports
without delay:

  (a)  If any unusual incident or circumstances lead the State to believe
  that there is or may have been loss of *nuclear material* that exceeds the
  limits to be specified for this purpose in the Subsidiary Arrangements; or
  (b)  If the containment has unexpectedly changed from that specified in
  the Subsidiary Arrangements to the extent that unauthorized removal of
  *nuclear material* has become possible.

### Amplification and clarification of reports

69. The Agreement should provide that at the Agency's request the State
shall supply amplifications or clarifications of any report, in so far as relevant
for the purpose of safeguards.

### INSPECTIONS

### General

70. The Agreement should stipulate that the Agency shall have the right to
make inspections as provided for in paragraphs 71-82 below.

Purposes of inspections

71. The Agreement should provide that the Agency may make ad hoc inspections in order to:

(a) Verify the information contained in the initial report on the *nuclear material* subject to safeguards under the Agreement;

(b) Identify and verify changes in the situation which have occurred since the date of the initial report; and

(c) Identify, and if possible verify the quantity and composition of, *nuclear material* in accordance with paragraphs 93 and 96 below, before its transfer out of or upon its transfer into the State.

72. The Agreement should provide that the Agency may make routine inspections in order to:

(a) Verify that reports are consistent with records;

(b) Verify the location, identity, quantity and composition of all *nuclear material* subject to safeguards under the Agreement; and

(c) Verify information on the possible causes of *material unaccounted for, shipper/receiver differences* and uncertainties in the *book inventory*.

73. The Agreement should provide that the Agency may make special inspections subject to the procedures laid down in paragraph 77 below:

(a) In order to verify the information contained in special reports; or

(b) If the Agency considers that information made available by the State, including explanations from the State and information obtained from routine inspections, is not adequate for the Agency to fulfil its responsibilities under the Agreement.

An inspection shall be deemed to be special when it is either additional to the routine inspection effort provided for in paragraphs 78-82 below, or involves access to information or locations in addition to the access specified in paragraph 76 for ad hoc and routine inspections, or both.

Scope of inspections

74. The Agreement should provide that for the purposes stated in paragraphs 71-73 above the Agency may:

(a) Examine the records kept pursuant to paragraphs 51-58;

(b) Make independent measurements of all *nuclear material* subject to safeguards under the Agreement;

(c) Verify the functioning and calibration of instruments and other measuring and control equipment;

(d) Apply and make use of surveillance and containment measures; and

(e) Use other objective methods which have been demonstrated to be technically feasible.

75. It should further be provided that within the scope of paragraph 74 above the Agency shall be enabled:

(a) To observe that samples at *key measurement points* for material balance accounting are taken in accordance with procedures which produce representative samples, to observe the treatment and analysis of the samples and to obtain duplicates of such samples;

(b) To observe that the measurements of *nuclear material* at *key measurement points* for material balance accounting are representative, and to observe the calibration of the instruments and equipment involved;

(c) To make arrangements with the State that, if necessary:

(i) Additional measurements are made and additional samples taken for the Agency's use;

(ii) The Agency's standard analytical samples are analysed;

(iii) Appropriate absolute standards are used in calibrating instruments and other equipment; and

(iv) Other calibrations are carried out;

(d) To arrange to use its own equipment for independent measurement and surveillance, and if so agreed and specified in the Subsidiary Arrangements, to arrange to install such equipment;

(e) To apply its seals and other identifying and tamper-indicating devices to containments, if so agreed and specified in the Subsidiary Arrangements; and

(f) To make arrangements with the State for the shipping of samples taken for the Agency's use.

### Access for inspections

76. The Agreement should provide that:

(a) For the purposes specified in sub-paragraphs 71(a) and (b) above and until such time as the *strategic points* have been specified in the Subsidiary Arrangements, the Agency's inspectors shall have access to any location where the initial report or any inspections carried out in connection with it indicate that *nuclear material* is present;

(b) For the purposes specified in sub-paragraph 71(c) above the inspectors shall have access to any location of which the Agency has been notified in accordance with sub-paragraphs 92(c) or 95(c) below;

(c) For the purposes specified in paragraph 72 above the Agency's inspectors shall have access only to the *strategic points* specified in the Subsidiary Arrangements and to the records maintained pursuant to paragraphs 51-58; and

(d) In the event of the State concluding that any unusual circumstances require extended limitations on access by the Agency, the State and the Agency shall promptly make arrangements with a view to enabling the Agency to discharge its safeguards responsibilities in the light of these limitations. The Director General shall report each such arrangement to the Board.

77. The Agreement should provide that in circumstances which may lead to special inspections for the purposes specified in paragraph 73 above the State and the Agency shall consult forthwith. As a result of such consultations the Agency may make inspections in addition to the routine inspection effort provided for in paragraphs 78-82 below, and may obtain access in agreement with the State to information or locations in addition to the access specified in paragraph 76 above for ad hoc and routine inspections. Any disagreement concerning the need for additional access shall be resolved in accordance with paragraphs 21 and 22; in case action by the State is essential and urgent, paragraph 18 above shall apply.

## Frequency and intensity of routine inspections

78. The Agreement should provide that the number, intensity, duration and 'timing of routine inspections shall be kept to the minimum consistent with the effective implementation of the safeguards procedures set forth therein, and that the Agency shall make the optimum and most economical use of available inspection resources.

79. The Agreement should provide that in the case of *facilities* and *material balance areas* outside *facilities* with a content or *annual throughput*, whichever is greater, for *nuclear material* not exceeding five *effective kilograms*, routine inspections shall not exceed one per year. For other *facilities* the number, intensity, duration, timing and mode of inspections shall be determined on the basis that in the maximum or limiting case the inspection régime shall be no more intensive than is necessary and sufficient to maintain continuity of knowledge of the flow and inventory of *nuclear material*.

80. The Agreement should provide that the maximum routine inspection effort in respect of *facilities* with a content or *annual throughput* of *nuclear material* exceeding five *effective kilograms* shall be determined as follows:

(a) For reactors and sealed stores, the maximum total of routine inspection per year shall be determined by allowing one sixth of a *man-year of inspection* for each such *facility* in the State;

(b) For other *facilities* involving plutonium or uranium enriched to more than 5%, the maximum total of routine inspection per year shall be determined by allowing for each such *facility* $30 \times \sqrt{E}$ man-days of inspection per year, where E is the inventory or *annual throughput* of *nuclear material*, whichever is greater, expressed in *effective kilograms*. The maximum established for any such *facility* shall not, however, be less than 1.5 *man-years of inspection*; and

(c) For all other *facilities*, the maximum total of routine inspection per year shall be determined by allowing for each such *facility* one third of a *man-year of inspection* plus $0.4 \times E$ man-days of inspection per year, where E is the inventory or *annual throughput* of *nuclear material*, whichever is greater, expressed in *effective kilograms*.

The Agreement should further provide that the Agency and the State may agree to amend the maximum figures specified in this paragraph upon determination by the Board that such amendment is reasonable.

81. Subject to paragraphs 78-80 above the criteria to be used for determining the actual number, intensity, duration, timing and mode of routine inspections of any *facility* shall include:

(a) The form of *nuclear material*, in particular, whether the material is in bulk form or contained in a number of separate items; its chemical composition and, in the case of uranium, whether it is of low or high *enrichment*; and its accessibility;

(b) The effectiveness of the State's accounting and control system, including the extent to which the operators of *facilities* are functionally independent of the State's accounting and control system; the extent to which the measures specified in paragraph 32 above have been implemented by the State; the promptness of reports submitted to the Agency; their consistency with the Agency's independent verification; and the amount and accuracy of the *material unaccounted for,* as verified by the Agency;

(c) Characteristics of the State's nuclear fuel cycle, in particular, the number and types of *facilities* containing *nuclear material* subject to safeguards, the characteristics of such *facilities* relevant to safeguards, notably the degree of containment; the extent to which the design of such *facilities* facilitates verification of the flow and inventory of *nuclear material*; and the extent to which information from different *material balance areas* can be correlated;

(d) International interdependence, in particular, the extent to which *nuclear material* is received from or sent to other States for use or processing; any verification activity by the Agency in connection therewith; and the extent to which the State's nuclear activities are interrelated with those of other States; and

(e) Technical developments in the field of safeguards, including the use of statistical techniques and random sampling in evaluating the flow of *nuclear material.*

82. The Agreement should provide for consultation between the Agency and the State if the latter considers that the inspection effort is being deployed with undue concentration on particular *facilities.*

### Notice of inspections

83. The Agreement should provide that the Agency shall give advance notice to the State before arrival of inspectors at *facilities* or *material balance areas* outside *facilities,* as follows:

(a) For ad hoc inspections pursuant to sub-paragraph 71(c) above, at least 24 hours, for those pursuant to sub-paragraphs 71(a) and (b), as well as the activities provided for in paragraph 48, at least one week;

(b) For special inspections pursuant to paragraph 73 above, as promptly as possible after the Agency and the State have consulted as provided for in paragraph 77, it being understood that notification of arrival normally will constitute part of the consultations; and

(c) For routine inspections pursuant to paragraph 72 above, at least 24 hours in respect of the *facilities* referred to in sub-paragraph 80(b) and sealed stores containing plutonium or uranium enriched to more than 5%, and one week in all other cases.

Such notice of inspections shall include the names of the inspectors and shall indicate the *facilities* and the *material balance areas* outside *facilities* to be visited and the periods during which they will be visited. If the inspectors are to arrive from outside the State the Agency shall also give advance notice of the place and time of their arrival in the State.

84. However, the Agreement should also provide that, as a supplementary measure, the Agency may carry out without advance notification a portion of the routine inspections pursuant to paragraph 80 above in accordance with the principle of random sampling. In performing any unannounced inspections, the Agency shall fully take into account any operational programme provided by the State pursuant to paragraph 64(b). Moreover, whenever

practicable, and on the basis of the operational programme, it shall advise the State periodically of its general programme of announced and unannounced inspections, specifying the general periods when inspections are foreseen. In carrying out any unannounced inspections, the Agency shall make every effort to minimize any practical difficulties for *facility* operators and the State, bearing in mind the relevant provisions of paragraphs 44 above and 89 below. Similarly the State shall make every effort to facilitate the task of the inspectors.

### Designation of inspectors

85. The Agreement should provide that:
   (a) The Director General shall inform the State in writing of the name, qualifications, nationality, grade and such other particulars as may be relevant, of each Agency official he proposes for designation as an inspector for the State;
   (b) The State shall inform the Director General within 30 days of the receipt of such a proposal whether it accepts the proposal;
   (c) The Director General may designate each official who has been accepted by the State as one of the inspectors for the State, and shall inform the State of such designations; and
   (d) The Director General, acting in response to a request by the State or on his own initiative, shall immediately inform the State of the withdrawal of the designation of any official as an inspector for the State.
The Agreement should also provide, however, that in respect of inspectors needed for the purposes stated in paragraph 48 above and to carry out ad hoc inspections pursuant to sub-paragraphs 71(a) and (b) the designation procedures shall be completed if possible within 30 days after the entry into force of the Agreement. If such designation appears impossible within this time limit, inspectors for such purposes shall be designated on a temporary basis.
86. The Agreement should provide that the State shall grant or renew as quickly as possible appropriate visas, where required, for each inspector designated for the State.

### Conduct and visits of inspectors

87. The Agreement should provide that inspectors, in exercising their functions under paragraphs 48 and 71-75 above shall carry out their activities in a manner designed to avoid hampering or delaying the construction, commissioning or operation of *facilities*, or affecting their safety. In particular inspectors shall not operate any *facility* themselves or direct the staff of a *facility* to carry out any operation. If inspectors consider that in pursuance of paragraphs 74 and 75, particular operations in a *facility* should be carried out by the operator, they shall make a request therefor.
88. When inspectors require services available in the State, including the use of equipment, in connection with the performance of inspections, the State shall facilitate the procurement of such services and the use of such equipment by inspectors.

89. The Agreement should provide that the State shall have the right to have inspectors accompanied during their inspections by representatives of the State, provided that inspectors shall not thereby be delayed or otherwise impeded in the exercise of their functions.

## STATEMENTS ON THE AGENCY'S VERIFICATION ACTIVITIES

90. The Agreement should provide that the Agency shall inform the State of:
    (a)  The results of inspections, at intervals to be specified in the Subsidiary Arrangements; and
    (b)  The conclusions it has drawn from its verification activities in the State, in particular by means of statements in respect of each *material balance area*, which shall be made as soon as possible after a *physical inventory* has been taken and verified by the Agency and a material balance has been struck.

## INTERNATIONAL TRANSFERS

### General

91. The Agreement should provide that *nuclear material* subject or required to be subject to safeguards thereunder which is transferred internationally shall, for purposes of the Agreement, be regarded as being the responsibility of the State:
    (a)  In the case of import, from the time that such responsibility ceases to lie with the exporting State, and no later than the time at which the *nuclear material* reaches its destination; and
    (b)  In the case of export, up to the time at which the recipient State assumes such responsibility, and no later than the time at which the *nuclear material* reaches its destination.
The Agreement should provide that the States concerned shall make suitable arrangements to determine the point at which the transfer of responsibility will take place. No State shall be deemed to have such responsibility for *nuclear material* merely by reason of the fact that the *nuclear material* is in transit on or over its territory or territorial waters, or that it is being transported under its flag or in its aircraft.

### Transfers out of the State

92. The Agreement should provide that any intended transfer out of the State of safeguarded *nuclear material* in an amount exceeding one *effective kilogram*, or by successive shipments to the same State within a period of three months each of less than one *effective kilogram* but exceeding in total one *effective kilogram*, shall be notified to the Agency after the conclusion of the contractual arrangements leading to the transfer and normally at least two weeks before the *nuclear material* is to be prepared for shipping. The Agency and the State may agree on different procedures for advance notification. The notification shall specify:

(a) The identification and, if possible, the expected quantity and composition of the *nuclear material* to be transferred, and the *material balance area* from which it will come;

(b) The State for which the *nuclear material* is destined;

(c) The dates on and locations at which the *nuclear material* is to be prepared for shipping;

(d) The approximate dates of dispatch and arrival of the *nuclear material*; and

(e) At what point of the transfer the recipient State will assume responsibility for the *nuclear material*, and the probable date on which this point will be reached.

93. The Agreement should further provide that the purpose of this notification shall be to enable the Agency if necessary to identify, and if possible verify the quantity and composition of, *nuclear material* subject to safeguards under the Agreement before it is transferred out of the State and, if the Agency so wishes or the State so requests, to affix seals to the *nuclear material* when it has been prepared for shipping. However, the transfer of the *nuclear material* shall not be delayed in any way by any action taken or contemplated by the Agency pursuant to this notification.

94. The Agreement should provide that, if the *nuclear material* will not be subject to Agency safeguards in the recipient State, the exporting State shall make arrangements for the Agency to receive, within three months of the time when the recipient State accepts responsibility for the *nuclear material* from the exporting State, confirmation by the recipient State of the transfer.

**Transfers into the State**

95. The Agreement should provide that the expected transfer into the State of *nuclear material* required to be subject to safeguards in an amount greater than one *effective kilogram,* or by successive shipments from the same State within a period of three months each of less than one *effective kilogram* but exceeding in total one *effective kilogram,* shall be notified to the Agency as much in advance as possible of the expected arrival of the *nuclear material,* and in any case not later than the date on which the recipient State assumes responsibility therefor. The Agency and the State may agree on different procedures for advance notification. The notification shall specify:

(a) The identification and, if possible, the expected quantity and composition of the *nuclear material*;

(b) At what point of the transfer responsibility for the *nuclear material* will be assumed by the State for the purposes of the Agreement, and the probable date on which this point will be reached; and

(c) The expected date of arrival, the location to which the *nuclear material* is to be delivered and the date on which it is intended that the *nuclear material* should be unpacked.

96. The Agreement should provide that the purpose of this notification shall be to enable the Agency if necessary to identify, and if possible verify the quantity and composition of, *nuclear material* subject to safeguards which has been transferred into the State, by means of inspection of the consignment at

the time it is unpacked. However, unpacking shall not be delayed by any action taken or contemplated by the Agency pursuant to this notification.

## Special reports

97. The Agreement should provide that in the case of international transfers a special report as envisaged in paragraph 68 above shall be made if any unusual incident or circumstances lead the State to believe that there is or may have been loss of *nuclear material*, including the occurrence of significant delay during the transfer.

## DEFINITIONS

98. "Adjustment" means an entry into an accounting record or a report showing a *shipper/receiver difference* or *material unaccounted for*.

99. "Annual throughput" means, for the purposes of paragraphs 79 and 80 above, the amount of *nuclear material* transferred annually out of a *facility* working at nominal capacity.

100. "Batch" means a portion of *nuclear material* handled as a unit for accounting purposes at a *key measurement point* and for which the composition and quantity are defined by a single set of specifications or measurements. The *nuclear material* may be in bulk form or contained in a number of separate items.

101. "Batch data" means the total weight of each element of *nuclear material* and, in the case of plutonium and uranium, the isotopic composition when appropriate. The units of account shall be as follows:

    (a) Grams of contained plutonium;

    (b) Grams of total uranium and grams of contained uranium-235 plus uranium-233 for uranium enriched in these isotopes; and

    (c) Kilograms of contained thorium, natural uranium or depleted uranium.

For reporting purposes the weights of individual items in the *batch* shall be added together before rounding to the nearest unit.

102. "Book inventory" of a *material balance area* means the algebraic sum of the most recent *physical inventory* of that *material balance area* and of all *inventory changes* that have occurred since that *physical inventory* was taken.

103. "Correction" means an entry into an accounting record or a report to rectify an identified mistake or to reflect an improved measurement of a quantity previously entered into the record or report. Each correction must identify the entry to which it pertains.

104. "Effective kilogram" means a special unit used in safeguarding *nuclear material*. The quantity in "effective kilograms" is obtained by taking:

    (a) For plutonium, its weight in kilograms;

    (b) For uranium with an *enrichment* of 0.01 (1%) and above, its weight in kilograms multiplied by the square of its *enrichment*;

    (c) For uranium with an *enrichment* below 0.01 (1%) and above 0.005 (0.5%), its weight in kilograms multiplied by 0.0001; and

(d)  For depleted uranium with an *enrichment* of 0.005 (0.5%) or below, and for thorium, its weight in kilograms multiplied by 0.00005.

105. "Enrichment" means the ratio of the combined weight of the isotopes uranium-233 and uranium-235 to that of the total uranium in question.

106. "Facility" means:

(a)  A reactor, a critical facility, a conversion plant, a fabrication plant, a reprocessing plant, an isotope separation plant or a separate storage installation; or

(b)  Any location where *nuclear material* in amounts greater than one *effective kilogram* is customarily used.

107. "Inventory change" means an increase or decrease, in terms of *batches*, of *nuclear material* in a *material balance area*; such a change shall involve one of the following:

(a)  Increases:

(i)  Import;

(ii)  Domestic receipt: receipts from other *material balance areas*, receipts from a non-safeguarded (non-peaceful) activity or receipts at the starting point of safeguards;

(iii)  Nuclear production: production of special fissionable material in a reactor; and

(iv)  De-exemption: reapplication of safeguards on *nuclear material* previously exempted therefrom on account of its use or quantity.

(b)  Decreases:

(i)  Export;

(ii)  Domestic shipment: shipments to other *material balance areas* or shipments for a non-safeguarded (non-peaceful) activity;

(iii)  Nuclear loss of *nuclear material* due to its transformation into other element(s) or isotope(s) as a result of nuclear reactions;

(iv)  Measured discard: *nuclear material* which has been measured, or estimated on the basis of measurements, and disposed of in such a way that it is not suitable for further nuclear use;

(v)  Retained waste: *nuclear material* generated from processing or from an operational accident, which is deemed to be unrecoverable for the time being but which is stored;

(vi)  Exemption: exemption of *nuclear material* from safeguards on account of its use or quantity; and

(vii)  Other loss: for example, accidental loss (that is, irretrievable and inadvertent loss of *nuclear material* as the result of an operational accident) or theft.

108. "Key measurement point" means a location where *nuclear material* appears in such a form that it may be measured to determine material flow or inventory. "Key measurement points" thus include, but are not limited to, the inputs and outputs (including measured discards) and storages in *material balance areas*.

109. "Man-year of inspection" means, for the purposes of paragraph 80 above, 300 man-days of inspection, a man-day being a day during which a single inspector has access to a *facility* at any time for a total of not more than eight hours.

110. "Material balance area" means an area in or outside of a *facility* such that:
    (a) The quantity of *nuclear material* in each transfer into or out of each "material balance area" can be determined; and
    (b) The *physical inventory* of *nuclear material* in each "material balance area" can be determined when necessary, in accordance with specified procedures,
in order that the material balance for Agency safeguards purposes can be established.

111. "Material unaccounted for" means the difference between *book inventory* and *physical inventory*.

112. "Nuclear material" means any source or any special fissionable material as defined in Article XX of the Statute. The term source material shall not be interpreted as applying to ore or ore residue. Any determination by the Board under Article XX of the Statute after the entry into force of this Agreement which adds to the materials considered to be source material or special fissionable material shall have effect under this Agreement only upon acceptance by the State.

113. "Physical inventory" means the sum of all the measured or derived estimates of *batch* quantities of *nuclear material* on hand at a given time within a *material balance area*, obtained in accordance with specified procedures.

114. "Shipper/receiver difference" means the difference between the quantity of *nuclear material* in a *batch* as stated by the shipping *material balance area* and as measured at the receiving *material balance area*.

115. "Source data" means those data, recorded during measurement or calibration or used to derive empirical relationships, which identify *nuclear material* and provide *batch data*. "Source data" may include, for example, weight of compounds, conversion factors to determine weight of element, specific gravity, element concentration, isotopic ratios, relationship between volume and manometer readings and relationship between plutonium produced and power generated.

116. "Strategic point" means a location selected during examination of design information where, under normal conditions and when combined with the information from all "strategic points" taken together, the information necessary and sufficient for the implementation of safeguards measures is obtained and verified; a "strategic point" may include any location where key measurements related to material balance accountancy are made and where containment and surveillance measures are executed.

# Statute of the International Atomic Energy Agency (Excerpts)

## ARTICLE II

*Objectives*

The Agency shall seek to accelerate and enlarge the contribution of atomic energy to peace, health and prosperity throughout the world. It shall ensure, so far as it is able, that assistance provided by it or at its request or under its supervision or control is not used in such a way as to further any military purpose.

## ARTICLE III

*Functions*

A. The Agency is authorized:

5. To establish and administer safeguards designed to ensure that special fissionable and other materials, services, equipment, facilities, and information made available by the Agency or at its request or under its supervision or control are not used in such a way as to further any military purpose; and to apply safeguards, at the request of the parties, to any bilateral or multilateral arrangement, or at the request of a State, to any of that State's activities in the field of atomic energy;

B. In carrying out its function, the Agency shall:

1. Conduct its activities in accordance with the purposes and principles of the United Nations to promote peace and international co-operation, and

in conformity with policies of the United Nations furthering the establish-ment of safeguarded world-wide disarmament and in conformity with any international agreements entered into pursuant to such policies;

2. Establish control over the use of special fissionable materials received by the Agency, in order to ensure that these materials are used only for peaceful purposes;

## ARTICLE XII

### *Agency safeguards*

A. With respect to any Agency project, or other arrangement where the Agency is requested by the parties concerned to apply safeguards, the Agency shall have the following rights and responsibilities to the extent relevant to the project or arrangement:

1. To examine the design of specialized equipment and facilities, includ-ing nuclear reactors, and to approve it only from the view-point of assuring that it will not further any military purpose, that it complies with applicable health and safety standards, and that it will permit effective application of the safeguards provided for in this article;

2. To require the observance of any health and safety measures pre-scribed by the Agency;

3. To require the maintenance and production of operating records to assist in ensuring accountability for source and special fissionable materials used or produced in the project or arrangement;

4. To call for and receive progress reports;

5. To approve the means to be used for the chemical processing of irradiated materials solely to ensure that this chemical processing will not lend itself to diversion of materials for military purposes and will comply with applicable health and safety standards; to require that special fissionable materials recovered or produced as a by-product be used for peaceful pur-poses under continuing Agency safeguards for research or in reactors, existing or under construction, specified by the member or members concerned; and to require deposit with the Agency of any excess of any special fissionable materials recovered or produced as a by-product over what is needed for the above-stated uses in order to prevent stockpiling of these materials, provided that thereafter at the request of the member or members concerned special fissionable materials so deposited with the Agency shall be returned promptly to the member or members concerned for use under the same provisions as stated above;

6. To send into the territory of the recipient State or States inspectors, designated by the Agency after consultation with the State or States con-cerned, who shall have access at all times to all places and data and to any person who by reason of his occupation deals with materials, equipment, or

facilities which are required by this Statute to be safeguarded, as necessary to account for source and special fissionable materials supplied and fissionable products and to determine whether there is compliance with the undertaking against use in furtherance of any military purpose referred to in sub-paragraph F-4 of article XI, with the health and safety measures referred to in sub-paragraph A-2 of this article and with any other conditions prescribed in the agreement between the Agency and the State or States concerned. Inspectors designated by the Agency shall be accompanied by representatives of the authorities of the State concerned, if that State so requests, provided that the inspectors shall not thereby be delayed or otherwise impeded in the exercise of their functions;

7. In the event of non-compliance and failure by the recipient State or States to take requested corrective steps within a reasonable time, to suspend or terminate assistance and withdraw any materials and equipment made available by the Agency or a member in furtherance of the project.

B. The Agency shall, as necessary, establish a staff of inspectors. The staff of inspectors shall have the responsibility of examining all operations conducted by the Agency itself to determine whether the Agency is complying with the health and safety measures prescribed by it for application to projects subject to its approval, supervision or control, and whether the Agency is taking adequate measures to prevent the source and special fissionable materials in its custody or used or produced in its own operations from being used in furtherance of any military purpose. The Agency shall take remedial action forthwith to correct any non-compliance or failure to take adequate measures.

C. The staff of inspectors shall also have the responsibility of obtaining and verifying the accounting referred to in sub-paragraph A-6 of this article and of determining whether there is compliance with the undertaking referred to in sub-paragraph F-4 of article XI, with the measures referred to in sub-paragraph A-2 of this article, and with all other conditions of the project prescribed in the agreement between the Agency and the State or States concerned. The inspectors shall report any non-compliance to the Director General who shall thereupon transmit the report to the Board of Governors. The Board shall call upon the recipient State or States to remedy forthwith any non-compliance which it finds to have occurred. The Board shall report the non-compliance to all members and to the Security Council and General Assembly of the United Nations. In the event of failure of the recipient State or States to take fully corrective action with a reasonable time, the Board may take one or both of the following measures: direct curtailment or suspension of assistance being provided by the Agency or by a member, and call for the return of materials and equipment made available to the recipient member or group of members. The Agency may also, in accordance with article XIX, suspend any non-complying member from the exercise of the privileges and rights of membership.

## ARTICLE XIV

*Finance*

A. The Board of Governors shall submit to the General Conference the annual budget estimates for the expenses of the Agency. To facilitate the work of the Board in this regard, the Director General shall initially prepare the budget estimates. If the General Conference does not approve the estimates, it shall return them together with its recommendations to the Board. The Board shall then submit further estimates to the General Conference for its approval.

B. Expenditures of the Agency shall be classified under the following categories:

1. Administrative expenses: these shall include:

(*a*) Costs of the staff of the Agency other than the staff employed in connexion with materials, services, equipment, and facilities referred to in sub-paragraph B-2 below; costs of meetings; and expenditures required for the preparation of Agency projects and for the distribution of information;

(*b*) Costs of implementing the safeguards referred to in article XII in relation to Agency projects or, under sub-paragraph A-5 of article III, in relation to any bilateral or multilateral arrangement, together with the costs of handling and storage of special fissionable material by the Agency other than the storage and handling charges referred to in paragraph E below;

2. Expenses, other than those included in sub-paragraph 1 of this paragraph, in connexion with any materials, facilities, plant, and equipment acquired or established by the Agency in carrying out its authorized functions, and the costs of materials, services, equipment, and facilities provided by it under agreements with one or more members.

C. In fixing the expenditures under sub-paragraph B-1 (*b*) above, the Board of Governors shall deduct such amounts as are recoverable under agreements regarding the application of safeguards between the Agency and parties to bilateral or multilateral arrangements.

D. The Board of Governors shall apportion the expenses referred to in sub-paragraph B-1 above, among members in accordance with a scale to be fixed by the General Conference. In fixing the scale the General Conference shall be guided by the principles adopted by the United Nations in assessing contributions of Member States to the regular budget of the United Nations.

## ARTICLE XIX

*Suspension of privileges*

B. A member which has persistently violated the provisions of this Statute or of any agreement entered into by it pursuant to this Statute may be suspended from the exercise of the privileges and rights of membership by the General Conference acting by a two-thirds majority of the members present and voting upon recommendation by the Board of Governors.

## ARTICLE XX

*Definitions*

As used in this Statute:

1. The term "special fissionable material" means plutonium-239; uranium-233; uranium enriched in the isotopes 235 or 233; any material containing one or more of the foregoing; and such other fissionable material as the Board of Governors shall from time to time determine; but the term "special fissionable material" does not include source material.

2. The term "uranium enriched in the isotopes 235 or 233" means uranium containing the isotopes 235 or 233 or both in an amount such that the abundance ratio of the sum of these isotopes to the isotope 238 is greater than the ratio of the isotope 235 to the isotope 238 occurring in nature.

3. The term "source material" means uranium containing the mixture of isotopes occurring in nature; uranium depleted in the isotope 235; thorium; any of the foregoing in the form of metal, alloy, chemical compound, or concentrate; any other material containing one or more of the foregoing in such concentration as the Board of Governors shall from time to time determine; and such other material as the Board of Governors shall from time to time determine.

# Participation in Safeguards Agreements, June 30, 1972

| Country | IAEA Member | Tlatelolco Party | NPT Party | IAEA Safeguards Agreements | | |
|---|---|---|---|---|---|---|
| | | | | Misc. | TL-SSA | NPT-SSA |
| | (1) | (2) | (3) | (4) | (5) | (6) |
| Afghanistan | M | | P | | | d,N |
| Albania | M | | | | | |
| Algeria | M | | | | | |
| Argentina | M | S | | PA(2), STA | | |
| Australia | M | | S | STA(2) | | |
| Austria | M | | P | STA | | F |
| Bahrain | | | | | | |
| Bangladesh[1] | A | | | | | |
| Barbados | | P | S | | d | |
| Belgium | M | | S | | | Nce |
| Bhutan | | | | | | |
| Bolivia | M | P | P | | d | d |
| Botswana | | | P | | | d,N |
| Brazil | M | SR | | STA | | |
| Bulgaria | M | | P | | | F |
| Burma | M | | | | | |
| Burundi | | | P | | | |
| Byelorussian S.S.R. | M | | | | | |
| Cameroon | M | | P | | | d |

| Country | IAEA Member | Tlate-lolco Party | NPT Party | IAEA Safeguards Agreements | | |
|---|---|---|---|---|---|---|
| | | | | Misc. | TL-SSA | NPT-SSA |
| | (1) | (2) | (3) | (4) | (5) | (6) |
| Canada | M | | P | STA(3) | | F |
| Central African Republic | | | P | | | d |
| Ceylon | M | | S | | | |
| Chad | | | P | | | |
| Chile | M | S | | PA | | |
| China, People's Republic of | ?* | E(ii) | | | | |
| China, Republic of [Taiwan] | xM* | | P | STA*, USS* | | d* |
| Colombia | M | P | S | STA | | |
| Congo, People's Republic of [(B)] | | | | | | |
| Costa Rica | M | P | P | | d | d,N |
| Cuba | M | E | | | | |
| Cyprus | M | | P | | | d,S |
| Czechoslovak Socialist Republic | M | | P | | | F |
| Dahomey | | | S | | | |
| Denmark | M | | P | STA(2) | | F |
| Dominican Republic | M | P | P | | d | |
| Ecuador | M | P | P | | d | d,N |
| Egypt [United Arab Republic] | M | | S | | | |
| El Salvador | M | P | S | | d | |
| Equatorial Guinea | | | | | | |
| Ethiopia | M | | P | | | d |
| Fiji | | | | | | |
| Finland | M | | P | PA(2) | | F |
| France | M | E(i,ii) | | STA | | |
| Gabon | M | | | | | |
| Gambia | | | S | | | |
| German Democratic Republic | | | P | | | F |
| Germany, Federal Republic of | M | | S | | | Nce |
| Ghana | M | | P | | | d,N |
| Greece | M | | P | PA, STA | | pF |
| Guatemala | M | P | P | | d | d,N |
| Guinea | | | | | | |
| Guyana | | | | | | |
| Haiti | M | P | P | | d | d |
| Holy See | M | | P | | | S |
| Honduras | xM | P | S | | d | |
| Hungary | M | | P | | | F |

| Country | IAEA Member | Tlate-lolco Party | NPT Party | IAEA Safeguards Agreements | | |
|---|---|---|---|---|---|---|
| | | | | Misc. | TL-SSA | NPT-SSA |
| | (1) | (2) | (3) | (4) | (5) | (6) |
| Iceland | M | | P | | | d,Nc |
| India | M | | | STA(2) | | |
| Indonesia | M | | S | PA, STA | | |
| Iran | M | | P | PA, STA | | d,N |
| Iraq | M | | P | | | F |
| Ireland | M | | P | | | F |
| Israel | M | | | STA | | |
| Italy | M | | S | | | Nce |
| Ivory Coast | M | | S | | | |
| Jamaica | M | P | P | | d | d,N |
| Japan | M | | S | PA, STA(5) | | |
| Jordan | M | | P | | | d,N |
| Kenya | M | | P | | | d,N |
| Khmer Republic [Cambodia] | M | | | | | |
| Korea, People's Democratic Republic of | | | | | | |
| Korea, Republic of | M | | S | STA | | |
| Kuwait | M | | S | | | |
| Laos | S | | P | | | d,N |
| Lebanon | M | | P | | | d,N |
| Lesotho | | | P | | | d,Nc |
| Liberia | M | | P | | | d |
| Libyan Arab Republic | M | | S | | | |
| Liechtenstein | M | | | | | |
| Luxembourg | M | | S | | | Nce |
| Madagascar | M | | P | | | |
| Malawi | | | | | | d,N |
| Malaysia | M | | P | | | F |
| Maldives | | | P | | | d,N |
| Mali | M | | P | | | d,N |
| Malta | | | P | | | d,N |
| Mauritania | | | | | | |
| Mauritius | | | P | | | d,Nc |
| Mexico | M | P | P | PA | F | d,Nc |
| Monaco | M | | | | | |
| Mongolia | | | P | | | d,Nc |
| Morocco | M | | P | | | d,N |
| Namibia [South-West Africa] † | | | | | | |

| Country | IAEA Member | Tlatelolco Party | NPT Party | IAEA Safeguards Agreements | | |
|---|---|---|---|---|---|---|
| | | | | Misc. | TL-SSA | NPT-SSA |
| | (1) | (2) | (3) | (4) | (5) | (6) |
| Nauru | | | | | | |
| Nepal | | | P | | | F |
| Netherlands | M | E(i) | S | | | Nce |
| New Zealand | M | | P | | | F |
| Nicaragua | xM | P | S | | d | |
| Niger | M | | | | | |
| Nigeria | M | | P | | | d,N |
| Norway | M | | P | | | F |
| Oman | | | | | | |
| Pakistan | M | | | PA(2), STA | | |
| Panama | M | P | S | | | |
| Paraguay | M | P | P | | d | d |
| Peru | M | P | P | | d | d |
| Philippines | M | | S | PA,STA | | |
| Poland | M | | P | | | d,S |
| Portugal | M | | | STA | | |
| Qatar | | | | | | |
| Rhodesia [Southern] † | | | | | | |
| Romania | M | | P | | | d,S |
| Rwanda | | | | | | |
| San Marino | | | P | | | d |
| Saudi Arabia | M | | | | | |
| Senegal | M | | P | | | d,N |
| Sierra Leone | M | | | | | N |
| Singapore | M | | S | | | |
| Somalia | | | P | | | d,N |
| South Africa | M | | | STA | | |
| Spain | M | | | PA, STA | | |
| Sudan, Democratic Republic of the | M | | S | | | |
| Swaziland | | | P | | | d,N |
| Sweden | M | | P | STA | | d,N |
| Switzerland | M | | S | STA | | |
| Syrian Arab Republic | M | | P | | | d |
| Tanzania, United Republic of | | | | | | |
| Thailand | M | | | STA | | |
| Togo | | | P | | | d |
| Tonga | | | P | | | N |
| Trinidad and Tobago | | S | S | | | |
| Tunisia | M | | P | | | d,N |

| Country | IAEA Member ber | Tlate- lolco Party | NPT Party | IAEA Safeguards Agreements | | |
|---|---|---|---|---|---|---|
| | | | | Misc. | TL- SSA | NPT- SSA |
| | (1) | (2) | (3) | (4) | (5) | (6) |
| Turkey | M | | S | STA | | |
| Uganda | M | | | | | |
| Ukranian S.S.R. | M | | | | | |
| U.S.S.R. | M | E(ii) | P | | | |
| United Arab Emirates | | | | | | |
| United Kingdom | M | P(i,ii) | P | STA(2) | | (N) |
| United States | M | P(ii) | P | STA(24) | | (N) |
| Upper Volta | | | P | | | d |
| Uruguay | M | P | P | PA | d,Sp | d,S |
| Venezuela | M | SR | S | STA | d | |
| Vietnam, People's Republic of | | | | | | |
| Vietnam, Republic of | M | | P | PA, STA | | d,N |
| Western Samoa | | | | | | |
| Yemen, People's Republic of [South] | | | S | | | |
| Yemen Arab Republic | | | S | | | |
| Yugoslavia | M | | P | PA | | d,S |
| Zaire [Congo (N)] | M | | P | PA | | d,S |
| Zambia | M | | | | | |

1 The possible succession of Bangladesh to membership in various organizations of which, and to participation in treaties to which, Pakistan is a party has not yet been determined.

* On December 9, 1971, the Board of Governors of the IAEA decided that the Nationalist government should no longer represent China in the Agency and that the Government of the People's Republic should be invited to do so. The consequences of that decision on China's membership in and agreements with the Agency and the reaction of the People's Republic have not yet been determined.

† International status in dispute.

### Legend

| | |
|---|---|
| A | applicant |
| E(i,ii) | eligible to become party to (protocols I and II to) Tlatelolco Treaty, but has not yet signed |
| d | delinquent in obligation to conclude SSA |
| F | in force |
| M | member |
| N | negotiations commenced |
| Nc | negotiation commenced |
| Nce | negotiations conducted jointly with Euratom commission and other |

|          |                                                                                                            |
| -------- | ---------------------------------------------------------------------------------------------------------- |
|          | Euratom non-nuclear-weapon states and concluded in July 1972                                               |
| *(N)*    | negotiations of quasi-NPT-SSA commenced                                                                     |
| *NPT-SSA*| Safeguards Submission Agreement for Non-Proliferation Treaty                                                |
| *P*      | party                                                                                                       |
| *PA*     | IAEA Project Agreement                                                                                      |
| *P(i,ii)*| Party to (protocols I and II to) Tlatelolco Treaty                                                          |
| *pF*     | provisionally in force                                                                                      |
| *S*      | signatory                                                                                                   |
| *S(i,ii)*| signatory of (protocols I and II to) Tlatelolco Treaty                                                      |
| *Sp*     | signed Tlatelolco protocol to NPT-SSA                                                                       |
| *SR*     | signed and ratified, but without waiver of conditions permitting immediate entry into force of Tlatelolco Treaty |
| *STA*    | Safeguards Transfer Agreement (transferring bilateral safeguards to the IAEA)                               |
| *T-SSA*  | Safeguards Submission Agreement for Tlatelolco (Latin American Nuclear Free Zone) Treaty                    |
| *USS*    | Unilateral Safeguards Submission Agreement                                                                  |
| *xM*     | former member                                                                                              |

# Notes on Contributors

*Bernhard G. Bechhoefer* is a practicing lawyer in Washington, D.C. From 1946 to 1958 he served as a senior officer of the Department of State specializing in questions of arms control and the peaceful uses of the atom and as an adviser to U.S. representatives in various United Nations commissions. He served as a consultant to The Brookings Institution from 1959 to 1969. Mr. Bechhoefer is the author of *Postwar Negotiations for Arms Control* (1961) and coauthor of *Arms Control Agreements* (1968). He received his law degree from Harvard University.

*Bennett Boskey* is a practicing lawyer in Washington, D.C. He was formerly Deputy General Counsel of the U.S. Atomic Energy Commission. He has written on the Supreme Court and on various aspects of atomic energy and is coeditor of *Nuclear Proliferation: Prospects for Control* (1970). Mr. Boskey received his law degree from Harvard University.

*Victor Gilinsky* was a member of the physics department research staff of the RAND Corporation at the time of his contribution to this volume. He is now Special Assistant to the Director of Regulation of the U.S. Atomic Energy Commission. Dr. Gilinsky holds a Ph.D. degree in theoretical physics from the California Institute of Technology.

*Edwin M. Kinderman* is currently the Director of Marketing for the Physical Sciences of the Stanford Research Institute, having served in several technical and management positions at the Institute over the past sixteen years. He is Chairman of the Subcommittee on Research and Development of the Committee on Material Safeguards of the Atomic Industrial Forum. He has been a chemist and senior scientist at General Electric Company, instructor and associate professor at the University of Portland, and a chemist in the radiation laboratory at the University of California. He has published a number of articles in scientific and industrial journals. He holds a Ph.D. degree in physical chemistry from Notre Dame University.

*Lawrence Scheinman* is Professor of Political Science at Cornell University. He has taught political science at the University of Michigan and the University of California, Los Angeles, and has been a visiting research scholar for the Carnegie Endowment for International Peace and a research associate at the Center for International Affairs at Harvard University. His publications in the field of nuclear policy include *Atomic Energy Policy in France under the Fourth Republic* (1965) and the articles "EURATOM: Nuclear Integration in Europe" and "Nuclear Safeguards, the Peaceful Atom, and the IAEA." He received the Ph.D. degree in political science from the University of Michigan.

*Henry D. Smyth* is Joseph Henry Professor of Physics Emeritus, Princeton University. From 1949 to 1954 Dr. Smyth was a Commissioner of the U.S. Atomic Energy Commission. From 1961 to 1970 he served as U.S. Ambassador to the International Atomic Energy Agency. He has also served as a consultant to various U.S. government agencies and industrial concerns. He is the author of *Atomic Energy For Military Purposes* (1945), the official U.S. government report on the development of the atomic bomb. In 1968 he received the Atoms For Peace award and in 1970 the Distinguished Honor award of the U.S. Department of State.

*Paul C. Szasz* is a member of the General Legal Division of the United Nations. He served previously in the Legal and the Safeguards divisions of the International Atomic Energy Agency and in the legal department of the International Bank for Reconstruction and Development. His extensive publications on IAEA safeguards include a book, *The Law and Practices of the International Atomic Energy Agency* (1970). Mr. Szasz received his law degree from Cornell University.

*Theodore B. Taylor* is President of International Research & Technology Corporation, which he founded in 1967. He has served as a consultant to the U.S. Atomic Energy Commission, the International Atomic Energy Agency, the Organization for Economic Cooperation and Development, and a number of other groups. In 1964-1965 he served as Deputy Director (Scientific) of the Defense Atomic Support Agency. He has served as a staff member of the Los Alamos Scientific Laboratory and the General Atomic Division of General Dynamics Corporation. Dr. Taylor was the recipient of the Ernest O. Lawrence Memorial Award of the Atomic Energy Commission in 1965 for his work on the development of nuclear weapons and the TRIGA research reactor. He received the Ph.D. in theoretical physics from Cornell University.

*Mason Willrich* is Professor of Law and Director of the Center for the Study of Science, Technology and Public Policy at the University of Virginia. He was Assistant General Counsel of the U.S. Arms Control and Disarmament Agency from 1962 to 1965 and has served on the U.S. delegations to the conference of the Committee on Disarmament in Geneva and to the Safeguards Review Working Group of the International Atomic Energy Agency.

Mr. Willrich has served as a consultant to the RAND Corporation, the U.S. Arms Control and Disarmament Agency, and the Naval War College. His books include *Global Politics of Nuclear Energy* (1971) and *Non-Proliferation Treaty: Framework for Nuclear Arms Control* (1969). He is the editor of *Civil Nuclear Power and International Security* (1971) and coeditor of *Nuclear Proliferation: Prospects for Control* (1970). Mr. Willrich received his law degree from the University of California, Berkeley.

# The American Society of International Law Panel on Nuclear Energy and World Order

## Members

Bernhard G. Bechhoefer
Bennett Boskey
Robert R. Bowie
George Bunn
Joseph I. Coffey
John T. Conway
Richard A. Falk
Adrian S. Fisher
Victor Gilinsky
Edwin M. Kinderman
Robert Leachman
Franklin A. Long
Henry R. Myers
Ashton J. O'Donnell

John G. Palfrey
Jaroslav G. Polach
George W. Rathjens, Jr.
Leonard S. Rodberg
Matthew Sands
Lawrence Scheinman
Herbert Scoville, Jr.
Henry D. Smyth
Louis B. Sohn
Eric Stein
Paul C. Szasz
Theodore B. Taylor
Alvin M. Weinberg
Mason Willrich
Christopher Wright

## Research Work Assisted

Mason Willrich, *Non-Proliferation Treaty: Framework for Nuclear Arms Control* (1969).

Bennett Boskey and Mason Willrich, eds., *Nuclear Proliferation: Prospects for Control* (1970). Contributors: Bernhard G. Bechhoefer, David B. Brooks, George Bunn, Joseph I. Coffey, Richard A. Falk, Adrian S. Fisher, Victor Gilinsky, Henry R. Myers, John G. Palfrey, George W. Rathjens, Jr., Lawrence Scheinman, Herbert Scoville, Jr.

Mason Willrich, *Global Politics of Nuclear Energy* (1971).

# Index

## A

Acceptability of safeguards, 13, 16-18, 20, 43, 225, 226
Activities proscribed, 86-87
Administration of safeguards, 116-25
Agreements, safeguards: bilateral, prior to NPT, 32, 225, 236; bilateral, and transfer to IAEA/NPT system, 34, 40, 133-34; Euratom, 34-35; failure to conclude, 110-13; IAEA members, 292-97; non-NPT, 82-86, 89-90; project agreements, 28-29, 31, 33, 82-86; structure and content of IAEA, 37, 261-68; U.S., 25, 32, 34
Arbitration in safeguards disputes, 112-13
Argentina, 62, 67
ASIL Panel on Nuclear Energy and World Order, 301
Atomic Energy Act of 1954, U.S., 25, 144
Atomic Energy Commission, U.S., 12-14, 17, 142-50, 181, 216; contracts, 149-50; Division of Nuclear Materials Safeguards, 147, 149; Division of Nuclear Materials Security, 149; Office of Safeguards and Nuclear Materials Management, 147
Atoms for Peace, 24-25, 26, 144, 214
Auditing, 96, 177, 188, 205-6, 209; in U.S., 148-49
Australia, 62, 64, 164
Austria, 61, 65, 94n
Authority. *See* Legal basis for safeguards

## B

Balance of interests, 222-23
Baruch Plan, 22-27, 28
Belgium, 61, 65
Boskey, Bennett, 298
Brazil, 61, 62
Breeder reactors, 49, 54, 56, 59, 180-81, 209-10
Brinks robbery, 188
British Nuclear Fuels, Ltd., 217
Brockville Trust and Savings Co. robbery, 189
Brookhaven National Laboratory, 126

## C

Canada, 60, 61, 62, 65, 66, 67, 68, 237
Chemical reprocessing, 30, 36, 53-54, 58, 59, 65-66, 68, 204, 212-13
China, 62, 63, 69, 160, 162, 164, 243
Clandestine nuclear facilities, 95, 168, 241. *See also* Diversion, nuclear
Cohen, Benjamin V., 23-24
Commercial and industrial data, 41, 109, 118, 131-32, 213-15, 219, 239, 262
Containment of nuclear material, 97, 98, 101, 194-95, 262
Contracts, U.S. AEC, 149-50
Control systems, 221-22
Conversion plants, 50
Coordination of NPT safeguards with other systems, 9-10, 19, 132-40, 263
Costs, 13, 18, 20, 75, 104, 265-66, 290; capital, 48-54 passim; distribution of,

303